Drapham Dzong

Ministry of Home and Cultural Affairs, Bhutan
Department of Culture
Archaeology Section under the Division for Conservation of Heritage Sites

and

SLSA
Swiss Liechtenstein Foundation for Archaeological Research Abroad
Zurich, Switzerland

Werner Meyer

Drapham Dzong

Archaeological Excavation of a Himalayan Fortress in Central Bhutan

Research Report
Bhutan-Swiss Archaeology Project

NIYOGI
BOOKS

Imprint

Author:
Werner Meyer

Translation from German into English:
Linda Cassens Stoian, Basel/Switzerland

Translation from English into Dzongkha:
Sonam Gyeltshen

Book design:
Elizabeth Hefti, Winterthur/Switzerland

Typesetting:
Claudia Rossi and Elizabeth Hefti

Photography:
Werner Meyer, and Jorrit Britschgi,
Eberhard Fischer, Peter Fux, Jorge Osatinsky,
Silvia Scheuerer, Valeria Wyler

Drawing:
Werner Meyer, and Giovanni Buzzi, Kuenga Wangmo, Dominique Oppler, Jorge Osatinsky, Silvia Scheuerer, Sonam Tashi, Anita Springer, Gaby Weber, Valeria Wyler

Colour separation:
Thomas Humm, Matzingen/Switzerland

Production monitoring:
Eberhard Fischer, Peter Fux, Daniel Schneiter

NIYOGI BOOKS
Block D, Building No. 77,
Okhla Industrial Area, Phase-I,
New Delhi-110 020, INDIA
Tel: 91-11-26816301, 26818960
email: niyogibooks@gmail.com
website: www.niyogibooksindia.com

ISBN: 978-81-933935-7-4
Publication: 2017

Printed in India at Niyogi Offset Pvt. Ltd., New Delhi

Table of Contents

Preface

The archaeological excavation project at Drapham Dzong commenced under the initiative of the Ministry of Home and Cultural Affairs of the Royal Government of Bhutan. In a letter dated March 29, 2005, addressed to Werner Külling, Secretary General of Helvetas Swiss Intercooperation, H.E. Jigme Y. Thinley expressed the request «to initiate for the first time in the country's history archaeological projects in Bhutan». The same letter states that «the site of the ruins of Drapham Dzong in the district of Bumthang has been selected as the first project site», and suggests that «experienced professionals (from Switzerland) provide support to undertake this first archaeological project and more importantly provide training in situ to locals.» In a subsequent letter dated May 13, 2005, the Home Minister informs the head of the Division for Conservation of Architectural Heritage that it is «His Majesty the King of Bhutan's personal wish to one day initiate archaeological projects in Bhutan». The letter notes further that this first undertaking will have special importance as «a leading example to many such projects that are planned for implementing in the country in future» and that the department hopes «to receive possible support for this significant and pioneering project» from Helvetas and/or from Switzerland.

This correspondence was subsequently passed on to the office of the Swiss-Liechtenstein Foundation for Archaeological Research Abroad (SLSA), of which I am the Secretary General. Unfortunately, it took some time before we in Switzerland realized the importance of this high-level initiative from Bhutan. Nevertheless, in November 2006 I accepted the invitation of Helvetas Coordinator Dr Walter Roder to visit Bhutan and, accompanied and guided by Namgyel Tshering, Head of Administration, I visited Drapham Dzong. In my report to the trustees of the SLSA, I stated that (1) the Government of Bhutan was sincerely interested in a joint archaeological venture with Swiss archaeologists and intended to institutionalize archaeology as a new discipline, and (2) the ruined Drapham Dzong merited a three-year excavation campaign.

When the scientific committee of the SLSA discussed such a long-term archaeological undertaking in Bhutan, they unanimously agreed that such a project would best be led by Professor Emeritus Dr Werner Meyer, long-time head of the Department of History at the University of Basel, since he had excavated the most important castles and fortresses in Switzerland over the course of several decades and had also achieved success at the famous site of Krak des Chevaliers in Syria. The SLSA trustees invited him to lecture on his most recent excavations, and during this occasion I spoke to him about Bhutan, the beauty and singularity of the country, the Bhutan Government's sincere interest in an archaeological endeavour, and in particular Drapham Dzong, with its superb situation and the magnificence of the ruin. A few months later, at the end of October 2007, we travelled with Dr Jorrit Britschgi of the Museum Rietberg Zurich to Bhutan to visit the site of Drapham Dzong. Dorji Yangki, Nagtsho Dorji, and Kuenga Wangmo of the Division for Conservation of Heritage Sites accompanied us on this short but rather exacting trip. By this time the hill crest site had been roughly cleared by order of the Department of Culture, and Professor Meyer sketched a first site plan and showed us where he saw the potential for and limitations of an excavation. (For instance, he recommended concentrating on the hilltop fortress rather than on the ruins at the foot of the hill or the impressive walled paths along the slope intended for the transportation of water).

Professor Meyer was now determined to undertake and lead the Drapham Dzong exploration and asked me to organize the first archaeological excavation in Bhutan for Autumn 2008. An excavation budget for that year and the following two years was then accepted by the SLSA executive board. During the first campaign, the project's participants were already able to map the basic structure of the fortress, which extends more than 9,000 square meters, and shift enormous amounts of stone, rubble, and debris. Slowly the structure of the once magnificent fortress became visible!

In 2009 and 2010, during two more very intense autumn campaigns, when it was reasonably dry in Central Bhutan and the local farmers were free of agricultural obligations and could be helpful, Professor Meyer worked at Drapham Dzong with his team: his former students Jorge Osantinsky, Silvia Scheuerer, Gaby Weber, Valeria Wyler, and (in 2010) Dominique Oppler, most of whom had become professional archaeologists by then. The team was strengthened in the second campaign by three more archaeologists: Kuenga Wangmo, Anita Springer, and Peter Fux. I myself participated in the first campaign for five strenuous weeks, as did my friend Namgyel Tshering, administrator of the Helvetas Bhutan office, who was from the beginning the soul of the entire enterprise. He took charge not only of all the logistics, equipment for the site camp, and recruitment and payment of the cooks and local workers, but also the general well-being of all, both Swiss and Bhutanese, and actively participated in the excavation work!

Three medical doctors from Switzerland joined the archaeological team: Dr Urs Lütolf (2008), Dr Stefan Obrist (2009), and Dr Karin Hartmann. Fortunately, none of the archaeologists or workers at the site ever needed serious medical help, but because of our interaction with the local community, the medical advice and treatment offered at our camp were greatly appreciated. We are grateful for their participation.

The SLSA was joined in the financing of this archaeological undertaking by the Royal Government of Bhutan. The Share Foundation of Mrs Elena Probst kindly sponsored the initial visit of Professor Meyer to Bhutan; the University of Basel, through the FAG Foundation (Voluntary Academic Society), contributed to the salaries of the Basel alumni during the 2009 and 2010 campaigns; and the authorities of the Museum Rietberg Zurich granted Jorrit Britschgi, Peter Fux, and me leave to participate in the project. I also acknowledge with thanks the participation of Helvetas Swiss Intercooporation: Dr Walter Roder, Mrs Tashi Pem, and Dr Pema Gyamtsho took an active interest in the project and permitted the Helvetas Head of Administration, Namgyel Tshering, to participate in the work for several weeks each season.

Of greatest importance for the success of the project was the participation of the Bhutanese Department of Culture, part of the Ministry of Home and Cultural Affairs under Lynpo Minjur Dorji and Secretary Dasho Penden Wangchuk. Aum Nagtsho Dorji, Head of the Division for Conservation of Heritage Sites, organized and administered the project, and it was thanks to her diligence and perseverance that the project proceeded smoothly. She saw to it that Phase I of the «Bhutan Swiss Archaeology Project» (the excavation of Drapham Dzong) was established, that funds were allotted from the Royal Government for clearing and fencing the site, that a camp with barracks and facility huts for the team could be built, and that a number of Bhutanese architects and engineers were allowed to participate in the training and practical archaeological fieldwork. From her division, Sangay Kinga, Sonam Tenzin, and (in 2010) Karma Tenzin proved most supportive in the office and in the field.

The actual fieldwork on Drapham Dzong ended in December 2010, and for each year from 2007 to 2010 reports on the excavations were published in the SLSA's annual report. The finds—potsherds, bones, stones, and a few metal and porcelain artefacts—were shipped to Switzerland for conservation and analysis. Because Professor Meyer had retired and could not avail himself of institutional support, the analyses at the University of Basel laboratories took much longer than expected. However, by October 31,

2014, all the finds had been professionally cleaned, the necessary conservation work completed, and the finds photographed, drawn, and analysed. They were then returned to Bhutan, where they arrived well packed and were «checked thoroughly with the inventory.... All artefacts were received safe and stored by the newly formed Archaeology Section under DCHS» (as reported by Karma Tenzin and Sonam Gyeltshen).

The only task remaining was for Professor Werner Meyer to write the monograph, which would include selected photographs and numerous plates, most of them hand drawn by the author himself. The publication before you is the completed work. The text, originally written in German, was carefully translated by Linda Cassens Stoian. Peter Fux and in the final stage Daniel Schneiter helped to assemble the various parts and worked with the author to properly align the illustrations with the text. Thomas Humm prepared scans from the original drawings and photographs and placed the many numbers and letters at the right spots. And Elizabeth Hefti, who for years has produced the SLSA's annual reports, designed the book with great care and also saw to its production. I thank all the contributors for this fine result and am happy that the book appears in this form under the auspices of the SLSA and the Department of Culture of Bhutan.

On behalf of the President of the SLSA, Dr Hans Heinrich Coninx, I offer my congratulations to Professor Werner Meyer for this important contribution to the study of Drapham Dzong, the first ruined fortress of Bhutan to be excavated. I would also like to express my gratitude and sincere thanks to the Royal Government of Bhutan, in particular to Dorji Tshering, former Director General of the Department of Culture; to Aum Nagtsho Dorji and the entire staff of the Division for Conservation of Heritage Sites; and to my friend Namgyel Tshering of Helvetas for this joint venture of excavating and documenting the Drapham Dzong ruin, which was carried out in such a pleasant atmosphere of good will and mutual understanding.

Eberhard Fischer Secretary General
Swiss-Liechtenstein Foundation for Archaeological Research Abroad

1

1. Foreword

On April 23, 2007, at the annual meeting of the Swiss-Liechtenstein Foundation of Archaeological Research Abroad (SLSA), where I gave a lecture about my excavations at Krak des Chevaliers in Syria, I was asked by Dr Eberhard Fischer, Secretary General of the Foundation, if I would be interested in the archaeological investigation of a ruined fortress in Bhutan. After briefly thinking it over, I agreed, not knowing exactly all that I would be confronted with.

Having focused my historical and archaeological research on the Occident and the Near East for decades, I felt certain that an excavation project in the Himalayas would mean not only plunging into a foreign world, but also treading unchartered scientific territory since Bhutan was one of the few countries in the world without a tradition of archaeological research—even though its settlement history reaches back to the Neolithic Era. I was aware of all this when, in the autumn of 2007, I made a reconnaissance trip with a small Swiss-Bhutanese task force to inspect the site in Central Bhutan in order to plan the first stage of research, which was intended to begin in 2008.

The journey from the national capital of Thimphu, which took several hours, was already adventurous enough. The curvy mountain road took us past sanctuaries, fortification compounds (Dzongs), and picturesque villages before we arrived at the Swiss Guest House of Jakar, where we were hospitably welcomed by Fritz Maurer. After a laborious ascent, we finally reached the sea of ruins of the Drapham Dzong, lying at approximately 3,000 metres above sea level. The sight that greeted our eyes was both fascinating and daunting: discontinuous remnants of walls overgrown by a dense mountain jungle. J. L. Stephens must have had a similar experience in the 19th century when he first caught sight of the ruins of the Mayan culture in the Central American jungle and had no idea what he was looking at in front of him.

Beginning in 2008, work proceeded on schedule. Thanks to a barracks camp, which the Bhutanese had built in the saddle below the fortress hill, the whole team had endurable accommodations, and apart from a few rainy days, even the weather cooper-

Fig. 1 Overall view of Chamkhar Valley. In the middle, Drapham Dzong. View down the valley towards southwest. J.O.

Fig. 2 The remains of the Utse (central tower) of Drapham dzong, November 2006. E.F.

2

ated, although after sunset the night spread a blanket of bitter cold over us. The proximity of a diverse array of animals living all around was a special experience for us Swiss city dwellers; these included trusting ravens, yaks driven past the camp by nomads, and bears secretly visiting our camp at night.

The work was designed as a communal effort, to whose success many locals and people from afar contributed. As the project's scientific director and the person ultimately responsible for the outcome of the research, I extend my sincere thanks to all the individuals and institutions that supported the work in some way. While it is beyond the scope of this foreword to mention all here by name, I would like to emphasize that without the support of the authorities of Bhutan—especially the Ministry of Home and Cultural Affairs and the district administration of Bumthang—as well as of Helvetas and the SLSA, the project could never have been realized. The small core group of specialists from Switzerland, consisting of experts from the University of Basel and the SLSA, in conjunction with the team of engineers organized by the Ministry were indispensable in accomplishing the tasks of management, organization, and documentation. Finally, a most hearty thanks is extended to the many men and women from the valley—up to 50 each working day—who undertook the painstaking exposure work, often under difficult conditions. The occasional celebration of a holiday with dart throwing, feasting, dancing, and singing was no more than an appropriate recognition of the enormous contribution on-site.

Fig. 3 Provisional ground plan of the site, 2007. W.M.

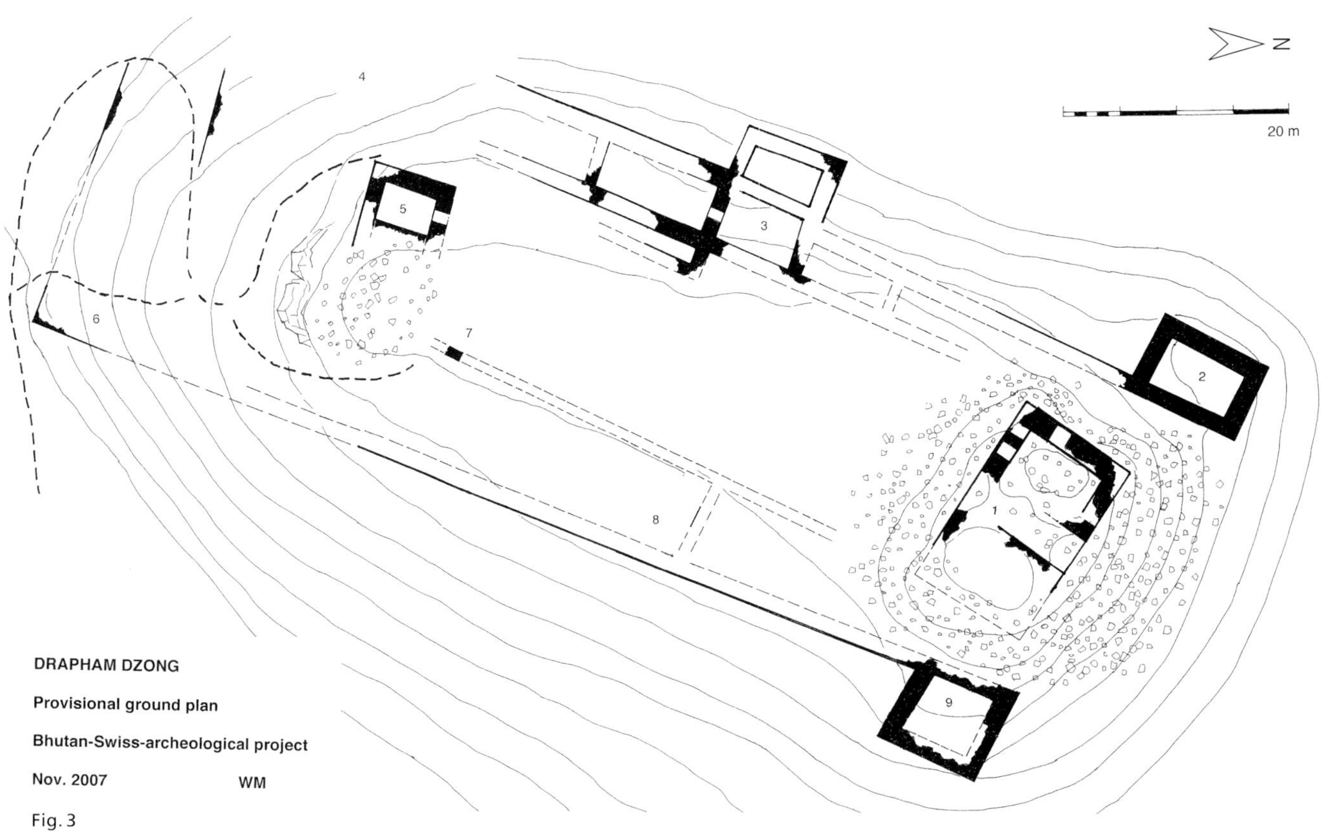

Fig. 3

Fig. 4 View of main fortress covered with debris before beginning of excavation and after removal of bushes. View towards northeast. W.M.

Fig. 5 Part of wall of a building leaning inside to the eastern fortified wall (pos. 7), 2007. J.B.

4

5

One of the things that motivated the team to face the hardships and inconveniences of daily life in the camp and on the rough terrain of the excavation site was the general interest with which the archaeological work was greeted. Not only were we visited by wandering lamas and trekking tourists from all over the world, but we even had the great honour of welcoming His Majesty the King of Bhutan Jigme Khesar Namgyel Wangchuck, as well as several of his ministers and governors, who wished to be kept informed of our results.

When the excavation came to an end in late autumn 2010 and the Swiss team was preparing for departure, our feeling of pride and joy at having mastered a difficult task was tinged with the sense of melancholy that often arises when it's time to say goodbye to those who have become cherished co-workers, acquaintances, and friends.

A scientific excavation is only finished once the results have been evaluated and published. Under certain conditions this may take several years, especially when the finds and findings prove to be rich, diverse, and difficult to interpret. Therefore, after each year of working, provisional articles about the excavations at Drapham Dzong were published in the annual reports of the SLSA and professional journals.

It is my hope that the present work will serve as the basis for future archaeological enterprises in Bhutan.

Werner Meyer December 2014

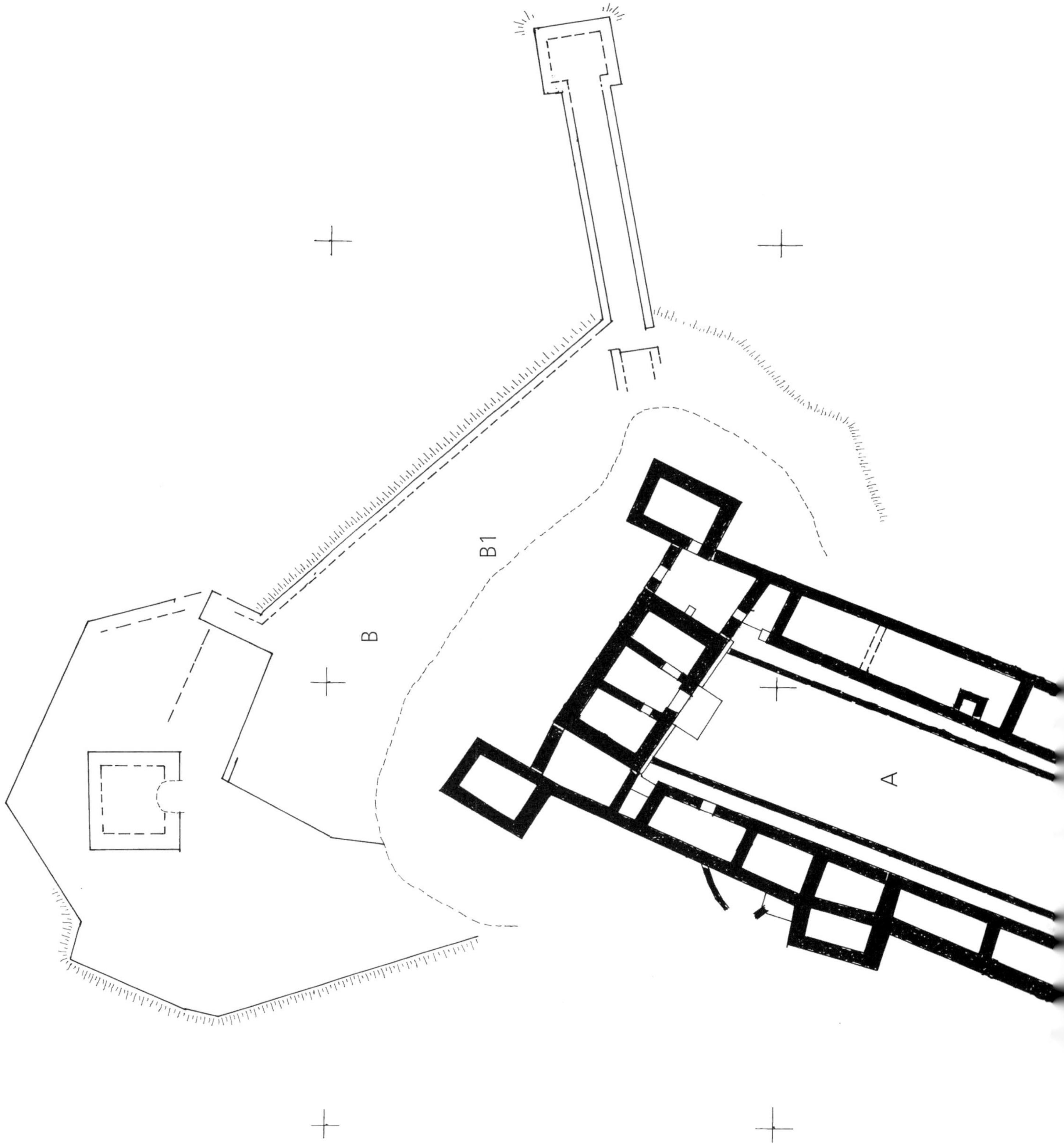

B1
B
A

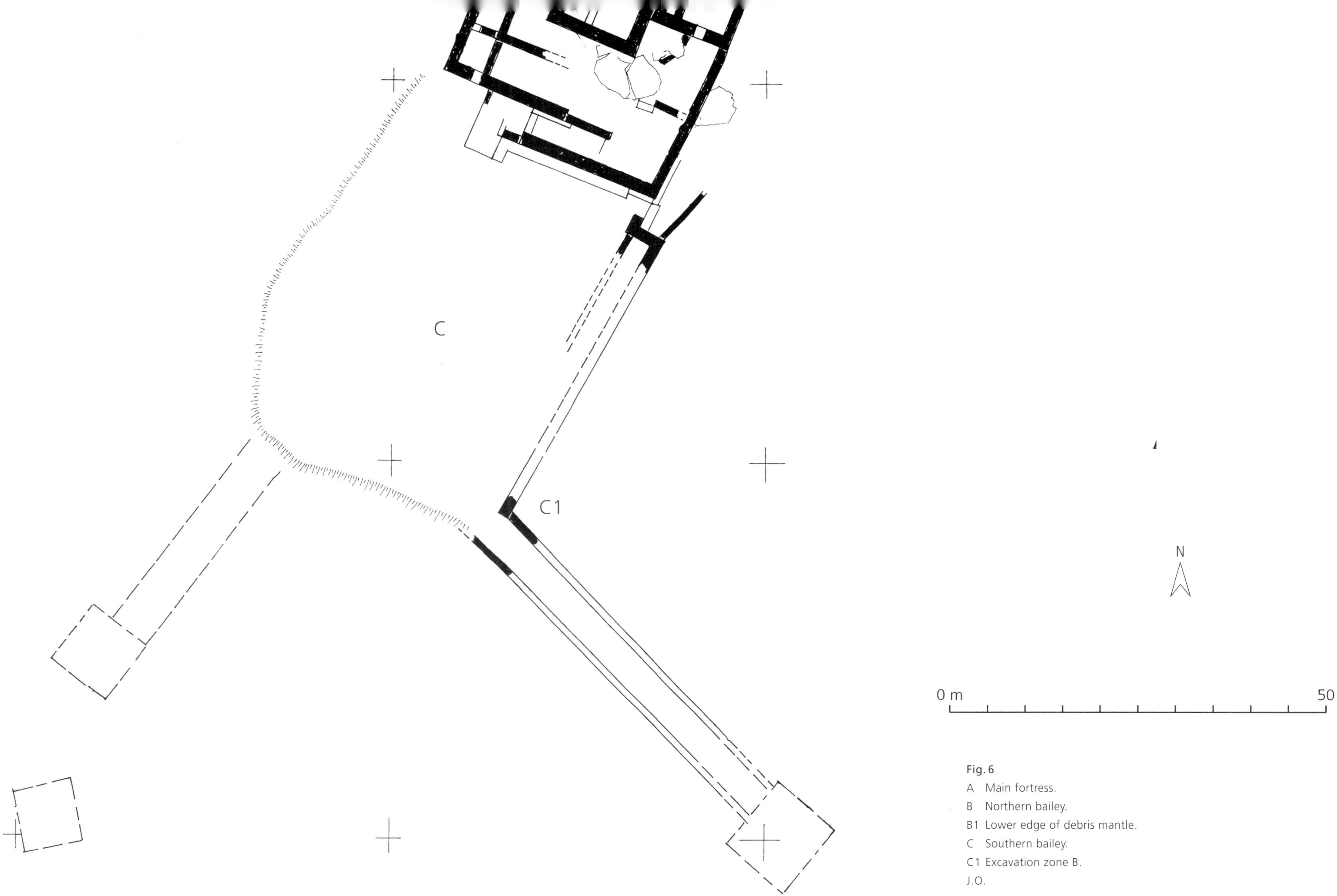

Fig. 6
A Main fortress.
B Northern bailey.
B1 Lower edge of debris mantle.
C Southern bailey.
C1 Excavation zone B.
J.O.

Eb
8/1a
Ec
8/1b
Ea
E
8/1d
Ee
8/1c
N
9/60
Tf
9/41a
9/41d
8/2
8/19
Ta
Td
Ka
9/39
Tb
9/41c
T
Ud
8/15a
9/40
9/47
8/6c
Kb
9/49
K
Ti
Tc
10/65a
Ue
Kc
Th
8/15b
8/6b
Te
9/41b
9/48
U
Kd
8/6d
8/15d
10/64a
N
10/65b
Ua
Nb
Tg
10/64a
9/45
8/15d
9/33
9/43
Na
9/46
9/59
Ub
8/5a
9/44b
8/3a
9/44a
8/3b
Uc
8/5b
9/43
Fc
8/4
Fb
8/5c
8/3c
Fa
Ff
Wa
Fd
F
9/57c
Fe
8/9c
9/33

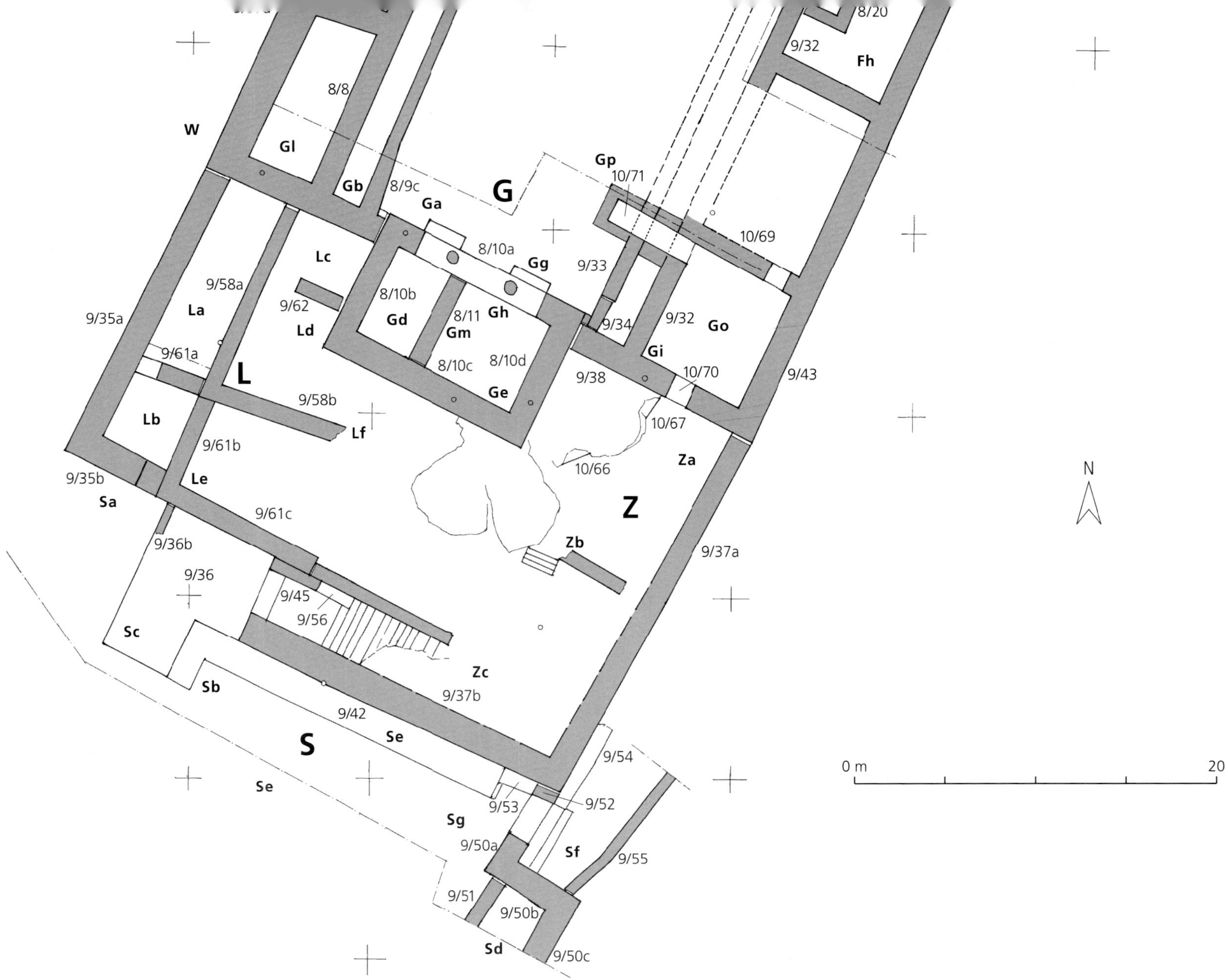

Fig. 7 Main fortress, ground plan of walls
W: Wall
W8f.: year of excavation (2008–2010)
W8/1f. wall number
J.O.

2. Introduction

Fig. 8 View from Drapham dzong into the upper Bumthang valley, November 2006. W.M.

2.1. Drapham Dzong Location

The ruins of Drapham Dzong are located on a mountain ledge approx. twelve km north of the center of Jakar, the capital of the Bumthang district in Central Bhutan.

Precise Location:
N 27° 39′ 15.4″
E 90° 45′ 14.9″
Altitude: approximately 2,930 m a.s.l.

The fortress compound rises high above the bottom of the valley, which lies 300 m below where the Chamkhar Chhu meanders. Fed by numerous watercourses, the river's source is located near the border to China/Tibet. (In tourist maps the Chamkhar Chhu is also referred to as Bumthang Chhu.[1]) Near Drapham Dzong, the valley is terraced, and the expanse of its floor has a width ranging from 150 to 600 m. On both sides of the river, there are small settlements, hamlet-like groups of houses that are oriented to sacral buildings and water-powered mills. A number of crops flourish on the agricultural land, primarily barley, buckwheat, and potatoes, whereas above Jakar the cultivation of rice is absent. Near the groups of houses, vegetable gardens and fruit trees can be found. Barren grassy grounds serve as grazing land for cattle and sheep. Arable fields and pasturelands are divided by stonewalls.

Isolated, small huts with woven walls rise up out of the landscape. Stretching across the terrain not used for farming—namely, the steep mountain slopes and deeply incised stream and river ravines—, are vast forests consisting of bamboo thickets and other bushes as well as tall deciduous and coniferous trees. These forests reach up to the peak regions of the mountains, which surround the valley on both sides with heights of more than 4,000 m. Looking from Drapham Dzong, these mountain ridges block the view beyond to the northern peaks of the Himalayans, which tower 6,000 and 7,000 m.

At the foot of the mountain ledge, on which Drapham Dzong lies, the Chamkhar Chhu makes a sharp bend. Coming from the northwest, where several hamlets are strung together at the wide bottom of the valley, the river turns in a tight curve to the southwest and flows through a narrow, approx. 5-km-stretch of the valley, which is largely uninhabited, but can be clearly seen from Drapham Dzong.

8

1 The spelling of the names of settlements, localities, streams, rivers, etc., is in accordance with the map series «Topographic Maps 1:50 000, sheets 78 I/10, Trongsa/Bumthang (1999)» and «78 I/14, Trongsa Province (1967).»

Fig. 9 View of hill of Drapham Dzong from southwest, with valley road in foreground. W.M.

The main road leading today from Jakar to here up the valley runs on the right side of the river. When the excavations were in progress from 2008 to 2010, the road ended approx. 2 km above the river bend at the groups of houses called Sangsangma and Drumphe at a narrow suspension bridge. This assumedly marks an old river crossing, because the original valley trail, a footpath of different widths, changes here to the other shore. An old pass route, the pathway crosses the dividing line to China/Tibet, at Man La (or Karchung La) between the peaks of Melaghi Kang and Chisanang Ri, and, following the course of Chamkhar Chhu, leads to Jakar. The nomadic yak herders of the region still use this path today for their seasonal migrations.

From the suspension bridge mentioned above, the valley trail rises to the southeast, past the hamlet of Ngang Lhakhang, upwards to the saddle east of Drapham Dzong–where the camp was set up for the excavation team–and descends to the bottom of the valley south of the fortress hill near Sang Ling. Here the traditional routes separate. Running along the left bank, the valley trail follows the course of Chamkhar Chhu until reaching Jakar, while a secondary route leads in an easterly direction over the 3,360 m a.s.l. Phophe La Pass into the Tang valley. Exactly how old these routes and settlement structures are, would still have to be clarified archaeologically. What can be stated with certainty, however, is that Drapham Dzong was erected around the mid-16th century (see 5.2.2.), and, that it did not emerge in an uninhabited area, but arose out of an old cultural landscape.

2.2. Objectives and Critical Questions

The excavation at Drapham Dzong literally meant venturing into uncharted scientific terrain.[2] In 2007, as a prospection on-site of several days was conducted to serve as the basis of the preparation, there were no pre-existing experiences available that could have been used for organizational and archaeological planning purposes.[3]

It was clear from the outset that the excavation objectives and critical questions could not be solely oriented according to the always unlimited needs of research, but rather had to conform to parameters, which were pre-determined by the resources available in terms of time, finances, and personnel. Archeologically, in order to completely expose the ruins area, which occupies a total area of approx. ten hectares, an excavation venture working for years would be required, combined with a solidly established organization with permanent staff and a continuously renewed annual

9

2 The first archeological prospections and probes in the valley of Bumthang (also at Draham Dzong) were undertaken by Reto Blumer. See Reto Blumer, Luc Braillard, *Forgotten Archaeological Sites of the Choskar Valleys in Central Bhutan: the Batpalathang Site near Jakar and the Potential of Bhutans Archaeological Heritage*. SLSA Annual Report 2000.

3 Werner Meyer (in collaboration with Eberhard Fischer and Jorrit Britschgi), *The Bhutan-Swiss Archaeological Project. The Fortification Drapham Dzong in Central Bhutan*. SLSA Annual Report 2007; – Division for Conservation of Architectural Heritage: Drapham Dzong. Bumthang District. Proposal for Conservation of the Site. Department of Culture, Ministry of Home and Cultural Affairs, Bhutan 2007.

10

Fig. 10 Panoramic view of the fortress hill from the west. J.O.

budget. Such prospects were beyond the scope of the means available and would also have been poorly compatible with the pilot nature of the intention of the excavation.

Since the project had to be defined according to the available means, the critical questions, with respect to the scientific level of the investigation, had to be limited to what probably would be attainable. However, because there were no previous experiences upon which the planning could be based, in other words, because there were no comparable research results to be consulted throughout entire Bhutan, the necessity of adjusting the original objectives and critical questions on an ongoing basis with respect to the actual status of the work, was unavoidable. For instance, it soon became clear that the initially intended probes in the areas of the baileys and the valley settlement could not be carried out for various reasons. Therefore, questions concerning these peripheral areas of the compound could not be answered satisfactorily. Accordingly, the excavation of areas had to be limited to the upper fortress zone.

While the objectives defined on the basis of the available means were solidly prescribed from the beginning, in the course of exposure work, further, limiting factors became apparent. The poor condition of the masonry, especially in the area of the Utse (see 3.2.2. and 3.3.2.) made it compulsory to forego the complete removal of masses of debris, which had piled up inside of the rooms that were becoming visible. In certain areas, unexpectedly such a danger of collapse so predominated, despite supporting constructions, that further dismantling of the debris had to be stopped. As a result, several questions, which were connected with the interior of the Utse, had to be subordinated under safety precautions, so that, unfortunately, the curiosity of the researcher remained unfulfilled.

Another aspect affecting the planning also became apparent only as the exposure work progressed. The crowns of the masonry, which had been built with clay as a binder, proved to be very prone to weathering and erosion. Consequently, comprehensive exposure of all the wall crowns—which would have been required in order to be able to draw the top views—had to be foregone. At hand in many places, a humus cover penetrated by grass roots protected the masonry so well, that its removal didn't seem sensible. In any case, through such measures no significant loss of information is incurred.

After the reconnaissance expedition of 2007, which was accompanied by a provisionary primary documentation, the excavation objectives and critical questions could be roughly sketched out. Two offensive directions clearly emerged. On one hand, central concerns were those typical key issues underlying every excavation, namely, dating; the sequence of the settlement and building history; and, the cultural assignment of the findings (see below). On the other hand, however, fundamental aspects of archeology in Bhutan were to be considered. The excavations at Drapham Dzong were intended as a pilot project, which should not only serve the gathering of experience of an organizational nature, but also of basic archaeological knowledge. Thereby, the ruins of Drapham Dzong constituted the scene of a pioneer enterprise, in which almost every intervention in the ground meant a step into uncharted territory. Lacking archaeological experience as a basis, it was not possible to simply proceed according to tested

Fig. 11 Fortress hill as seen from the camp in the east with the workers during the climb before. W.M.

11

schemas, which were known and commonly practiced in well-researched regions. Many of the working procedures developed—that was clear from the outset—as a fast-forward button into the unknown. Uncertainty about the archaeological relevance of what was continuously coming to light and had to be destroyed, called for especially thorough and tightly woven documentation of the constantly expanding finding results.

The routine questions directly related to the excavation object were easily formulated. The primary concern was situating the ruins chronologically. When did the settlement emerge, when was it abandoned? Was the compound violently destroyed or gradually forsaken? The object of exposing the ground plan of the upper fortress structure should serve to clarify the sequence of the building history and the function of each volume.

Other questions were addressed to individual elements of the masonry, to doors, windows and other details, but above all to the anticipated settlement deposits with their inclusions. Beyond that, there was no idea as to what the ground would disclose in terms of finds—pottery, metal, bone, etc.—, as there were no comparable excavation findings, let alone pre-existing find objects. As a consequence, this condition meant that absolute dating, as in archeologically, well-developed regions, could not be supported by typological comparison of artifacts or building forms, but rather only upon natural scientific analyses of organic material. With respect to the complete lack of research-based find categories of ceramic up to this time, there was hope for a yield, which would make it possible to at least set up a provisional typology for Bhutan.

Further questions were also to be raised in relation to the amount, structure, and significance of the finds and findings. Some hoped for insights into everyday life at the Dzong included finding out something about diet, heating, or the water supply. In terms of the masonry, which was to be exposed in places down to the bottom edges of the foundation, information was expected not only which would reveal the building history sequence, but also would disclose building craft practices.

Whether it would be possible to more exactly specify the function of individual buildings or rooms, could only be proven in the course of the excavation, but the overall concept of the ground plan with access, residential, military, and agricultural buildings was to be conveyed by a comprehensive excavation of areas, at least in terms of the main features. What traces the religious life had left behind was an open question at the beginning of excavation, especially since written sources remained silent about a possible monastic settlement. In contrast, already on the occasion of the on-site inspection in 2007, visible remnants of walls hinted that military elements would emerge, after the defense value of the compound could be evaluated.

Rather vague hopes were directed to the possibility of information about the societal, economic, and cultural environment. Here the finds and findings had to speak, whose quality and extent could only be speculated about before the beginning of excavation. Clearly formulated was the aim to gather as much information about the history of Drapham Dzong, its inhabitants, and their way of life. Historical assumptions, which were based on the scanty and legendary literary sources, were not allowed to influence the course of excavations. The excavation results were not intended to provide any confirmation of the written records and oral tradition legends, but rather make their truthfulness verifiable.

What could be expected of the archaeological investigation of Drapham Dzong is that its results make a significant contribution to an evidence-based view of the history of Bhutan. Archaeology does not have the task to confirm myths, and certainly not to provide information about gold and art treasures to be uncovered, but rather to provide information about the past.

2.3. Procedure

The archaeological excavation project at the Drapham Dzong was initiated by the Ministry of Home and Cultural Affairs of the Royal Government of Bhutan in the year 2005. Eberhard Fischer had visited the place the following year and recommended its documentation.

In 2007, I travelled to Bhutan for the first time in order to get acquainted with the site of Drapham Dzong and also to see other relevant fortifications in Bhutan in order to start exploration. My team consisted of Dr. Eberhard Fischer (SLSA) and Dr. Jorrit Britschgi (Museum Rietberg Zurich), and we spent altogether ten days in Western and Central Bhutan (October 29 to November 7, 2007). Upon arrival in the capital Thimphu, we met with staff members of the several Departments of the Royal Government of Bhutan involved in this project. Our goal was to establish a legal and organisational framework within which such a project can be carried out in the future and to determine a three-year plan for such a scientific excavation of a fortress ruin.

12

Fig. 12 Exposure and documentation work in sector B1. View towards northwest. W.M.

13

14

Fig. 13 Superficial excavation of eastern enclosure wall at the time of the reconnaissance of 2007. W.M.

Fig. 14 Transporting stones to the stone deposits. S.S.

During our stay in Bhutan, we not only started to acquaint ourselves with the site, but also had a chance to extensively visit fortification structures similar to Drapham Dzong. These well-kept and renovated sites included the Drukgyel Dzong, the Trongsa Dzong with its adjacent Ta Dzong and the Jakar Dzong (all 16th century and later).

Our visit was made successful by Dorji Tshering (Director of the Department of Culture), Yangki Dorji (Head of the Division for Conservation of Architectural Heritage DCAH), Nagtsho Dorji (Architect, DCAH), Kuenga Wangmo (Archaeologist, PhD student at Cambridge) and Sangay Wangchuk (Culture Officer Bumthang). Helvetas Bhutan most generously rendered us logistical, organisational and financial support and hospitality, namely Werner Külling (Resident Coordinator), Dr. Pema Gyamtsho (Deputy Resident Coordinator) and Tashi Pem (Chief Programme Officer). In particular, Namgyel Tshering (Head of Administration) participated as Helvetas representative. In the field, Fritz Maurer and the staff of the Swiss Guesthouse were most helpful. The Elena Probst Fonds made this first exploration of the site possible with a travel grant.

For the first investigation of the ruin, only two and a half days were available. This tight time schedule forced us (Yangki Dorji, Nagtsho Dorji, Kuenga Wangmo, Namgyel Tshering, Dr. Eberhard Fischer, Jorrit Britschgi and me) to concentrate our activities on the hill crest and its building remains. Trees and bushes on a part of the hill top were cleared thanks to a team of local workers. This action did not only serve to make the still preserved stonework visible for a simple documentation, but also to protect it against further decay caused by roots.

Besides a first photographic survey of the site, the area was organised in several positions, and a provisional first site sketch 1:200 with the still visible walls and an approximate image of the topography was drawn. The south-western corner of the area had to be excluded since there was not enough time to clear this part of the hill top as well. The results of our first endeavour at Drapham Dzong and our proposal for an extensive excavation project was then published in the Annual Report of SLSA 2007: 29–42.

To contribute towards institutionalisation of archaeology in Bhutan and to strengthen the technical capacity of the Department of Culture in archaeology, early in 2008 the three-year Bhutan-Swiss Archaeology Project was jointly executed by the Ministry of Home and Cultural Affairs of the Royal Government of Bhutan and Helvetas, the Swiss Association for International Cooperation, in collaboration with the Swiss-Liechtenstein Foundation for Archaeological Research Abroad (SLSA).

The Drapham Dzong field campaign of 2008 started off in August 2008 with the Department of Culture constructing basic housing and service facilities near the exca-

15

16

vation site for the team consisting of a collective of approximately six Swiss archaeologists, three coordinators from SLSA and Helvetas and six Bhutanese counterparts from the Division for Conservation of Heritage Sites, as well as local technicians from Bumthang and Mongar Dzongkhags (Districts). The camp, beautifully located at the foot of the fortified hillock of Drapham Dzong on a large grazing ground for cattle and ponies, consisted of a U-shaped block of six tin-sheet roofed rooms, a small kitchen unit and several bathroom cubes. It was designed and the construction supervised by Sangay Kinga of the Department of Culture. Very rudimentary furniture, the equipment for kitchen and dining tent, and the basic foodstuff were purchased in Thimpu by Namgyel Tshering, Head of Administration Helvetas, Jorrit Britschgi and Eberhard Fischer and then transported to the camp. Later on, all rooms were furnished with small locally produced iron stoves which proved very important since the temperature fell to minus 6 degrees centigrade during the nights in November and even lower in December. Sleeping bags, some Swiss food, all technical equipment and locally unavailable archaeological tools necessary for excavation were shipped well in advance to the Helvetas office in Thimpu by sea cargo. All this equipment had to be transported via road to Jakar, from there on a farm road up to the Choekhor suspension bridge on a truck, and finally on horseback and by local helpers to the campsite. Water was tapped from a small river, and all camp installations were constructed after the Swiss archaeologists and their Bhutanese counterparts had arrived after a short stop-over in Thimpu and an overnight stay at the Swiss Guest House in Jakar where they were cordially welcomed by Fritz Maurer and his family.

Fig. 15 Opening ceremony at the beginning of the excavation. V.W.

Fig. 16 The excavation area at the beginning; view from the Utze, south-westward. W.M.

Fig. 17 Excavation works, zone E. W.M.

17

Fig. 18 Group photograph at the beginning of the excavation. P.F.

18

The first implementation phase of the archaeological excavation of the main structures of Drapham Dzong's citadel began with an elaborate traditional ceremony performed by local monks on October 15, 2008. The ceremony was attended by the Governor of Bumthang District, Dasho Karma Tshering, the team of Swiss archaeologists led by myself, representatives from Helvetas—coincidentally the board of directors including Helvetas President Peter Arbenz, former Resident Coordinator Werner Külling and the present Resident Coordinator Dr. Walter Roder—Dr. Eberhard Fischer, representative of SLSA and Dr. Jorrit Britschgi, Museum Rietberg Zurich; the entire Bhutanese team and the local community were also present. This intense ceremony was performed in order to appease the local deities to safeguard the site and to pray for the successful implementation of the project and the overall well being of all people involved in the project. Of great importance was furthermore the address of Dasho Karma Tshering, Governor of Bumthang, informing the local community about the importance of the archaeology project, requesting them to participate and offer their work skills: Historic knowledge is to be gained, and treasures not hunted!

Since the ruins of Drapham Dzong were overgrown by dense jungle, the foremost activity that followed the ceremony was to clear the site with the assistance of the local community. Besides the technical team from Switzerland and the Royal Government of Bhutan, the project employed as many local people as possible. Their number depended on availability of local human resources, because the harvest season was not over in the entire valley. The main objective of encouraging the participation of the local community was to raise awareness and implement a sense of ownership among them for the Drapham Dzong archaeological site. Women, men and youngsters of nearby villages worked five days a week from 8 a.m. to 5 p.m. with tea and lunch breaks. Their payment was in line with Government regulations. Twice on Sundays, the team organised feasts for all the local helpers on the campsite, hence providing the foodstuff for the women to cook while the men held a darts competition open to mixed teams.

While excavating the site, the Swiss team provided short on-site training sessions to the local technical counterparts on the methodology of excavation and documentation. Right from the beginning, I determined the areas of excavation and allotted the work sections to my crew. A small tent was erected in the center of the citadel under a tree for shade and protection against rain (we only encountered four days of rain during the seven-week work period). The equipment was stored over night in this tent that also provided space for my drawing table. Our regular meetings also took place here.

19

Fig. 19 Group photograph at the end of the excavation 2008. S.S.

It proved extremely useful that Prof. Dr. med Urs Lütolf, accompanied by his wife Beatrice, had joined the team as «archaeological volunteers» for a period of about two weeks to hold regular medical consultations for our local collaborators. Thanks to the generous gift of the pharmacy of the University Hospital Zurich, he was able to supply the resident community with the appropriate medicines which enhanced the goodwill the project received.

The entire team worked diligently from sunrise to sunset which eventually resulted in excavating a large area of the walls on the upper part of the hill. These excavated walls already provide a hint of an important fortification. Since we were also successful in locating and excavating several pieces of charcoal, the radiocarbon analysis of these charcoal pieces later assisted in determining the approximate age of this fortification. Furthermore, the project excavated several potsherds, animal bones and ceramics.

My team consisted of my former students from Basel University, Silvia Scheuerer (3.11.–7.12.), Valeria Wyler (12.10.–7.12.), Jorge Osantinsky (12.10. 7.12.) and Gaby Weber (12.10.–2.11.); from SLSA, Eberhard Fischer (3.10.–13.11.) and Barbara Fischer (19.10.–13.11.); from Museum Rietberg Zurich, Jorrit Britschgi (3.10.–20.10.) and Peter Fux (12.10.–7.12.). We were visited by Giovanni Antonio Buzzi (Politecnico di Milano) and Yvonne Kocherhans (University of Applied Sciences, Liestal) (3.11.–23.11.), Prof. Dr. Urs M. Lütolf, Medical Director University Hospital Zurich and his wife Beatrice Lütolf-Keller (19.10.– 6.11.).

The Bhutanese part of the team was led by Nagtsho Dorji, DCHS and Namgyel Tshering, Head of Administration Helvetas and comprised Sangay Kinga, DCHS, the engineers Kiba Wangchuk, Nidup Gyeltshen, Sangay Wangchuk, Tashi Lhendup, conservator and Kuenga Wangmo (Cambridge University) as volunteer.

The results of this campaign are discussed in the Annual Report of SLSA 2008, 25–52.

Prior to the second excavation season **in October and November 2009**, extensive preparatory work was carried out on-site. Under the direction of the Division for Conservation of Heritage Sites (DCHS), the archaeological staff's camp was doubled in size, thus providing a more comfortable excavation base. The new premises not only offered more bedrooms, but also an office and a canteen. Due to the camp's improvements it

Fig. 20 View from fortress hill onto excavation camp. In background, cultivated farmland. W.M.

Fig. 21 View over the excavation compound of main fortress. In the front (left), protective tent; in the background, the Utse. View towards north. W.M.

20

was possible to continue with documentation work and finish paper work in the evening hours. Besides the construction work at the camp, wide-ranging forest clearance was also carried out on the fortress hill.

On **October 7**, the excavation campaign of 2009 began with a traditional ceremony on the Drapham Dzong hill; monks from a local monastery performed it in the presence of the local workers and the excavation team.

This time, my team consisted of Anita Springer, Department of Archaeology of the Canton Basel-Land, Silvia Scheuerer, University of Basel, Jorge Osatinsky and Gaby Weber; Nagtsho Dorji, Head of the DCHS, was again project coordinator with Sonam Tashi, Nidup Gyeltshen, and Ugyen from Bumthang; Namgyel Tshering, Helvetas Bhutan, was in charge of organisation, finances and logistics. Our team was once again strength-

21

22

23

24

Fig. 22 Exposure work in sectors Ub/Uc. View towards southeast. W.M.

Fig. 23 Removal of the secondary debris in area Ua. In the background: south-eastern wall of the Utse. W.M.

Fig. 24 Removal of the wall debris in sector L. W.M.

ened by Kuenga Wangmo, University of Cambridge, and as medical doctor we could depend on Dr. med. Stefan Obrist from the University Hospital Zurich which again generously supplied the pharmacy. During this campaign, approx. 50 to 60 local workers and two cooks were regularly engaged.

At the beginning of November, a team led by Professor Armin Gruen of the ETH Zurich visited the excavation site for three days to conduct a photogrammetric survey with drone flights over the fortress area (Peter Fux, Henri Eisenbeiss, Maros Blaha and Martin Sauerbier). Their images were to be used to construct a 3-D model of the fortified hill. Furthermore, Eberhard Fischer, Walter Roder and his wife visited the excavation site.

Besides the archaeological exploration of the fortress, an additional archaeological site was inspected near Kenchosum/Jakar, which had been discovered recently: a cist grave (era unknown), apparently part of a large burial site. The tomb was subsequently documented by the archaeologists, and its scientific exploration was considered urgent and of high significance.

Provided that the daily excavation routine allowed for it, the three Bhutanese engineers were introduced to the on-going specialised works during the entire excavation process. In addition to the «learning by doing» procedures in the daytime, the archaeologist Anita Springer held theory classes in the evening to cover topics on excavation engineering and the basics of archaeology. She had these teaching units and examples of the daily excavation routine compiled as a manual and handed it out along with my general script at the end of the excavation stage.

After 45 days of work in seven weeks, the excavation campaign 2009 was concluded on November 25, 2009 with a feast for the workers. Upon return to Thimphu, the excavation team was invited to present the results of the campaign 2009 to a group of interested persons from the Department of Culture and Helvetas. The results of this 2009 campaign were subsequently published in the Annual Report of SLSA for 2009 (25–60). The actual research and results are published in the Annual Report of SLSA 2009, 25–60.

25

Fig. 25 The excavation team 2009.

26

Fig. 26 Tea break during the excavation. W.M.

In **autumn 2010**, the third and final excavation campaign took place at Drapham Dzong. Thanks to DCHS engineer Sonam Tashi, the camp—enlarged and improved in 2009—was ready for use when the Swiss team arrived and the workers were already recruited, so that work could start without delay.

On October 5, 2010, the final excavation stage formally opened with a traditional ceremony led by three monks at the Drapham Dzong site. Contrary to previous years, the weather proved to be relatively unstable, but the temperatures only fell below zero at night. The workers and the residents extended a very warm welcome to the Swiss team and once again were highly committed to making the project successful.

Two festivities were organised for the workers and their families at the camp. During the Tsechu festival in the neighbouring village at Nga Lhakhang, the excavation team was invited to witness this religious festivity.

This time, the Swiss team comprised Silvia Scheuerer, Jorge Osatinsky, Dominique Oppler, Valeria Wyler and my daughter Gaby Weber, and the team from Bhutan assigned by Nagtsho Dorji, Head of the DCHS as Project Coordinator, consisted of Sonam Tashi, Sangay Kinga, Sumay Tshering, Nidup Gyeltshen, Sonam Gyeltshen and Ugyen Norbu. Our special guest as research associate was Kuenga Wangmo, University of Cambridge, whilst Namgyel Tshering, Helvetas Bhutan, led the project's administration. Approximately 50–60 local workers were employed and two cooks engaged. Dr. med. Karin Hartmann from the Cantonal hospital of Chur accompanied the team as medical doctor. Once again, the excavation pharmacy was provided by the pharmacy of the University Hospital Zurich. Luckily, this excavation stage also proceeded without any notable medical emergencies, so that Dr. med. Karin Hartmann was able to fully devote her time to the patients from the entire valley.

In 2010, we were again able to welcome interested visitors to the excavation site. At the beginning of November, we were honoured by the visit of the King of Bhutan, His Majesty Jigme Khesar Namgyel Wangchuck, and his court, accompanied by the Prime Minister H.E. Jigme Yoser Thinley, the Minister of Agriculture and Forests, H.E. Pema Gyamtsho, and the Minister of Home and Cultural Affairs, H.E. Minjur Dorji. Eberhard Fischer, SLSA project coordinator, his wife and Namgyel Tshering were requested by the Prime Minister to accompany His Majesty.

27

28

Fig. 27 Removal of a layer rich in finds at Du, north of the Utse. W.M.

Fig. 28 Exposure of the staircase to the Utse and the courtyard. W.M.

Fig. 29 Excavation team 2010. W.M.

In addition to the further scientific documentation of the Dzong, several Bhutanese engineers were trained during the on-going fieldwork. Due to the fact that the fieldwork had to be completed in 2010, no evening lessons were held as much time was spent on documentation and inventory work.

After 52 working days, on November 25, 2010, this final excavation season was concluded at Drapham Dzong. We said goodbye to our workers and the Maurer family at the Swiss Guesthouse. Back in Thimpu, the excavation team presented its new results to the Secretary Dasho Penden Wangchuk and the Department of Culture. This brought an end to the third and last campaign of excavating and documenting Drapham Dzong.

The results are published in the Annual Report of the SLSA for the year 2010, 223–244.

29

3. Features

3.1. Overview of the Fortress Compound

3.1.1. Drapham Dzong at the Beginning of Excavation

Immediately before the beginning of excavation in the fall of 2008, what could still be seen of Drapham Dzong were only man-made changes to the terrain and disjointed remnants of walls, which, although suggesting the rough forms of the expansive area of the site, did not indicate any constructional coherence, not to mention a clear ground plan. The dense Himalayan jungle covering the entire site made the task of gaining an overview immensely difficult. Only after clearance of hampering vegetation—« high-trunk » or tall coniferous and deciduous trees and all kinds of head-high thicket had to be removed—were the full dimensions of the compound evident, and in the fragments of walls that were still visible, it was possible to discern an outline of the main architectonic and topographical features.[4]

As expected, a clearly perceptible *upper* or *main fortress* extended on the elongated, highest knoll of the rocky fortress hill. Numerous traces of walls evidenced dense building development. Discernible was the course of a turreted enclosure wall that seemed to inscribe a rectangle. There were no signs of a gate system to be discovered, on the other hand, the outlines of two towers lying on the longitudinal axis of the main fortress could be distinguished. One tower, the smaller, was positioned on the southern small side (zone G), while the other, the larger one—probably the most dominant building of the entire compound, still with the highest rising remains of walls—was situated at the northern periphery (sector T). Its interior having been filled with debris, on top, stood a hut with two parts, which had been erected several years earlier by a Buddhist hermit, who, shortly before the start of excavation work, abandoned the dwelling.

On two terraces lying approx. 10 m lower, expansive bailey areas of the site joined north and southwest of the highest knoll, at whose edges remnants of turreted enclosure walls were distinguishable. Within the interior, on the other hand, only very uncertain traces of any building development were visible. Coursing to the north and south of the bailey areas of the site as they branched off radially on the slope, connecting walls ended at the protruded square towers. At the southeastern corner of the southwestern bailey, another (also tower-fortified) course began, which meandered down in zigzag fashion over the steep, southeastern mountain flank on a terrace at the foot of the fortress hill. With its remnants of walls and a skirting trench, this terrace formed a fortified *valley settlement*. Along its longest axis running from the northeastern bailey outwards to the southeast until reaching the valley settlement, the entire compound of Drapham Dzong measured approx. 500 m.

After removal of the vegetation from the main fortress area, it was clear that voluminous masses of debris extended across its surface. Although only a few remnants of walls were still visible above the ground, this did not mean that the individual buildings had been removed except for a few layers of stone, but rather that most of the masonry must have remained untouched, embedded in the debris. It could therefore be expected that after the removal of the masses of debris that a spectacular ruin with walls several meters high would emerge.

The piles of debris and soil erosion on the steep slopes of the fortress hill seemed to have extensively obliterated the original topography. Outcroppings of natural rock formations occasionally emerged, but definite traces of the former fortress path could not be detected. Although some man-made terracing was apparent on the northern flank below the bailey area of the site, this could not be considered as the remains of the main access, especially since the gate system discovered in 2009 at the southwestern corner of the main fortress (sector Sd) led to the conclusion that the original ascent from the saddle at the eastern foot of the fortress hill approximately corresponded to the alignment of the trail by which the fortress compound can be reached today.

[4] The traces of a small test trench or probe, which R. Blumer had undertaken, were still visible. In 2008 there was no documentation available. R. Blumer, L. Braillard: *Forgotten Archaeological Sites of the Choskar Valley in Central Bhutan: the Batpalathang Site near Jakar and the potential of Bhutan's Archaeological Heritage.* SLSA Annual Report 2000.

Whether individual retaining walls that accompany the current ascent on the slope side date back to the period of the fortress or are more recent, remains an unanswered question.

Thanks to referrals from the local population, a large slag heap on the mountain-side slope opposite Drapham Dzong, about 500 m further to the north could be located (see 4.1.). This was also densely overgrown, but enabled conclusions to be drawn about the existence of an intensively operated means of mining iron. Therefore, this had to be integrated into the surveying part of the project.[5]

3.1.2. Name of the Fortress

Administratively and officially, the defense compound is called *Drapham Dzong*. Whether this designation is historically correct, is questionable, especially since the sources, which are imbued by legends, only enable uncertain statements. In fact, it is not possible to exactly determine, which mentions are even to be correlated with our fortress.[6]

The problem of the name of the fortress is addressed by Yonten Dargye as follows:

> The biography of Gyalse Tenzin Rabgye (1638–1696; r. 1680–95) authored by the 6th Je Khenpo Ngawang Lhundrub (1670–1730, r. 1724–30) mentions the name of the dzong as ‹Drabel› (written as: Gra-sbal), which in the literal sense has no direct meaning. I am [of] the opinion that the author of the biography, while writing his work, must have rendered the local pronunciation incorrectly; so the word ‹drabel› seems to be the corrupt rendition of ‹Drapey› (written as: Brag-phe), the name by which the dzong is locally known.
>
> A caretaker at Threlsaby Lhakhang vehemently argues that the dzong is known only as Draphey Dzong, and that it is not known by any other name. According to Bumthang dialect, the word ‹Brag› means ‹cliff› and ‹phe› means ‹edge› or the one that is ‹the edge of a sheer cliff.›
>
> Some are of the opinion that the name could be ‹Drakbel› (written as: brag sbal): ‹brag› denotes ‹cliff/ridge› and ‹sbal› denotes ‹frog/tortoise›, so the meaning would be: ‹Dzong, which is located on the frog-shaped cliff/ridge.› To be sure, when we look from the other side, we can see that the whole ridge where the dzong was built resembles the shape of a frog.
>
> According to another version, the dzong is called ‹Drapham› (dGra-pham). Drapham literally means a ‹defeated enemy.› It is said that the Choekhor Depa, who revolted against the central government in the 17th century, was defeated by the forces of Choetse Penlop Mingyur Tenpa, after which the dzong was named Drapham Dzong or ‹Fortress of the Defeated Enemy.› However, this version does not seem to be a likely derivation for the name, since the dzong is thought to have been built in the late 9th century.[7]

Considering the uncertain circumstances of the sources, it seems advisable for the time being to use the name *Drapham Dzong* in scientific and scholarly literature.

3.1.3. Documentation and Systematic

In archeology, the following basic principle applies: *Documentation is not everything, but everything is nothing without documentation.* Accordingly, during the three stages of excavation at Drapham Dzong not only was the actual exposure work continuously documented, but also the preparations, everyday life in the camp, and cleanup operations. The Bhutanese and Swiss cadre shared the responsibility for this multifaceted task.

Documentation involved the following aspects:

1. Technical journal
2. Scientific journal (conducted by the project manager)

[5] D. Oppler, R. Soulagnac, V. Serneels: *Entdeckung einer metallurgischen Industrie am Fusse des Hochhimalayas*. Hochwald 2013.

[6] Concerning the written and oral news about Drapham Dzong, see Michael Aris, 2009, Ugyen Norbu, n.d.

[7] Y. Dargye: *Fortress of the Defeated Enemy*. Kuensel, March 29 and 30, 2013.

3. Photo documentation, including intermittent accompanying of the work with video filming
4. Basic surveying of the excavation site at a scale of 1:100
5. Detailed drawings (stone-by-stone) of stratigraphic profiles as well as ground plan and elevation views of built structures at the scales of 1:10, 1:20, or 1:50 (Vertical and horizontal angles were measured and documented using 1/100 gradian or gon unit system.)
6. Accompanying documentation of finds and probes in a photographic inventory
7. Storage of organizational and administrative (selective) records

In 2009 a team headed by Prof. A. Grün (ETH Zurich) created a photogrammetric aerial view of the fortress hill, which formed the basis for a 3D model.[8]

For each excavation stage, the plans and drawings were classified, ordered, and filed according to three categories: overview surveys (V8/1ff.), stratigraphic profiles and wall elevations (P8/1ff.), and stone-by-stone ground plans (8/1ff.).

As a prerequisite for an orderly and overseeable documentation procedure and results, a viable system had to be developed for the documentation process during the excavation. The partially precipitous terrain of the site and disjointed remains of the walls prohibited subdivision of the excavation area of the site according to the frequently applied principle of an abstract grid system staked out in orthogonal fields. Instead, in adapting to the topography and the still recognizable remains of walls spread across the ground, the excavation site was divided into zones of unequal size and shape. For years this system has proven to be suitable for full excavations of fortresses built on hilltops in Europe. The individual zones were designated by uppercase letters, beginning with B. Within the zones, sectors were staked out, which were marked with lowercase letters. The outlines of these sectors, e.g., Ud, were determined in a way that their boundaries followed the trajectory of the slope or abutted the still visible wall courses at a right angle, which ensured optimum monitoring of the stratigraphy, namely the connections or the layers to the masonry.

For naming individual buildings, the already established, common terms in Tsonka and the analogous designations of German/English fortress terminology were used.

The numbering of the individual layers was conducted per sector in Arabic numbers from top to bottom (e.g., Ud. 3), while the individual wall courses were specified according to the succession of their detection, with the letter W (for *wall*) and the year of the excavation stage in order of discovery (e.g., W8/2). Angled walls that nonetheless belonged together were given the same number, but an additional distinction was made by using lowercase letters (e.g., W8/10a). The step-by-step, ongoing expansion of the excavation documentation during the three stages from 2008 to 2010 was based on this flexible system of identifying zones, sectors, layers, and walls.

Statistical compilation of small finds and probes for laboratory tests had to be integrated into the excavation documentation. Since the layers rich in finds were hardly ever deposited horizontally, on account of the uneven topography, there was no need to take a reading of the height per find and probe. It was sufficient to record the affiliation of the layer of the individual pieces, and according to the pre-specifications of the individual layers, to order the entire material in find compoundes (see 4.1. and 4.3.).

Since the small finds material (in particular, the ceramic ones) provided no means of dating—due to the lack of comparative typological material—, the scientific method of radiocarbon dating was particularly important. Probes were processed at the University of Groningen NL.[9]

The scientific requirement that all statements, interpretations, and dating assessments would have to be attested to and verifiable on the basis of the documentation of finds and features is met in full by the system of documentation applied at Drapham Dzong.

[8] A. Gruen, H. Eisenbeiss, M.Blaha, M. Sauerbier, P. Fux, N. Tshering: *UAV Photogrammetry Project Drapham Dzong, Bhutan*. SLSA Annual Report 2009.

[9] J. van der Plicht, Faculty of Mathematics and Natural Sciences, Isotope Research — Energy and Sustainability Research Institute Groningen, University of Groningen.

30

Fig. 30 Stratigraphic profile in sector Nb. Under the wall debris, humus settlement deposit and light-colored building horizon. Underneath, dark backfilling of the foundation pit and natural subsoil. W.M.

3.2. Overview of the Finds

3.2.1. General Remarks Concerning the Stratigraphy

The layer relationships of all the excavation areas of the main fortress were very straightforward. Because Drapham Dzong was occupied for just a single period, there were no complex sequences of settlement or destruction horizons to be found. Stratigraphic disturbances were distinguished only in the uppermost layers. In the interior of the Utse, where during the late 20th century a lama had constructed a solitary hermitage, wall debris had been relocated to the surface. In addition to this disturbance, in the surroundings of this hut there were six postholes extending up to 1.2 m in depth into the debris, apparently traces of poles onto which prayer banners had once been fastened. At the start of the excavation, two of these banner poles were still standing upright. Furthermore, other disturbances were caused by the root system of large trees and also tunnels burrowed through the ground by small mammals, namely mice. All of these disturbances, however, did not impinge upon the archaeologically relevant features in any significant way, as they only affected the uppermost parts of the wall debris.

The whole area of the main fortress was covered with a rather loose, humous, brownish-black forest soil, 0.2–0.5 m in thickness. Soil removal was impeded by the dense root system. Large deciduous and coniferous trees had to be chopped down, and tree-ring dating indicated that they were up to 200 years old. This means that the humous cover constituting the forest soil first settled in the late 18th century, and by that time the walls of Drapham Dzong had already reached their present extent of deterioration.

Secondary debris, consisting mainly of wall stones and clay, appeared beneath this mantle of humous forest soil. It ranged from 0.3 to 8 m in thickness and was divided into flatter or steeper and occasionally cone-shaped debris heaps, which had formed along the decayed walls. In parts, these heaps completely covered the deteriorating walls, but in other areas the uppermost stone layers remained visible. Only the exterior side of the western section of the Utse protruded above the debris mantel—up to a height of about 5 m. Dispersed throughout the secondary debris were small, charred remnants of wood; these may have stemmed either from the interior finishing or from roof girders, but no definite constructive correlations could be established. Moreover, humous lenses, which frequently crop up in ruins and indicate a slow, incremental decay, were not present in the deposits of the secondary debris. The composition and stratification of the secondary debris suggest that the collapse of the buildings and walls at Drapham Dzong occurred relatively rapidly, so that no intermediary humous layers caused by vegetation could even form. A further point to be considered is that after the fortress was abandoned, the walls had no roofs to protect them and may have started to collapse within only a few decades—excluding the consideration of any acts of human violence.

Under the secondary debris resulting from the deterioration of the masonry were sporadic patches of primary debris, which had settled immediately after the fortress had been abandoned, i.e., in the course of its destruction. The primary debris was particularly and markedly pronounced in the interior of the Utse, which was destroyed by fire. Intense heat had reddened the clay and stones. In addition, the primary debris in the Utse also contained several scorched chunks of clay plasterwork and numerous, also larger remnants of charred wood. The actual burnt layers, which were created through the collapse of the wooden construction during the blaze of the fire, are also to be counted as primary debris. For the most part, these layers had metamorphosed into ash and a black charred substance. At the site larger pieces of wood in the burnt layers partially reveal the construction of door and window cladding as well as of the intermediate floors. In addition to the remains of the wooden interior finishing, there were remnants of collapsed substance consisting of clay and pebbles, which had been used to construct the attics of the upper levels.

The primary debris covered the settlement layers, i.e., sedimentations that had formed while Drapham Dzong was still used and inhabited. These layers proved to be of different intensity in character—the thickness varying from 0.01 to 0.3 m—, but they could be detected at most of the excavation areas. There was only one unique layer always to be found, which consisted of grayish-brown or grayish-black, compact and phosphate-rich soil. This layer contained a variety of inclusions, albeit in variable quantities. Practically all animal bones and artifacts as well as precipitated, organic ultrafine particles appeared in these settlement sedimentations. Most markedly pronounced and richest in finds were the settlement layers outside of the enclosure walls (Sa, Na/Nb, and Ud) and which may be regarded as actual garbage disposal sites. In contrast, settlement layers over clay floors installed in the interiors of buildings and over stone paving levels proved to be comparatively shallow and poor in finds. An exception was a settlement deposit in the interior of the small tower (find complex Gm.4), which entailed the remains of a cooking hearth that had collapsed from an upper story. Ground-level hearths, recognizable by their dense concentration of charred wood particulate matter, are also to be attributed to the settlement sedimentations.

Man-made, ground level, walkway horizons are to be considered as a separate stratigraphic category. Two distinct types were observed: stone slab paving and clay floors. The latter consisted of a 10-cm-thick, firmly trodden clay layer interspersed with pebbles about 3 cm in diameter. Such clay floors were mainly installed in roofed rooms, also on upper floors, while stone slab paving stretched over open areas and along gate passageways. Larger stone slabs with irregular contours were artfully arranged to cover one area. The stone slab paving in the inner courtyard (Doche) appeared to have been partially torn away when Drapham Dzong was destroyed. In individual areas (i.a., Go/Gp, Ua/Ue, Ub), the walkway level was created by man-made-leveling of the surface of the natural subsoil.

In terms of the history of construction, one important, but often little regarded layer category is represented in an especially impressive way on the Drapham Dzong site: This pertains to the adding of material laterally to level out a surface and filling in holes, crevices, or sunken areas in short, material that had been brought onto the natural surfaces to create terrace-like leveling of the fortress compound. The original topography was characterized by a narrow, high ridge, steeply sloping on all sides. Huge amounts of debris material must have been deposited inside of the rectangle-shaped enclosure wall—primarily at the longitudinal sides, but during Phase 2, also at the southern flank—to attain a horizontal walkway level for each room or courtyard. In total, an estimated 10,000 m^3 of material must have been dumped on the compound site, which consisted primarily of clay obtained from the immediate vicinity. The presence of scattered particles of charred wood as well as animal bone splinters and ultrafine ceramic fragments confirmed the man-made origins of these mounds. As excavation proceeded, it became increasingly clear that land augmentation had not only been carried out during the initial construction of Drapham Dzong, but also while it was inhabited, principally during Phase 2 of the construction. These subsequent level increases, lateral additions of material, and terracing could be observed mainly in the southern section of the compound (zone F, sector Go, zones L and Z) as well as in sectors Ua/e. Apparently, during Phase 2, the lower-lying ground floors, especially those at the eastern side, were augmented up to the level of the inner courtyard (see 3.3.8. and 3.3.11.). It was difficult to distinguish this lateral fill from the wall debris lying on top of it.

The secondary infill at the periphery of the main fortress, namely in zones, i.e., respectively sectors Fc, Fe, Fh, Ua, L, and Z, were difficult to interpret due to the erosion that occurred after the fortress had been abandoned. However, what only gradually became evident is that the upper settlement layers from Phase 2 together with vast cubic amounts of the underlying infill had been mostly carried, i.e., washed away. Burnt layers from the period of destruction may similarly have eroded away. On account of this

31

Fig. 31 Sector Fg. Walkway horizon of eastern loggia. Screed with erratic gravel. W.M.

Fig. 32 Remains of wooden lintel in shooting opening of room Tc (wall W9/41a of the Utse). W.M.

Fig. 33 Sector Th. Wall W9/41c of the Utse. Imprint in the western gate reveal or sconcheon of a round beam securing the wooden cladding of the gate. W.M.

erosion the spreading of the blaze of the fire, which ultimately led to the demise of Drapham Dzong, could not be completely grasped in terms of the stratigraphy (see 5.2.3.).

The content of the filled-in foundation trenches constituted a special category of infill. This consisted of a heterogeneous material, which clearly differed from the lighter-colored surroundings in terms of the planum and the profile. In places, the upper edge of the foundation trenches was marked by a thin construction horizon approx. 0.5 m in width. It was waste material from the construction process, somewhat distinguishable by particles of chalk whitewash. The foundation trenches had been dug to different depths in the natural subsoil, where this consisted of sandy clay or soft, unstable rock. At several places there was a firmer subsurface in the form of solid rock. This base had been left in its original state, i.e., respectively covered over with fill, or, if necessary, ground out or off, e.g., in the area of the Small Tower (zone G) or the inner gate (sector Gp). The diversity of the in-situ clay and rock reflects the complex composition of the geological structures in the part of the valley where Drapham Dzong is located, which is delineated by a sharp bend of the Chamkhar River. The natural subsoil consists of glacial moraine material, made up of heterogeneous clay interspersed with boulders of various sizes and geological origins (see 3.2.3.).

3.2.2. General Remarks Concerning the Masonry

Although Drapham Dzong's walls and buildings belong to two different phases, probably separated by several decades (see 5.2.2.), the overall impression of the masonry work is very coherent. Constructed of natural stone, the elements are cemented together using a slurry of clay mixed with water. Architecturally important components such as windows and doors (see below) were executed in wood, of which, however, only little pieces have been conserved. Wood was also used for various pieces of wall surfaces and the roof construction, of which nothing in situ has been preserved.

Stones for building the walls came from the nearby vicinity of the fortress compound, and due to the complex geology of this part of the valley, the stones represent different rock types. Considering this variety there are major qualitative differences with respect to the workability and susceptibility to weathering.

Raised walls were erected using a double shell. Foundations built into slopes, however, consisted of a single shell leaned against the rising embankment. The wall filling (or wall core) is striking on account of its abundant utilization of clay. Inserted in this core are horizontal layers of filler stones of various shapes and sizes. The wall shells are not rough hewn or stratified, but rather carefully assembled with only narrow in-between spaces. Stretchers and headers alternate in irregular intervals. In general, the individual stones are only slightly hewn; at most protruding heads on visible surfaces were struck off to achieve an exact vertical plane of the wall line. Exceptionally treated, certain wall elements were meticulously constructed, i.e., window and door openings as well as

32

33

34

corner bracings of the buildings and enclosure walls. Here the rectangular-hewn blocks are to be found in especially high-quality structures. Wherever the wall courses still extend to a height of several meters, the incline of the outer shells clearly measures three degrees.

The masonry work features outstanding butt joints at numerous locations, above all, where different wall courses converge. Only exceptionally few butt joints indicate different construction phases. Most merely reveal that the building stages were staggered. As will be illustrated in more detail later (see 5.2.1.), joints found in pairs in the course of the wall are relics of temporary openings needed for the transport of building materials.

The variable nature of the building ground precluded any uniform design of Drapham Dzong's foundations. In the case of solid bedrock, the masonry work with 3–10-cm-projecting foundation layers rests directly on the natural rock. Where the subsoil consists of sandy clay, the base of the wall sits in a foundation trench 0.3–2 m in depth. The wall shells of roofed structures were covered on both sides with a 3–5-cm-thick coat of clay plasterwork. Minimal residual paint reveals that the exterior walls, especially the enclosure walls and those of the flanking towers, were whitewashed respectively tinted black and reddish-brown.

As already mentioned, wall openings, such as doors, windows, and arrow slits or embrasures, were clad with woodworking. The supporting wooden lintels are, with one exception (sector Gp), either burnt or rotted, which led to severe damages from the collapse of the overlying masonry work. The same applies to the few wall alcoves situated in the interiors of individual buildings. Several door and window sconcheons displayed a striking overhang of three to four degrees. Wherever a doorway had to negotiate level differences, the threshold was divided in steps. These consisted of a core constructed of stones and clay with carefully laid treads out of large stone slabs. Remarkably, these constructions were not interwoven with masonry work of the adjacent walls, even though this would have certainly strengthened the building as a whole. In some places it appears that wooden treads were laid on top of the stone slab treads.

Small holes, approx. 10–15 cm in diameter, in the masonry work probably stem from the erection of the scaffolding, while the large, upright-aligned rectangular putlog or girder holes, with a side length of 20–40 cm and a depth of up to 1 m, suggest that they served to support the load-bearing girders of the intermediary floors in the interior and the balcony consoles at the exterior walls. For larger spaces one or two crossbeams supported the load-bearing girders. Such putlog or girder holes could be observed in the Utse, in the Small Tower as well as in the eastern and western tracts.

Since no notable amount of stone debris has been removed from the main fortress of Drapham Dzong after the abandonment, it's possible to calculate the original height

35

Fig. 34 Sector Nb. Lower edge of foundation of wall W9/59, erected on natural deposits. W.M.

Fig. 35 Sector Ud. Foundation area of wall W9/49. Dark coloration of backfilled foundation pit stands out from light-colored, natural subsoil. Building horizon is discernible as white band. View towards northwest. W.M.

Fig. 36 Sector Tc, interior of the Utse. Shooting niches in danger of collapse in wall W9/41b. Supporting wall rubble could not be removed further. W.M.

36

Fig. 37 Sector Gm. Stratigraphic profile with burnt debris of collapsed hearth in small tower. W.M.

37

of the most important buildings from the dimensions of the preserved walls as well as the volume of the wall debris (see 5.2.3.).

Also to be mentioned here is the fact that no walls made of stomped cast clay have been detected at the main fortress of Drapham Dzong, even though such walls are by no means unknown in Bhutan.

3.2.3. Natural Topography

The appearance of the Drapham Dzong hill before the construction of the fortress compound can only be broadly reconstructed. Certainly it can be stated that no precursor compound had ever stood on the knoll where the main fortress and both baileys are arranged in a stepping configuration. In contrast, the age of the valley settlement is still to be determined, but it is likely that some sort of settlement associated with the longstanding route over the pass could have existed before construction of the fortress began. Site excavations could shed further light on the issue.

Although there are outcroppings of bare rock in several places on the fortress hill, the compound as a whole does not consist of bedrock, but rather quaternary sedimentations, which consist of sandy, and, in part, compact layers of compressed clay interspersed with boulders of various sizes and shapes. Many rock types occur. Those that have been documented and identified, predominantly include gneiss, granite, coarse-grained white marble, and various types of slate. Apparently these represent so-called erratic boulders, which had been carried to the area by glaciers during the last ice age. Radiocarbon dating from the deposit material yielded a value of 38,000 ± 300 years.[10] Respectively, the entire fortress hill consists of moraine material composed of clay and boulders, whereby, as geological analyses have yet to be completed, it has still not been determined whether the hill is the remains of a ground or terminal moraine. In any case, its form is the result of post-glacial erosion, which converted the enormous moraine mass into a hill with steep slopes on all sides. Downpours during the annual monsoons as well as watercourses in the nearby vicinity could have equally contributed to this erosion. The present-day position of the erratic boulders can be explained partly by their sinking as the glacial ice melted and partly by erosion-induced deformations of the natural surface.[11]

In the lower regions of the valley, the Chamkhar River deposited massive layers of gravel, which consists of greatly rounded pebble stones, 10–20 cm in diameter.

The basic topographical shape of the fortress hill can largely be attributed to natural origins, i.e., to post-glacial erosion, even though man-made changes have been induced in various areas by the removal of clay and erratics. The trench at the northern foot of the hill appears to be of natural origins, as is the deeply incised stream ravine, which delimits the valley settlement on the eastern side. The terrain ribs, which the connecting walls extend across linking the two baileys with the protruded fortified towers, can also be described as natural relics of erosion. The tripartite division of the hill knoll, on which the main fortress and the two lower-lying baileys stand, also appears to be a natural formation, even though the present-day, extensively leveled surface could only have resulted from man-made lateral fill and removal of material. The deep trench enclosing the valley settlement towards the north, i.e., towards the higher lying terrain saddle, was certainly dug by hand. The volume of the excavated material might have amounted to almost 1,000 m^3 of debris.

Erosion damage was not observed in the foundation areas of the wall courses, at least not where the foundations could be exposed. Nevertheless, it seems odd that such an extensive compound with this extent of massive structures was built on ground that is quite unstable. This situation calls to mind several medieval fortresses in alpine Europe, which were erected not on bedrock, as one would expect, but rather on highly unstable moraine and landslide debris or on a debris mound. Quite a few of these compounds had to be closed prematurely due to the shifting of the terrain. Apparently, with

10 Radiocarbon sample 10/2: 38 290 BP, +330, -370.

11 For more information on the geology of Bhutan in general, see: A. Gansser, *Geology of Bhutan Himalayas*. New York, 1983. See also: M.C. Meyer et al., «Active tectonics in Eastern Lunang (NW-Bhutan): Implications for the seismic and glacial hazard potential of the Bhutan Himalaya,» *Tectonics* 25 (2006), doi: 10.1029/2005TC001858. In the Sangling Temple, the molar of a mammoth has been preserved.

respect to these structures as well as Drapham Dzong, there were criteria other than the stability of the terrain that determined the choice of location.

Since the fortress hill on which Drapham Dzong was built is covered today with dense, jungle-like vegetation—except for the areas cleared as part of the excavations—, the surface is well protected against erosion damage. The vegetation cover should therefore be disturbed as little as possible during all future undertakings to study and preserve the fortress compound, treating its protective effect with respect so that the existing, loamy, moraine scree is not lost to erosion.

3.3. Individual Excavation Zones and Sectors

3.3.1. Southwestern Front (Excavation Zone S)

3.3.1a. Exterior Gate (Excavation Sectors Sd and Sf)

Before the excavation began, there were no remnants of walls at the Drapham Dzong ruins site that clearly indicated the existence of a gate system. Therefore, a central aim of the excavation was to determine just how and where the main fortress had been entered.

Prior to the excavation traces of several wall courses could be seen along the steep footpath used today that extends up the steep incline from the ridge at the eastern foot of the fortress to the plateau of the southern bailey; however, it was not possible to recognize any overall coherence of the architectonic elements from these fragments. Only one wall angle could be identified, which must have been the southern corner of the enclosure wall (W9/37) surrounding the main fortress. Exposure work was completed in stages from 2009 to 2010. Not unexpectedly, this yielded evidence of a fortified or defensive gate system. Its location is remarkable in that it is situated at the same place where the fortress area is still entered today.

The masonry that was exposed was set partly on the steeply ascending bedrock to the northeast and partly in foundation trenches, which had been dug up to 1 m in depth in the natural sandy clay. The lowermost stone layers of enclosure wall W9/37 protruded over the rock by up to 0.8 m. The ascending masonry of the enclosure wall still showed traces of whitewash. In addition, the enclosure wall was preceded by a low outer wall or bulwark covered with stone slabs, nearly 1 m in width (W10/54).

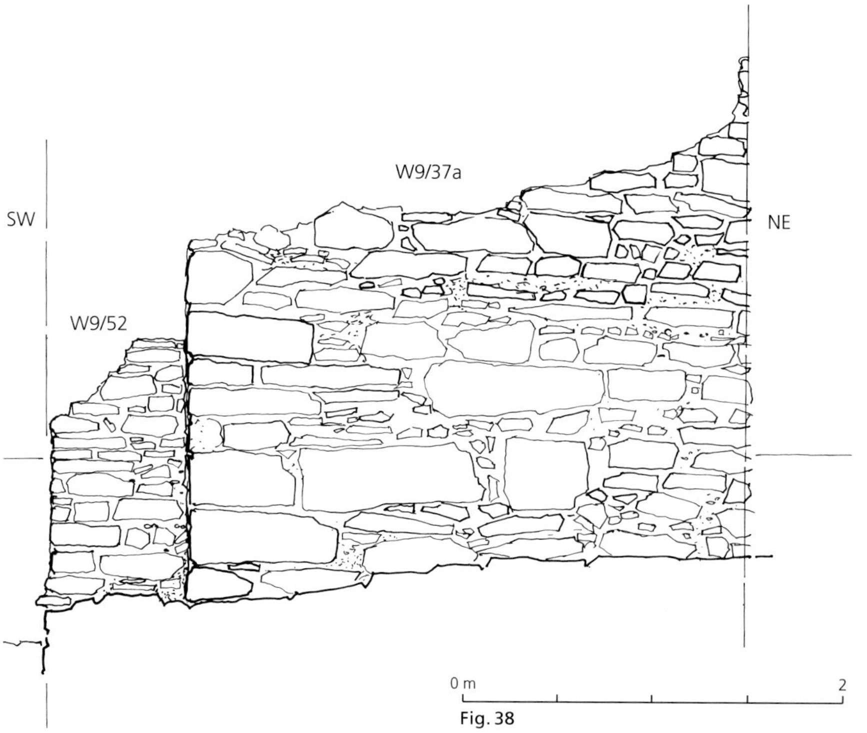

Fig. 38

Fig. 38 Sector Sf. Southern corner of enclosure wall W9/37a. D.O.

39

Fig. 39 Sector Sf. Exterior gate. View towards northwest. W.M.

The actual gate system was connected to the enclosure wall with butt joints (W9/37). The northeastern reveal consisted of a 0.9-m-thick wall stone (W9/52) abutting the enclosure wall. The southwestern reveal formed the end of an angling segment of wall (W9/50) that bends twice at 100°. This wall interlocked across the corner with the straight aligned encircling or ring wall of the southern bailey. In the middle segment of wall W9/50, which was turned towards the entrance, there were remnants of two simple conical (arrow) slits or embrasures oriented towards the gate system. The inner, better-preserved embrasure featured a unilateral, niche-like slot.

The gate opening itself had a clearance of 2.6 m. Its reveals showed no traces of a rabbet other feature for locking. The gate passageway was paved with slabs. Separated by a joint, this surface treatment continued inside the gate. It covered just a few square meters, however, before merging into the compacted clay walkway level of the southern bailey.

An entrance ramp about 3 m in width leading to the gate system ascended steadily from the northeast. It was paved with slabs and bounded on the downhill side by a retaining wall partially pushed out of alignment. Resting on this retaining wall, there was a parapet wall (W9/55) about 0.6 m in width, whose traces were only faintly recognizable. Three steps made of stone slabs led from the upper end of the entrance ramp to the gate opening.

At the southwest edge of excavation sector Sd, wall segment W9/51 emerged, which abutted wall W9/50, ran parallel to the enclosing wall of the southern bailey, and apparently belonged to an elongated building, approximately 4.5 m in width and 20 m in length. The building's walkway level corresponded with the aforementioned (arrow) slits or embrasures and lay about 1 m deeper than the presumed level of the rest of the bailey.

The stratigraphy of both excavation sectors Sd and Sf provided no important information. Secondary wall debris consisting of clay and stones appeared under the forest humus, which was interspersed with roots. This debris directly covered the floor and

40

41

Fig. 40 Sector Sd. Exterior gate. Shooting opening in wall W9/50b. View from interior towards northeast. W.M.

Fig. 41 Sector Sf. Exterior gate system, overview towards south. W.M.

stair steps joined by slabs, without there having been any possibility to observe a settlement layer. Such a layer appeared only on the irregular stone steps at the foot of enclosing wall W9/37 in sector Sf. The humous, dark grey layer, which was only a maximum of 5–10 cm in depth, contained isolated animal bones, a porcelain fragment as well as several iron arrowheads (find complex Sf.3).

According to various butt joints, the gate system must have been erected as part of several construction stages and segments. The majority of these most likely were part of Phase 2. The appearance of the entrance during Phase 1 remains unknown. It may be assumed, however, that the alignment of the entrance path and location of the first gate were not significantly changed by the construction activities of Phase 2.

The stone wall remnants of the gate opening imply wood cladding. Nothing of this, however, has survived. Also lacking is any evidence of destruction by fire, which might become of interest in reconstructing the process of the abandonment of the fortress (see 5.2.3.).

Fig. 42 Sector Se. Outlet opening of drainage channel in walls W9/37b and W9/42. View towards northeast. W.M.

3.3.1b. Stepped Ramp, Second Gate, and Southern Enclosure Wall (Excavation Sectors Sb, Sc, Se, Sg, and Zc)

At the start of the excavation, the southern, narrow end of the rocky hill upon which the main fortress had stood, was covered by a mantel of debris steeply sloping towards the south bailey. Halfway up, disjointed remnants of masonry were distinguished, which could be attributed to a ring/encircling or enclosure wall. Already an initial provisional sketch of the plan completed in 2008 revealed that these wall traces did not follow a single course but rather belonged to two parallel wall segments separated by a gap approx. 4 m in width. This initial feature seemed to imply the location of a gate construction, but an excavation of the area was required to obtain more exact, verifiable proof. This was initially tackled in 2009, but could only be finished in 2010, because, on a stretch approximately 8 m in length, the debris protecting the underlying masonry could only be removed after the excavated material from the southern part of the main fortress (zones L and Z) had been transported down over the steep slope in the bailey.

Exposing the remnants of the wall of the southern front of the main fortress not only led to proof of the expected gate system, but also to some constructional and stratigraphic surprises. As had already been suggested before the beginning of the excavation, a gap opened between the western and eastern segments of the enclosing wall (W9/35 and W9/37b), in which a gate opening had been built. The gate's walkway horizon lay clearly above the level of the bailey and must have been reached by means of a stepped ramp approximately 4 m in width, which abutted the western enclosure wall at a right angle. Only the massive plinth (W9/36) of the outer, i.e., southern part of the ramp, had survived. At both long sides, it consisted of a single-shell wall, and, at the core, a structure of clay and stone. Its surface ascended in steps. However, nothing remained of the stone slabs of the treads. With an estimated width of approximately 0.5 m per tread, the lower segment of the staircase plinth could have included ten steps. These led to the upper segment, namely to a landing measuring approximately 3×6.5 m, which abutted the ring wall (W9/35). The surface treatment of the landing, irregularly shaped but tightly laid stone slabs, had largely survived intact. At the northwestern corner of the landing and directly abutting the course of wall W9/35, the remnants of a 0.5-m-thick parapet wall (W9/36b) could also be distinguished, which probably ran along the entire northwestern edge of the staircase plinth. (There were no recognizable remnants of an analogous parapet wall on the other side of the plinth.)

From the stone-paved landing, the entrance angled 90° to the southeast in the gap between the two offset-running enclosure walls, where the remnants of the so-called second gate were visible. Two steps made of slabs led into the actual gate system cham-

42

43

ber. Its outer or southwestern reveal consisted of the inner course of enclosure wall W9/37, while the inner reveal consisted of a 0.6-m-thick outer wall or bulwark leaned against enclosure wall W9/35. On both sides in the reveals there were holes, recessed flush with the ground level and with a square cross section having a side length of approximately 0.4 m; these served to accommodate a massive wooden threshold and anchor the wooden gate frame. The distance between the gateposts may have measured nearly 2 m.

The gate chamber, approximately 4 m in length, was paved with stone slabs. To the left, i.e., the northeastern side, a lower stretch of wall (W9/56) clad with slabs followed the course of the gate chamber for a length of approximately 2 m, being flush with the reveal, but separated from it as well as from the enclosure wall by a joint.

At the interior end of the gate chamber, a straight flight of stairs led up to the southern plateau of the main fortress. The individual steps—thirteen total—were almost 0.5 m in width. Towards the top, the state of preservation of the steps was increasingly poorer. Towards the northeast, i.e., towards the interior of the fortress, the staircase connected with a retaining wall (W9/38), which continued the course of the western enclosure wall with butt joints, however, with only a thickness of 0.9 m. The wall ended at the uppermost step, where the entrance turned off to the northeast and opened onto a walkway level of compacted clay at the southern plateau of the main fortress (excavation sector Zc). This lay almost 0.3 m beneath the surface of the forest floor and was covered with humous clay. There was no settlement layer present.

To the southwest, facing the southern bailey, the staircase abutted enclosure wall W9/37b with joints. The fusion, however, was still only apparent at the three lowest steps. Further up, the loamy fill, upon which the staircase rested, had slid down over the crown of the badly deteriorated enclosure wall and had carried most of the staircase construction along with it.

At the outer shells of both enclosure walls W9/35 and W9/37b, some special constructive features important for understanding the compound as a whole were man-

Fig. 43 Zone S. Middle gate complex with stepped ramp W9/36. View towards east. W.M.

Fig. 44 Sector Sc. Staircase ascent behind middle gate. View towards southeast. W.M.

Fig. 45 Main fortress, southern front with end wall W9/37b, after conclusion of excavation. View towards northeast. W.M.

44

ifest. At the crown area of the tapered western wall W9/35, a door opening leading into room Lb (see 3.3.6.) was evident. Underneath the threshold level of this door, there were three putlog holes inserted in the outer shell of the wall. Their upper edge corresponded with the landing level of the staircase base or plinth, whereby, however, this covered the third, southeastern putlog hole.

A plinth-like outer wall or bulwark approximately 0.85 m in width and 0.5 m in height (measuring from the lower edge of the foundation) had been built in front of the eastern, protruded enclosure wall (W9/42) along nearly its entire length. The plinth-like outer wall started to the east just inside of the exterior gate (excavation sector Sd) and could be reached from the paved level of the gate by climbing two steps. The outer

45

wall with joints led along the entire length of enclosure wall W9/37 and bent at a 90° angle at the western end to follow the stepped ramp. It ended flush with the ramp's southwestern course.

Enclosure wall W9/37 must have been built in two stages, because in the extension of the gate chamber, evidenced by a step, a distinct butt joint was visible, which, however, was braced or secured by a large stretcher stone. Features midway along the entire length of the wall course proved to be even more informative. Here, at the outer shell of the enclosure wall, approximately 0.4 m above the level of the outer wall or bulwark, a carefully constructed outlet of a canal, approximately 0.2 m in width and 0.25 m in height, appeared. The slab cladding of the bottom and sidewalls protruded approximately 0.15 m beyond the wall course. To catch the water flowing out of the outlet, a collection basin made of slabs had been set into the surface of the bulwark, from which the covered canal ran straight through the outer wall into the open, i.e., over the clay level of the bailey. A gully, approximately 0.4 m in width and 0.1 m in depth, filled with blackish alluvial humus indicated the direction that the water had originally flowed. However, later from the outlet of the canal in the outer wall, a runoff or outflow clad and covered with slabs was created, which diverted the water to the southwest. Apparently this water outlet was the lower end of the canal that had already been observed at the Doche (inner courtyard) and small tower (see 3.3.3.).

The existence of holes at irregular intervals in the ascending parts of both ring walls W9/35 and W9/37 for anchoring scaffolding is only briefly mentioned here for the sake of completeness.

The observation of the stratigraphy generated only occasional insightful features. The entire terrain of excavation zone S, which steeply slopes to the south, was covered by a layer of forest humus, 20–50 cm in thickness, permeated by dense roots, under which lay wall debris consisting of clay and stones. To the south underneath the staircase, the debris also contained flat slabs, which appeared to stem from loosened staircase steps that had slid down the slope. In the middle part of the excavation sector (Se, Sg), the debris contained clay from the collapsed manmade infill from the southern plateau of the main fortress. Aside from the garbage disposal deposits in excavation sector Sa (see 3.3.1c.), there was no trace of any settlement layer anywhere. The secondary wall debris lay directly over the ruins of the wall crowns and slab-paved floors, or respectively, the staircase steps. A humous sedimentation was only present in excavation sector Sb underneath the lower edge of the foundation of outer wall W09/42. This layer, approximately 20 cm in thickness, contained a few anthropogenic inclusions, thereby providing proof that the southern front had been built during a more recent phase. For the most part, the foundations of the wall courses identified in zone S rested on a natural substrate of sandy clay and boulders.

In the angle between the stepped ramp and enclosure wall W9/37 directly over the natural rock level (here elevated), a deposit of round stones, each approx. 10 cm in diameter, appeared, comparable to the feature in excavation sectors Ua and Ue (see 3.3.10b.).

Also to be mentioned here is an important detection: In the entire area of the southern front with ring walls, gate system, ramp, gate passage, and staircase, there were no traces of a blaze, neither in the form of burnt layers nor heat-induced reddening of the masonry.

The dovetailing and butt joints of the masonry indicate that there were various stages and segments of construction. First, enclosure walls W9/35 and W9/37 were erected. At the same time fill material was brought to the southern plateau of the main fortress (zones Z and L). During the next stages both gates in Sd and Sb/Zc were constructed. Finally, the stepped ramp with its platform as well as the outer wall W9/42 were built. All building activities took place, as established elsewhere (see 5.2.2.), in Phase 2 of the entire compound.

Fig. 46 Settlement deposit in sector Sa. Clearly recognizable animal bone remains in situ. W.M.

3.3.1c. Garbage Disposal Deposit in Front of Enclosure Wall (Excavation Sector Sa)
In the angle between enclosure wall W9/35 and the stepped ramp (W9/36), a stratigraphic feature appeared, which was not necessarily to be expected. Before the beginning of excavation, very little of the masonry was visible. The stepped ramp was completely covered with debris, and only a few stone layers jutted out from under the forest soil. After the removal of the debris stratum, which sloped down towards the southwest, i.e., south towards the bailey, a blackish-grey settlement layer (layer Sa.3) appeared. Its rich abundance of finds was surprising. With a thickness of 15–30 cm, it was nestled against the footing of walls W9/35 and W9/36, and, therefore, must have been deposited after their construction in Phase 2. Towards the west and south, i.e., towards the plateau of the bailey, the layer tapered off with a diminishing concentration of finds. Consequently covering an area of approximately 9 m², the layer contained a multitude of finds (find complex Sa.3), primarily animal bones and coarse ceramic fragments. Strikingly, many bones formed coherent skeletal parts, which indicated they were slaughtering waste. Among the ceramics there were many join sherds, whereas metal objects—among them, an iron arrowhead is worth mentioning—were exceptionally rare.

46

Appearing directly beneath the settlement deposit, whose stratigraphy could not be further divided, there was natural clay dispersed among the boulders. Its surface appeared to be coarsely eroded and under the foundations of walls W9/35 and 36 was articulated in steps.

The composition and state of the find material support addressing settlement deposit Sa.3 as a garbage disposal deposit. However, the location is rather to be considered as unexpected. Situated immediately next to the representational entrance staircase that led to the second main gate, a stinking heap of garbage—imagining the stench of decomposing animal cadavers—seems unusual to say the least.

Conducted down to the foundation area, the excavation of wall W9/35 did not expose any masonry at the wall's southwestern corner that could be attributed to an enclosure wall of the southern bailey. Therefore, what the architectonic interconnection between the southern bailey and the main fortress at its southwest corner looked like remains open.

3.3.2. Utse or Main Tower (Excavation Zone T)
Even before the start of the excavation, it seemed obvious that the remnants of an important and once towering building must be hidden in the mighty heap of debris at the northeastern periphery of the main fortress. Wall courses were only discernible in

47

the western part of the heap of rubble, so that the complete ground plan only became manifest during the course of the exposure work.

The parts of the wall that had been visible before excavation—as became evident later, belonging to the second floor—were in very poor condition, especially in the crown area. The corner stones had become chipped, which increased the instability of the remnants of the wall all the more. With individual battlements looming between them, deep breaches appeared to have been caused by the collapse of the woodwork destroyed by fire or decay, robbing the structure of its supporting elements.

Fig. 47 Western section of the Utse. Temporary support of the northwestern wall and first conservation work on southern edge (2008). W.M.

Outside the building, the debris was piled up into a great cone, which reached the uppermost layers of the preserved wall parts. The interior of the building was filled with debris allowing only a few pieces of the wall to be discerned. The fractured points of the breaches demonstrated—not least of all, the destructive impact of the tree roots—all the signs of advanced disintegration. The horizontal course of the wall crown lay underneath a protective humous layer overgrown with grass, which we did not want to remove in order to not expose the wall surfaces to the risk of erosion.

The removal of the debris took place in stages, first (2008 and 2009), from the entire interior surface down to the floor level of the second story, at the outer side, down to approximately 1 m above the presumed height of the threshold of the entrance in wall W9/41c. In a second stage of work (2009 and 2010), the partial exposure of the walkway levels inside and outside of the building took place. This way of proceeding had several advantages: first of all, with the removal of the upper debris layers, it was unnecessary to be concerned about archaeologically relevant features; secondly, the interruption of work on the upper removal levels made the documentation of the high-lying wall parts easier. Moreover, removal in stages guaranteed increased protection against the collapse of the unstable debris profile and provided more efficient removal of the excavated material, which consisted of stones and clay.

While attempting to remove the lower masses of debris in the interior of the building, as well as before the northeast front from the entire surface area down to the original walkway level, respectively to the natural substrate, difficulties emerged, which forced ending the project earlier than had been planned. Aside from the disintegrating state of the northeastern wall (see 3.3.5a.), the cause was the obvious extremely bad condition of the masonry, namely, the window niches at the ground floor, which were in severe danger of collapsing internally. Upper, partially overhanging segments of the wall, which had shifted from their original positions, could be temporarily stabilized with wooden stays. Completely uncovering the building interior without extensive safety precautions—for which we lacked any means—would have entailed the risk that the ruins might collapse with catastrophic consequences. Therefore, we had to be content with creating a planum halfway up the debris layers and only excavating down to the original walkway level in places where there was no safety risk (see 3.3.2c.). The dangerousness of the situation was apparent in 2009 during the removal of the debris in sector Tc when the wall mantle above the (arrow) slit or embrasure niches in the southeastern wall (W9/41b) suddenly collapsed, whereby, with the debris gone, the decaying wall lost its support. Luckily, no one was injured.

The removal of the debris at the upper level inside and outside of the building allowed its general form to clearly emerge: a rectangular structure, approx. 17.4 × 11.4 m with an outer wall thickness of 1.8 m (W9/41a–d). Two transverse walls (W9/39 and W9/40) divided the interior into three nearly equally sized rooms (excavation sectors Ta, Tb, and Tc). The outer shells of the building were inclined 3°, which is typical for tower structures in Bhutan. Extending to the uppermost, still preserved segments, the inner wall shells—stones, clay, and clay plaster—were heavily discolored red to a depth of 4 cm, obvious evidence of a devastating fire, of which the traces were to become even more distinct in the deeper layers overlying the walkway levels of the ground floor (see 3.3.2e. and 3.3.2d.).

With a wall thickness of 1.8 m, the building was the sturdiest of all the structures belonging to the main fortress. The height of the still preserved walls as well as the volume of the mass of the debris suggests an estimated height of nearly 25 m (see 5.2.3.). Accordingly, the building can be acknowledged as the main tower (Utse).

In the remaining part of 3.3.2., the features will be presented section-by-section relative to the individual excavation sectors, which are nevertheless sometimes separate from each other and sometimes interconnected.

3.3.2a. Open Staircase and Forecourt (Excavation Sectors Te and Tg)

The side of the Utse facing the inner courtyard (Doche) was exposed along its entire length, so that excavation sectors Te and Tg were connected to the adjacent sectors Kc and Ub. Under the steeply ascending wall debris lying against the wall of the Utse (W9/41c), which was removed in two stages in 2009 and 2010, a number of important features emerged that essentially contributed to understanding the Utse both in terms of its construction as well as function.

Underneath the wall debris, the entire exposed area of the inner courtyard in Te and Tg (6 m in width and 15 m in length) was fitted with a carefully paved slab flooring. The individual slabs, irregularly shaped and unequal in size, were tightly arranged. To the northwest and southeast they abutted with joints against the low and narrow coursing walls W8/9c and W9/33 (see below), yet extended under the plinth of the open staircase, which led to the entrance of the Utse. At the base this flight of stairs defined a rectangle measuring 6.5×3.2 m and encompassed five steps, each ranging from 20–25 cm in height and with a width of 35 cm. The individual steps, made of slabs, were damaged to varying degrees, yet their original shape was still clearly discernible. The entire plinth of the staircase was more than 1 m in height, the uppermost step lay at the same height as the stone threshold of the entrance to the Utse, which was separated from the threshold by a joint.

Fig. 48 Sectors Te, Tg, Ti. Forecourt of the Utse with open staircase and entrance. W.M.

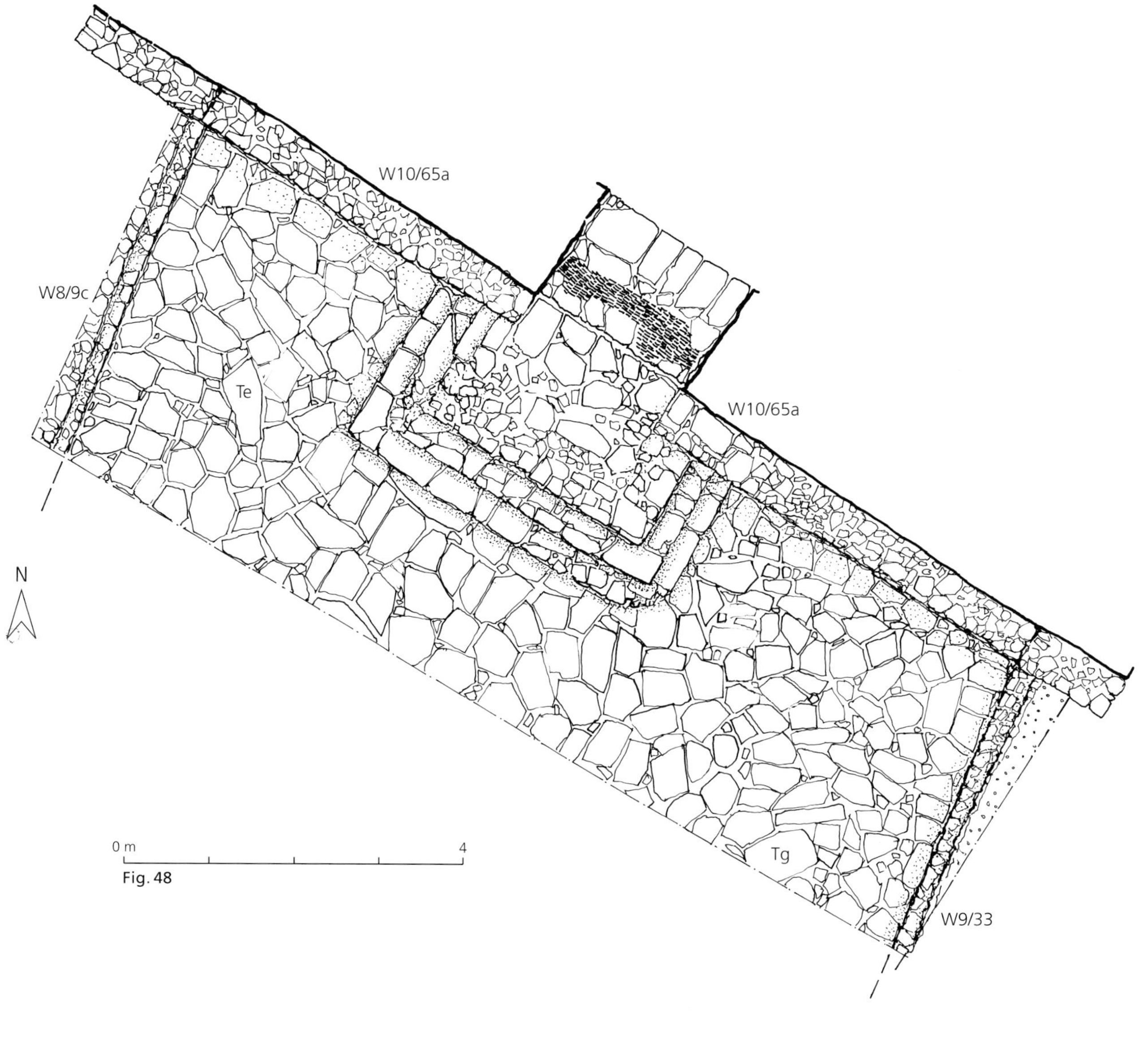

Fig. 48

Fig. 49 Utse, overall view, looking towards northwest. W.M.

Fig. 50 Stratigraphic profile in forecourt of the Utse, sector Te.
A Removal level 2009,
B Upper edge of open staircase,
C Slab paving of interior courtyard.
1 Secondary debris.
2 Primary debris, clay with burnt particles.
3 Burnt layer. Overheated clay, charred wood.
4 Settlement layer, humus.
W.M.

49

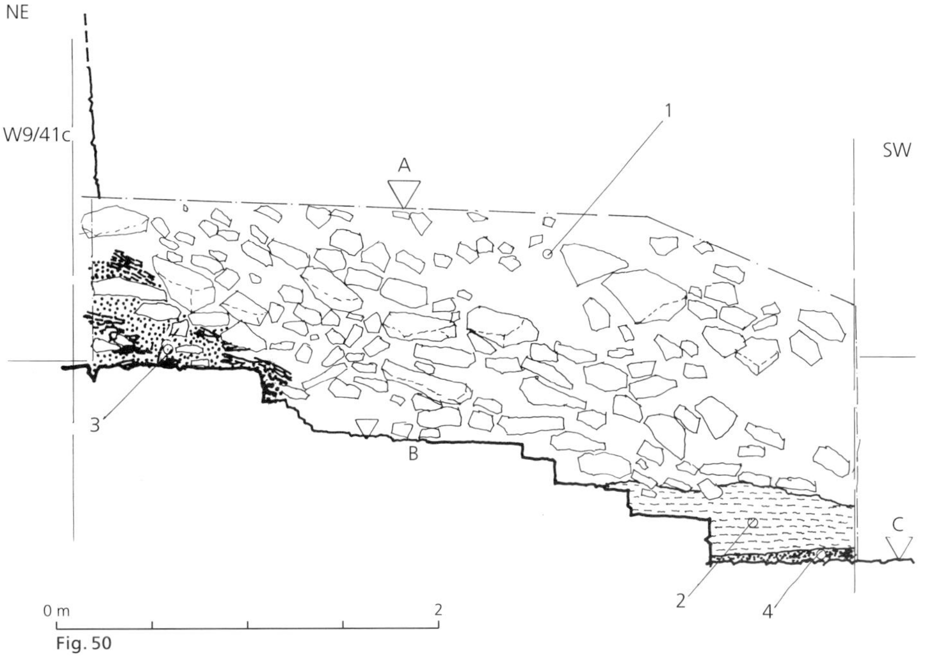

Fig. 50

The slab steps of the staircase plinth were interlocked with the adjacent left and right walls W10/65a and W10/65b. These two wall courses, 65 cm in thickness, nestled with butt joints against wall W9/41c of the Utse. Their height, measured from the slab paving, amounted to only approx. 1 m, which somewhat corresponded to the level of the uppermost stair step. Since a 5-cm-thick humous settlement layer lay on parts of the wall crown, it cannot be assumed that both walls were once higher. Both wall courses abutted the courtyard paving slabs with joints. Originally W10/65a and W10/65b did not run along the entire length of the Utse wall W9/41c, but ended with a cleanly joined front before walls W8/9c and W9/33, which extended to the foot of the Utse. These two narrow, parallel-running walls formed the northern end of the foundations observed further south in zones F and G, upon which the wooden structures of the protruding loggia corridors of the eastern and western wings rested. The courtyard-side notch for securing the threshold beam was still clearly visible. Later, after both walls W10/65a and W10/65b had been extended to the corner of the Utse (W10/68a and W10/68b), the threshold beams were incorporated into the new wall structure, of which two putlog holes with wood traces still remain.

51

52

Fig. 51 Sectors Te and Tg. Representatively designed forecourt of the Utse. Plinth walls on both sides of open stairs assumedly served for setting up sacral equipment. View towards east. W.M.

Fig. 52 Sectors Te/Tg. Final exposure work on the open staircase to the Utse. View towards northwest. W.M.

From these features the following relative chronology of the construction sequence in sectors Te and Tg could be construed: First, the wall of the Utse (W9/41c) is erected. This is followed by the two foundation walls of the loggia corridors W8/9c and W9/33. During the next period of work, i.e., simultaneously in several different areas of work, the courtyard paving, the plinth of the staircase and corollary walls W10/65a and 65b are created. The last step of the work includes the extensions (W10/68a and 68b) of the corollary walls to the corners of the Utse.

The stratigraphy of excavation sectors Te and Tg yielded little information about the sequence of construction, but some hints as to the demise of Drapham Dzong (see 5.2.3). Lying under the secondary and primary debris, a burnt layer, tapering out to the southwest, originated from the interior of the Utse (see 3.3.2e). The lower steps of the staircase were directly covered with primary debris. In contrast, appearing elusively only in part in the joints between the stone slabs, a thin, 1–5-cm-thick settlement layer of greyish-black soil extended out over the slab pavement of the courtyard and on corollary wall W10/65. As a whole, rather poor in finds, in excavation sector Te there were small fragments of porcelain and imitation porcelain vessels, and in excavation sector Tg, a dozen lead musket balls of various calibers, some of which were misshapen (find complex Te. 4). No artifacts were found in the burnt layer on the uppermost steps.

3.3.2b. Northwestern Interior Room (Excavation Sector Ta)

As previously suggested, only the first upper floor in the northwestern interior space of the Utse was excavated completely. The upper parts of the masonry were in bad condition and had to be secured with wooden stays. The window opening in the northwestern wall (W9/41d) was closed up using a dry-stone method, thereby protected from imminent collapse.

The inner wall shells showed clear traces of an intense blaze. The stones and the clay mortar had been heat-reddened up to 4 cm below the surface, the stones of the mantel, more or less disintegrated by fire depending on the resistance of the rock type. There were no plaster remnants on any masonry surfaces.

At the height of the material removal level in excavation sector Ta, no parts of northeastern wall W9/41 had been preserved. At the edge of the excavation sector, where the coursing wall might have been expected, it was necessary to excavate deeper so that at least parts of the vanished course could still be registered. An image of advanced destruction emerged through the feature. Due to a crack, the inner edge of wall W9/41a had loosened at the corner abutting W9/41d and was tilted outward along its whole length. Therefore, further exposure appeared too risky. The most important feature was delivered in the northeastern inner corner of room Ta, where outer wall W9/41a and inner wall W9/39 intersected. In the part where the two walls merged, the latter showed a cleanly joined front side, thereby indicating that it must have been built later against—at this height, in the meantime vanished—the outer wall (W9/41a). In the exposed lower layers the two wall courses, however, displayed an obvious dovetail, which, however, was badly damaged as a result of the tilting of wall W9/41a. The feature enabled important conclusions to be drawn about the construction process (see 5.2.1.).

In the southwestern wall of the room, seven putlog holes had been inserted, which marked the partition height between the ground floor and the first upper story. The putlog holes exhibited heavy fire damage, but their alignment, as far as could be discerned, corresponded to the ceiling construction of room Tc (see 3.3.2d.).

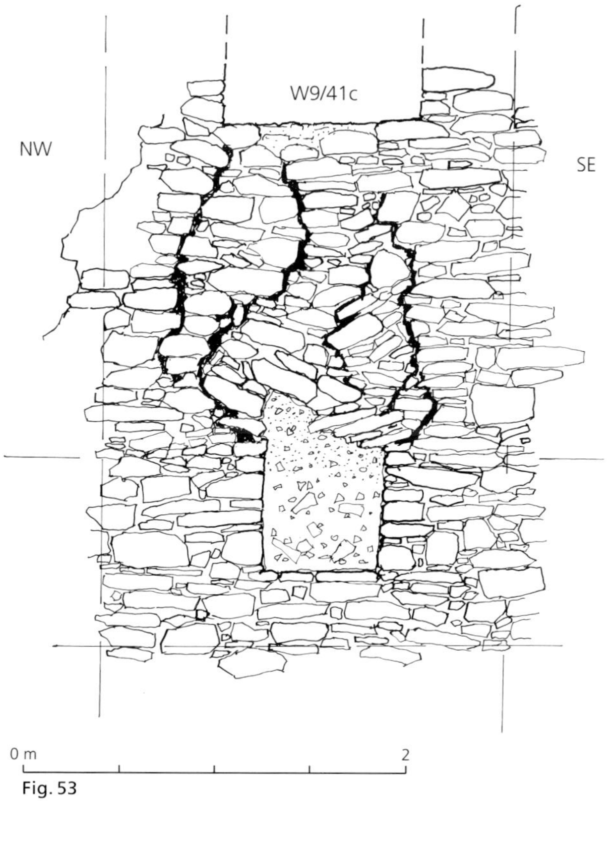

Fig. 53

Fig. 53 Southwestern outer wall W9/41c of the Utse. Window opening to room Ta. Collapsed lintel. A.S.

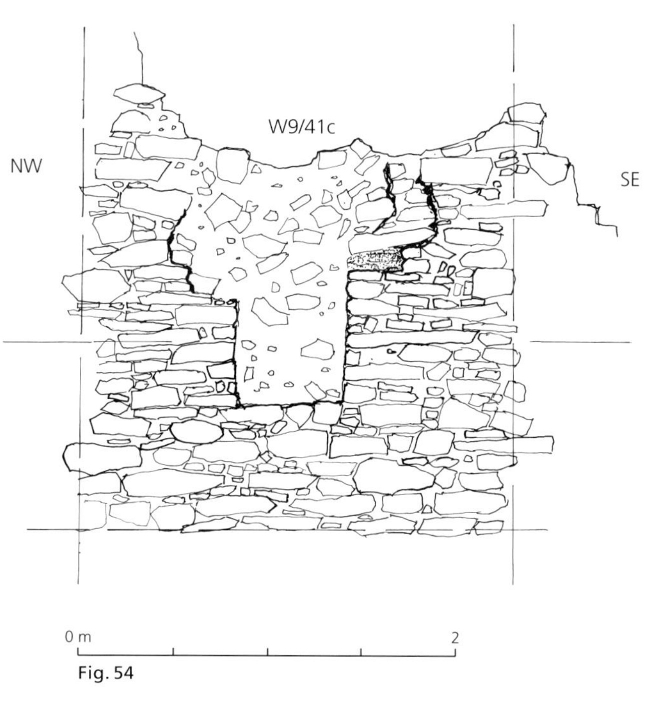

Fig. 54

Fig. 54 Southwestern outer wall W9/41c of the Utse. Window opening to room Tc. Collapsed lintel. A.S.

55

Fig. 55 Interior of the Utse, northwestern interior room Ta. In the front (right), interior wall W9/39. View towards southwest. W.M.

In the southwest and northwest walls (W9/41c and 41d) at the first upper story level, there were two very heavily damaged window openings. They opened to the outside, not in (arrow) slits or embrasures, their reveals intersecting the wall transversely along its entire width. There were no preserved traces of wooden cladding, namely, of the window lintels, which by their loss—probably as a consequence of the fire—could have led to the collapse of the entire wall structure lying at a higher level. The sill of the window opening in the southwestern wall W9/41c contained a step flush with the outer casing, approximately 0.2 m in width and 0.1 m in height, while the window sill in the northwestern wall W9/41d was so badly damaged that no more details could be observed.

Room Ta also possessed two window openings at the height of the ground floor, a narrow (arrow) slit or embrasure in northwestern wall W9/41d and a square window in southwestern wall W9/41c. Both openings were visible only from the exterior, therefore, no statement can be made about their condition in the interior or the shape of the window niches.

At a fracture in the crown area, northwestern wall W9/41d indicated an opening, which could not be more precisely defined. Positioned high above the floor level of the first floor, this feature could possibly be the remnants of a flue.

3.3.2c. Middle Interior Room (Excavation Sector Tb)

The entrance to the Utse, which lay directly on the main tower's transverse axis, led into the middle interior room, which at the beginning of excavation was filled to such an extent with wall debris that only slight remnants of the sidewalls, the interior partitioning walls W9/39 and W9/40, were visible. The northeastern end, the middle part of wall W9/41a, was no longer to be seen at all, not even after the removal of 3 m of debris. The same fire damage that was present in the adjacent sectors Ta and Tc was also observed on the wall shells of room Tb. Only a few surviving remnants of the southwestern outer wall (W9/41c) protruded out of the debris, because over the collapsed entrance, which

Fig. 56 Sectors Th and Ti, Entranceway of the Utse. Burnt layer,
1 upper frame of joists,
2 lower frame of joists.
W.M., G.W.

only emerged during the course of the excavation, there was a huge, gaping breach. Since also only deeply embedded remnants of the northeastern outer wall survived, no holes for the ceiling beams between the ground floor and first upper floor could be observed in the middle room. Two putlog holes lying across from each other in the interior partitioning walls W9/39 and W9/40 may have stemmed from a joist, which—analogous to the construction in room Tc—had supported the ceiling beams (see 3.3.2d.).

The two internal partitioning walls W9/39 and W9/40 evidenced large, deeply extending breaches at their southern ends. These were caused by the collapse of the wall structure over the doors leading from room Tb at ground level into rooms Ta and Tc (see 3.3.2e.).

3.3.2d. Southeastern Interior Room (Excavation Sector Tc)

Before the beginning of excavation, the contours of the southeastern interior room were no longer visible. After they were uncovered (2009), it became apparent that the room had the same dimensions as room Ta. Accordingly, the tripartite division of the Utse followed the principle of axial symmetry along the northeastern-to-southwestern transverse-running middle axis.

For reasons already mentioned, the exposure of room Tc had to be ended prematurely. Nevertheless, some important details of the masonry could be observed and documented. As in the other two rooms, the inner shells of all the wall courses displayed the characteristic damage and discoloration caused by the effects of fire. In the window openings of the first upper floor, which had survived—albeit without lintels—in the southeastern and southwestern walls, clear remnants of the wooden cladding could be detected. The position of the wood traces indicated paneling along the reveals and a wooden wall spanning the window opening.

The floor of the first story was supported by seven beams, whose notches, in the form of square holes in the southwestern wall of room Tc, were still completely intact, although heavily damaged by fire. On the opposite side, where wall W9/41 had eroded down to well under the level of the load-carrying beams, there were no corresponding putlog holes. On the contrary, in walls W9/41b and W9/40 the slots for two joists could still be verified, which had served to prevent the roof construction from sagging. Whether the joists were further supported by columns, as was evidenced in excavation sectors Ka and Go, had to remain open, because the walkway level of the ground floor in room Tc could not be cleared.

From the exterior, at the height of the ground floor, wall course segments W9/41b and W9/41c exhibited various window openings, a narrow (arrow) slit or embrasure in the southeastern wall, and two small rectangular windows in the southwestern wall. Unfortunately, the window niches could not be explored from the room's interior. With the slit or embrasure in the southwestern wall, when trying to expose the window niche—which had been robbed of its wood supports—the entire upper wall structure threatened to cave in, which made immediate emergency stabilization measures mandatory and necessitated abandoning an analogous plan for [exposing] the window niches in the southwestern wall.

Only a very few remnants of the northeastern wall (W9/41a) of room Tc survived. From within excavation sector Ud, these could at least be partially cleared of debris, whereby at the ground floor level a (arrow) slit or embrasure appeared, whose constructive details deserved special attention. In terms of the typology, it corresponded

57

Fig. 57 Sector Tc. Southeastern interior space of the Utse. Shooting opening in wall W9/41a. View towards southeast. W.M.

Fig. 58 Sector Th. Entrance to the Utse. Above the slab level, charred remains of wooded threshold. W.M.

to the same type of (arrow) slit or embrasure that could be observed in excavation zones F, S, and U. Although the lintel was missing, several wooden remnants were preserved in the bearing supports at the side over the reveals. A large piece of a beam was striking, as it seemed separated, flush with the reveal—and not somewhat mutilated by fire—an observation, which should prove important for the interpretation of the destruction process (see 5.2.3.).

The sidewalls of the (arrow) slit or embrasure niche as well as its bottom, including a step before the conical tapered mouth, were coated with clay plaster, 3–4 cm in thickness. This had survived throughout, but its blackish-red discoloration clearly indicated traces of high heat. There were only a few stones from the (arrow) slit or embrasure preserved *in situ*, but these still enabled recognition of the exact shape of the (arrow) slit or embrasure mouth.

In sector Tc the walkway level of the ground floor could not be reached anywhere. No artifacts were found in the dismantled layers of the secondary and primary debris.

3.3.2e. Entranceway (Excavation Sectors Th and Ti)

58

From beyond the entrance in the Utse (excavation sector Th) in the area of the middle room Tb, an area of approximately 3 × 3.5 m could be excavated down to the walkway level of the ground floor (excavation sector Ti)—despite the risk of the collapse of the wall and debris masses. The excavation not only permitted observations of the lower parts of the masonry, namely the entrance area and the two doors in the side rooms, but also of the burnt layers, which had been deposited by the destruction of the Utse.

The masonry entrance to the Utse, accessible from the Doche (inner courtyard) via an open staircase (see 3.3.2a.), was 2.5 m in width, a span, however, that did not correspond to the width of the door opening. In the reveals there were putlog holes, which didn't serve in locking the wings of the door—even though they were mutually offset—but in securing wood cladding. This also included a wood threshold, approximately 35 cm in width, for which a base assembled from small stone slabs had been carefully prepared in the middle of the passage.

At the upper edge of the reveals, signs of the support beams were visible, enabling the calculation of an estimated entrance height of approximately 3 m. The gate's 2.5-m width—not including the wooden cladding—rather suggests there was a two-winged door. Pivot bearings or door hinges did not surface, but were probably embedded in the wooden doorframes. The only surviving traces of the wood threshold were black burnt remnants on the stone base.

Excavation sector Ti in the interior of the Utse was defined at the sides by the internal partitioning walls W9/39 and W9/40, which, each 0.5 m from the inner edges of the gate opening, abutted with joints against the outside wall W9/41c of the Utse. Beneath the breaches, which had shifted the upper parts of the internal partitioning walls into a threateningly unstable state, two doors became apparent. At ground floor level they led from the middle room Tb beyond to the side rooms Ta and Tc. With widths of 1.5 m and 1.3 m respectively, they were clearly more modestly dimensioned than the entrance gate. Sizable, parallel-lying remains of charred wood from the lintel beam lay on the bearing above the reveals.

The stratigraphy of the lower layers observed in sector Ti was characterized by the very clearly burnt remnants. Lying under the secondary debris, 3–4 m in thickness, there was a layer of primary debris about 1 m in thickness, which contained numerous particles of charred wood along with stones and clay. The primary debris rested on an upper burnt layer of heterogeneous material discolored by heat, which consisted of burned stones and clumps of clay, fragments of burnt clay plaster, and larger pieces of charred, splintered wood. After being carefully exposed, the latter permitted a better understanding in planum of the interior fittings. Mainly stretching from the northeast to the southwest, numerous beam fragments showed an arrangement similar to what could

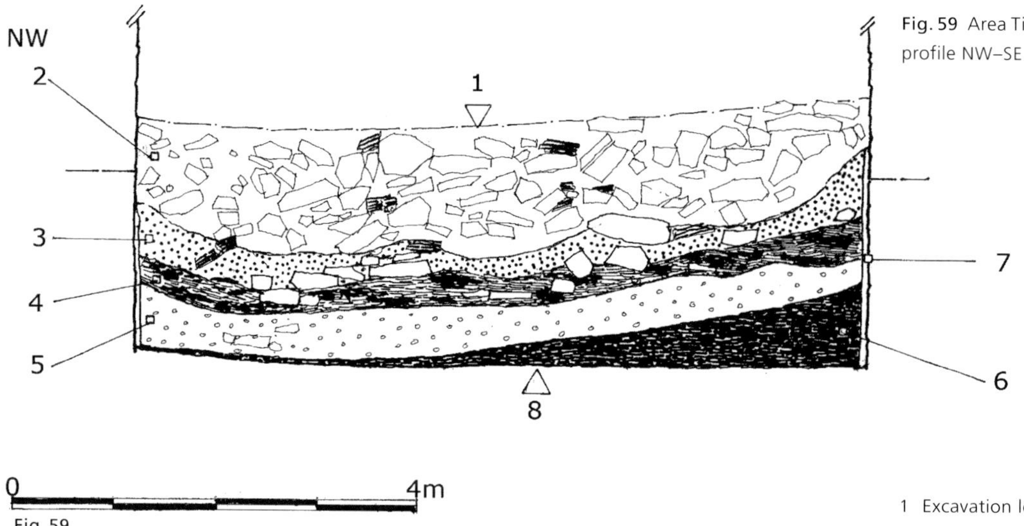

Fig. 59

Fig. 59 Area Ti, interior of the Utse, layer profile NW–SE. W.M., K.W.

1 Excavation level 2009.
2 Secondary debris.
3 Primary debris.
4 Upper burnt layer.
5 Discharged, yellow clay.
6 Lower burnt layer.
7 Clay plaster in situ.
8 Walking level made of clay and pebbles.

be deduced from the putlog holes in the laterally situated Ta and Tc rooms. The upper burnt layer continued through the gate opening, tapering off on the upper landing of the open staircase (see 3.3.2a.), where the wood remnants maybe originated from the bordering edge of the gate and not from the interior of the Utse.

The upper horizon of the burnt layer extended sideways along walls W9/39 and W9/40 up to 2 m above the walkway level. Up to this height there was clay plaster *in situ* on the walls. Through the heat of the fire, it had been variably discolored gray, black, and yellow-red to dark red. In places the plaster was crumbling and seemed about to come loose from the wall.

Lying underneath the upper burnt layer on the entire excavation sector Ti and tapering off over the gate threshold in excavation sector Th, there was a compact, yellow layer of clay approx. 20 cm in thickness. Dispersed throughout it were pebbles 2–3 cm in diameter. The layer must have been the remnant of an entire clay floor or screed that had collapsed from an upper story. Up to a depth of 3–4 cm, the upper horizon of the clay layer exhibited a reddening brought about by heat, proof that the material of the upper burnt layer must have still been glowing and burning when it fell onto the already collapsed clay floor.

The clay floor completely covered the lower burnt layer. Being 30–80 cm in thickness, it consisted solely of charred plant substance disintegrated into small particles. Structures or contours of individual elements were not discernible. The layer rested directly on the clay ground, which formed the walkway level of the ground floor. The clay of the floor was heavily strewn with pebbles. A settlement layer was not observed, however, in the interstitial area between the walkway level and the lower burnt horizon, occasional artifacts were found (find complex Ti.6). Even though the exposed excavation sector comprised only a fraction of the entire interior, it may be assumed that the Utse was completely emptied out before the fire.

The stratigraphy in the interior of the Utse allows the following reconstruction of the destruction process: The interpretation of the features are based on the analysis of documentation kindly provided by Lieutenant Colonel R. Bopp, Chief of the Basel-Stadt Fire Department. After the evacuation of movable goods and the partial removal of re-useable wooden structural elements, easily combustible material (straw, hay, brushwood, or something similar) are placed in the lower stories and set on fire, so that the building burns from bottom to top, causing the formation of lower burnt layers. Then, robbed of its supports, the clay floor or screed crashes down from an upper story as a compact mass, and finally the strong beam construction, namely, what is part of the roof construction, caves in. Thereby, the upper burnt layer is created. Through the still burning or glowing wooden elements, the surface of the already collapsed clay floor

Fig. 60 Sector Lf. Stratigraphic profile of front southeastern wall of small tower. W.M.

or screed is discolored red. At the end of the catastrophic fire, whatever had been damaged, but did not immediately collapse, eventually becomes detached and is deposited over the upper burnt layer as primary debris.

Based on the excavation features, the attribution of this sequence of destruction, which can be convincingly reconstructed from the stratigraphy, to the impact of a military conflict, can be accepted with a high degree of probability (see 5.2.3.). In any case, natural causes of fire, e.g., lightning, careless handling of an open flame, or some other unfortunate accident, have to be excluded as possibilities. What is certain, however, is that the Utse was never rebuilt after the fire.

3.3.3. South Ta Dzong or Small Tower (Excavation Sectors Gd, Ge, Gg, Gh, Gm)

The southwestern narrow side of the inner courtyard (Doche) was closed off by a building, whose remains—less well preserved than the walls of the Utse—appeared to originate from a tower (South Ta Dzong). As the reconnaissance in 2007 showed, individual parts of the wall had already been superficially exposed earlier, which is why in 2008 it seemed wise to start excavation of the sectors at this spot. The complete exposure of the building was carried out in the stages of 2009 and 2010.

With a wall thickness of 1.2 m, the building (W8/10a–d) delineated a rectangle with the length of its sides measuring approximately 12 × 8 m. The building lay exactly transverse to the longitudinal axis of the main fortress. All of the wall courses, which bordered South Ta Dzong—W9/57b and W9/62 on the northwestern and W9/38 on the southeastern narrow sides—abutted with continuous vertical joints and therefore must have been built later.

The height of the surviving trapezoidal, walled-in structure W8/15a–b and the volume of debris, both in- and outside the building, indicate a total height of 20 m (see 5.2.4.). Accordingly, the building possessed tower-like proportions, which justifies its name Ta Dzong or small tower (in contrast to the Utse).

1 Forest humus.
2 Wall debris.
3 Settlement deposit.
4 Naturally weathered clay.
5 Boulder.

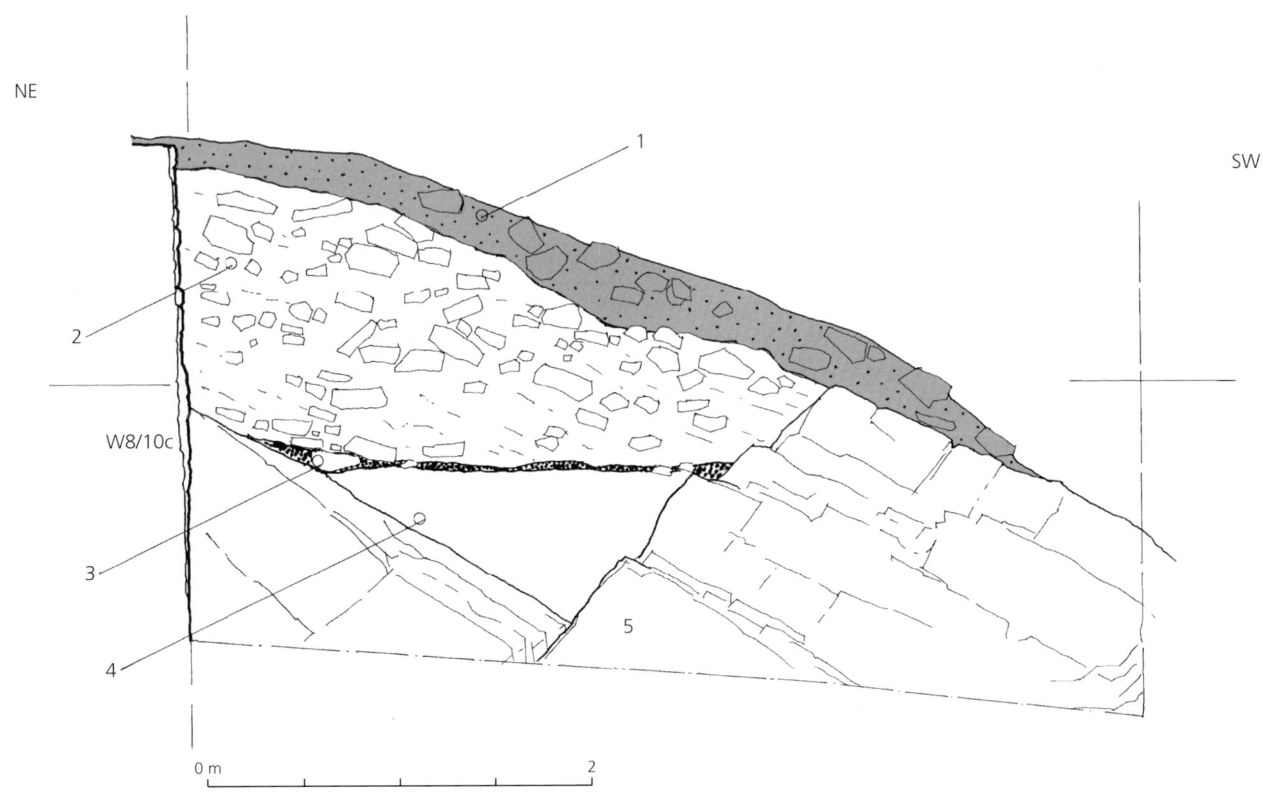

Fig. 60

An internal partitioning wall (W8/11) divided the interior of the building into two unequally sized rooms. In the outer walls several different openings could be observed. The southwestern and northwestern walls (W8/10c and W8/10d) were penetrated by two low-lying canals with an upright rectangular cross section. The orientation of their penetrations, which were slightly inclined towards the exterior, allowed them to be identified as drainage outlets. In the wall crown of the southwestern wall (W8/15c), small parts of a rectangular window niche was present, which corresponded to the walkway level of the ground floor. Unfortunately, the window's outer opening had not survived. An embrasure or (arrow) slit, situated low at the level of the cellar room, became visible in the same wall when the external heap of debris was removed. The embrasure or (arrow) slit had collapsed towards the interior, therefore, excavation was foregone for safety reasons.

The most important wall opening was located in the northeastern longitudinal wall (W8/15a) turned towards the Doche. It consisted of a gateway passageway 7.4 m in width, which—being symmetrically oriented—occupied more than half of the total wall length (12.2 m). The broad gate was obviously partitioned by two wood columns, of which the circular foundation plates of stone had been preserved *in situ*, dividing the opening into three passages—two narrow ones at the sides, and a wide one in the middle. The height of the entrance is no longer ascertainable. The middle opening, which had apparently been used as a thoroughfare, was preceded on the courtyard side by a pavement 1.3 m in width (W8/31). From the adjacent walkway level of the inner courtyard, only occasional slabs at this spot had survived. If a continuous paved surface once did exist, it would have been destroyed through dismantling (see excavation sector Gp). Positioned in front of the side entrance openings, which were located between the columns and gate jambs, there were two narrow wall courses (W8/17a and W8/17b) situated outside, flush with the threshold edge. Only a few stone layers had survived. The meager wall thickness of 0.6 m suggests a low height and is reminiscent of walls W10/65a and W10/65b, built to the front of the Utse (see 3.3.2a.).

On the southern segment of the inner courtyard, which was located in front of the small tower (excavation sector Gg), occasional stone slabs were found scattered about at the height of the walkway level, indicating extensive destruction of the courtyard's stone paving. Also fitting this scenario was the find of a vertical chute with a square cross section, whose sides measured approx. 20 cm in length. This was apparently a drain («gully»), through which rainwater from the courtyard was carried into a canal further south, which was verified at various spots (see below and 3.3.1.). The chute was originally covered by a stone slab with a round opening. When the courtyard paving was ravaged, this stone slab was broken. Half of it was still lying approx. 1 m from the gully.

The tower had been constructed on ground difficult to build on. The northwestern part had been placed on the steeply sloping-to-the-west moraine clay, while the southeastern area was built against a massive erratic boulder. This projected obliquely out of the clay soil and was marred by many fractures. Outside of the tower footprint, the boulder showed traces of workmanship in the form of a horizontal step. A jagged peak formed the highest point of the boulder, barely 0.5 m away from the southern corner of the tower. The external foundations W8/10c–W8/10d had been widened here in stages, thereby underpinning the overhanging rock.

In the interior of the tower, parts of the erratic boulder had been chiseled off, whereby space was created and filling material was gained. It eventually turned out that the aforementioned internal partitioning wall W8/11 had been built only up to the level of the ground floor and had served as a retaining wall for a cellar room, which had been dug into the rock and clay soil in the smaller northwestern part of the tower (excavation sector Gd). Above this cellar room, which was completely filled with debris, there was a wooden floor resting on seven girders. Their putlog holes were still

Fig. 61 Sector Gg in interior courtyard. Destroyed inlet opening of drainage channel. In the front, square-shaped chute; behind, battered cover slab with round hole. View towards south. W.M.

Fig. 62 Western wall of small tower with the outlet of drainage channel. View towards northeast. W.M.

61

62

Fig. 63 Layer profile WE in room Ge. K.W.

partially well preserved in the northeastern wall W8/10a. Unfortunately, the wooden substance, which was found inside of the putlog holes, proved to be too contaminated to deliver useful radiocarbon dating.

In the larger southeastern room (excavation sectors Ge, Gh, Gm), a sequence of layers was exposed, whose interpretation was only possible on the basis of the features in planum and in profile. (In the northwestern room, i.e., in excavation sector Gd, the stratigraphy had been destroyed by an earlier probe.) The secondary debris, overlain by forest humus with rootage, extended up to the crown of wall W8/10d. A distinct separation from the underlying primary debris was not discernible, but in the deeper layers of the wall debris, there were fewer stones and a higher proportion of clay than in the upper parts. The debris covered a settlement layer with a thickness of 5–25 cm. The layer consisted of grayish-black clay and filled the whole area of the southeastern room. It also extended over the crown of internal partitioning wall W8/11. Respective to the progressive excavation stages of 2008 to 2010, the layer was spread over excavation sectors Ge, Gh, and Gm.

Approximately in the middle of the room, the settlement layer was mixed with fine burnt debris, in which rectangular stone slabs were scattered. Their position did not indicate any deliberate arrangement, but rather a configuration, which could have resulted through crashing down from an upper story. The burnt layer—its diameter measuring approximately 3 m and tapered off in all directions—could thereby be interpreted as the remains of a hearth that had collapsed from an upper story. The numerous fragments of coarse pottery riddling the burnt layer (find complex Gm.4) supported the conjecture that a cooking hearth was involved. The abundance of join sherds from bellied cooking pots was striking. Other than the position of the hearth, respectively the burnt lenses, the settlement layer contained only occasional artifacts.

1 Forest layer.
2 Debris of walls: stones and loam.
3 Collapsed settlement layer.
4 Collapsed fireplace.
5 Limestone floor: ground niveau.
6 Back-filling: heterogenic, humus and limestone pockets.
7 Yellow loam.

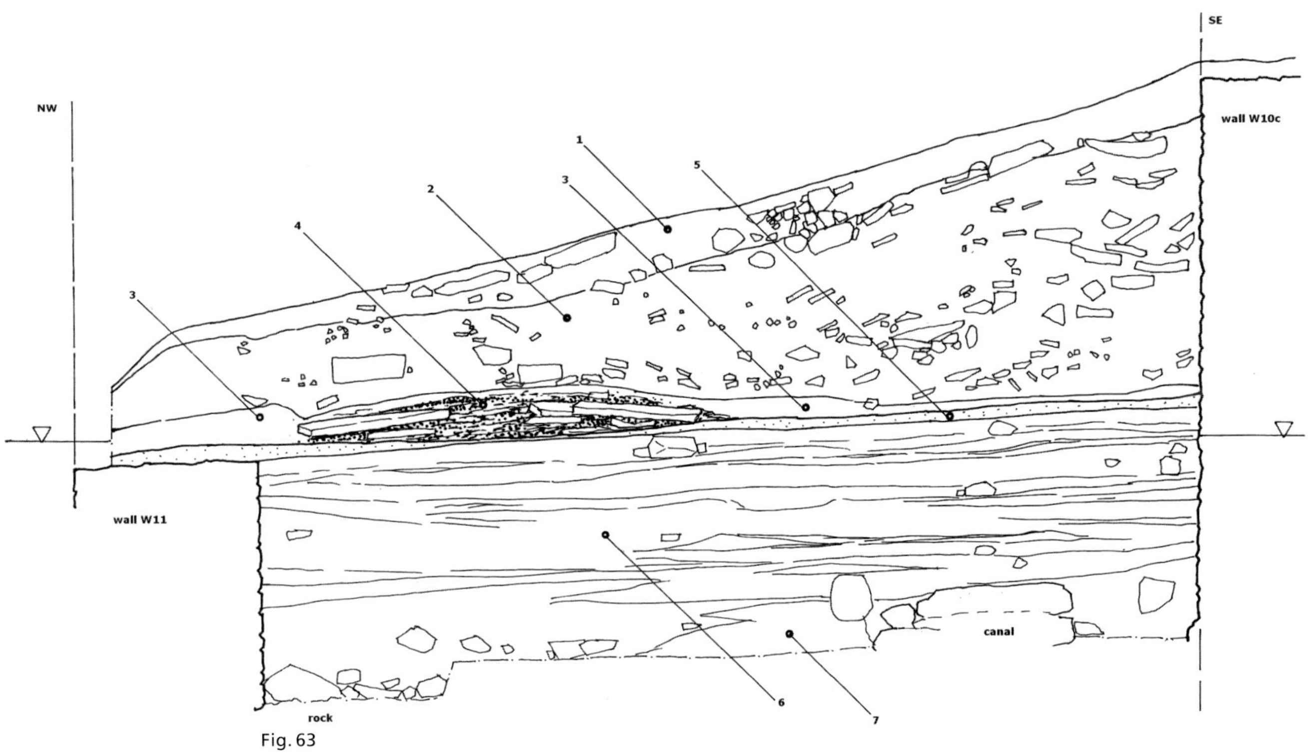

Fig. 63

64

65

Fig. 64 Sectors Ga and Gd. Entranceway of small tower. Foundation slab for supporting columns in gate opening of wall W8/10a. View towards northwest. W.M.

Fig. 65 Sector Ge, interior of small tower. Drainage channel across natural substrate. Slabs covering channel, partially removed. In stratigraphic profile to the left, heterogenous infill. View towards southeast. W.M.

The settlement layer covered another layer, approximately 10 cm in thickness, of white, coarse-grained and compact sand, which was accrued through the previously mentioned chiseling of the erratic boulder. Strikingly, this sandy layer—evidently the walkway level of the ground floor—also extended over the crown of internal partitioning wall W8/11, ending horizontally. The walkway level in the interior of the tower consisted respectively of firmly trodden sand in the southeastern part and wood flooring over the cellar room.

In the southeastern room, where in 2008 in excavation sector Ge a profile section was cut down to the natural substrate, a manmade infill appeared underneath the ground level walkway horizon. This infill was comprised of individual lenses, which consisted partly of whitish material that had been chiseled away from the erratic boulder, partly of re-located, often humous soil. In profile, the sequence of the heterogeneous lenses resembled a zebra pattern. At the bottom of the filling, directly over the natural rock surface, a canal made out of stone slabs surprisingly appeared. Its upright, rectangular cross section measured approximately 25 × 35 cm. In 2008, when it was discovered in excavation sector Ge, the beginning and end of the canal were not yet known (see 3.3.1b.). It began by the gully in excavation sector Gg, continued on under tower walls W8/10a and W8/10b, and opened up into the protruding foundations to the southwest. Covered over with thick slabs, the canal was hollow, the bottom covered by a fine layer of silt, 2–3 cm in thickness, without finds.

Fig. 66 Zone G. Overview of small tower. In the front, large entrance with two round basis slabs for supporting columns. Width of opening could indicate sacral use on ground floor. View towards southeast. W.M.

66

The constructional and stratigraphic features yielded the following chronological-relative building sequence: In an initial stage of work, the construction site is prepared by partly chiseling off the erratic boulder. The first constructive measure is the laying of the canal. Then tower walls W8/10a–d with their various openings are erected, whereby the ceiling beams are laid over cellar room Gd. Next, retaining wall W8/11 is built in the cellar area, whereupon the southeastern part of the tower is filled in with heterogeneous material so that a sandy surface can be added at the height of the walkway level. At the latest, now the wood floor is laid over the ceiling beams already in place. To conclude the process, the interior finishing of the upper floors is completed, including the wood paneling of the door opening. The only vestige of the upper floors to have survived is the collapsed cooking hearth.

Compared to the overall size of the façade, the three-part, oversized entrance suggests in the interior of the building, at least on its ground floor, that here there was a representational room for profane or religious ceremonies. In any case, the door opening does not correspond to any residential function that can be associated with the upper construction based on the collapsed cooking hearth. Indications of a major fire, which would have destroyed the interior of the small tower, are not to be concluded from the feature.

3.3.4. Northwestern Front (Excavation Zone N, Sectors Na/Nb, Nc, Nd)

During the reconnaissance of the excavation site in 2007, only limited parts of the wall could be recognized protruding from the debris of the slope on the elongated, northwestern periphery of the main fortress. In any case, once the vegetation had been removed, there was a course of what seemed to be an enclosure wall visible, out of which protruded a rectangular building, probably a flanking tower.

Strewn with wall debris, the site terrain fell steeply towards the northwest. Similarly, the debris mantle sloped down along the presumed enclosure wall from northeast to southwest. Given these pre-existing topographical conditions at the surface, it seemed advisable to deal with the debris in stages. The work, however, was delayed, because from time to time excavated material from excavation zones L, F, K, and sector Tf had to be temporarily stored on the removal terraces outside the enclosure wall, as these sizable masses of debris could not be disposed of other than on the northwestern slope.

During the excavation work, as the exterior side of the enclosure wall became more clearly visible, the question arose as to whether and to what length the foundation footing with the lower edge of the wall should be exposed. As it became evident, that the enclosure wall rested, not on stable bedrock, but on clay layers prone to weath-

67

Fig. 67 Zone N. Northern tower W8/1 and enclosure wall W8/2. In background, the Utse. View towards northeast. W.M.

ering (see below), we had to decide to not excavate the exterior side of the enclosure wall along its entire length down to the foundation, but rather to proceed in three steps to protect the residual debris from sliding down and the foundation area from weathering. However, sections were cut down to the natural subsoil in three places (see 3.3.4a., 3.3.4b., 3.3.4c.), and this allowed sufficient insight into the stratigraphic relationships at the wall footing as well as into its construction.

The enclosure wall, whose estimated exterior height from the foundation footing is still 4–5 m, was divided clearly into three segments. The northern segment (W8/2) stretched between the two protruding towers (excavation zone E and sectors Fc, Fb), the middle segment (W9/57a) abutted the sidewall of tower Fc, Fb (W8/3c) with a butt joint, and bent at the southern end to the southeast. The southern segment W9/35a was connected at the corner bond W9/57a–b. All three segments lay in a straight course, which, however, had a few slight bends. The southern segment bordered on the corner bond W9/57a–c with a distinct butt joint, which reached down to the foundation area, certain evidence that the segment had been constructed later. The courses of all three segments were inclined 5–6°.

Insofar as they had been freed of debris, the three wall segments contained only a few openings. Holes for anchoring scaffolding were not evident. In the northern segment (W8/2) there was an embrasure or (arrow) slit, which belonged to the non-excavated ground floor of annex room Tf (see 3.3.9.). In the middle segment (W9/57a), the outlet of a vertically aligned rectangular drainage canal was sighted, which came from room Gl (see 3.3.7.). In addition, embrasures or (arrow) slits were present in the ground floor of the protruding flanking tower Fc, one each in the northern, western, and southern walls (see 3.3.7.).

In the masses of removed debris, which reached nearly as far as the crown, there were no archaeologically relevant items. From the height of the still surviving masonry and from the volume of debris, the approximate height of the enclosure wall could be calculated, which is estimated to have been ca. 10–12 m.

The three test trenches, from the removal level of the wall debris down to the natural subsoil, have provided diverse and to some extent surprising features.

Fig. 68 Sectors Na and Nb. Waste disposal site in front of western enclosure wall. A: lower edge of waste disposal site. J.O.

3.3.4a. Excavation Sectors Na and Nb

In 2009 test trench (Na) was cut into the corner between flanking tower Fc, Fb (W8/3a) and enclosure wall W8/2. This revealed features that called for an extension of excavation sector (Nb) to the north, which was realized in the 2010 campaign.

In the angle between tower wall W8/3a and enclosure wall W8/2, the wall foundation W9/59 unexpectedly appeared, which rested on the natural subsoil and abutted with joints the tower and enclosure wall. Approximately 1.8 m in width and—measuring from the foundation's lower edge—about 1.2 m in height, the wall segment is probably to be construed as a supporting construction intended to prevent the enclosure wall, which is built on unstable subsoil, from sliding down. To the north an extraordinary appearing construction was joined to this wall plinth W9/59. It consisted of two wall courses (W10/64a and W10/64b), which extended obliquely to the enclosure wall, following the gradient of the slope, thereby, in ground plan defining a triangle with a base length of 7.5 m. Through butt joints the two wall courses respectively adjoined wall plinth W9/59 and enclosure wall W8/2. With a mere thickness of 0.6 m, the two walls could only have been of limited height.

Within the walled triangle, paving appeared, which had been executed using densely laid stone slabs. This rested on the natural clay subsoil, which followed the slope gradient. Thereby, the paving formed a slanting, steeply declining level extending from the foot of enclosure wall W8/2. Unfortunately, the western or end on the side of the slope, turned out—probably as the result of terrain slides—to be heavily disturbed, which is why the appearance of the corner section, where walls W10/64a and 64b met, could no longer be determined.

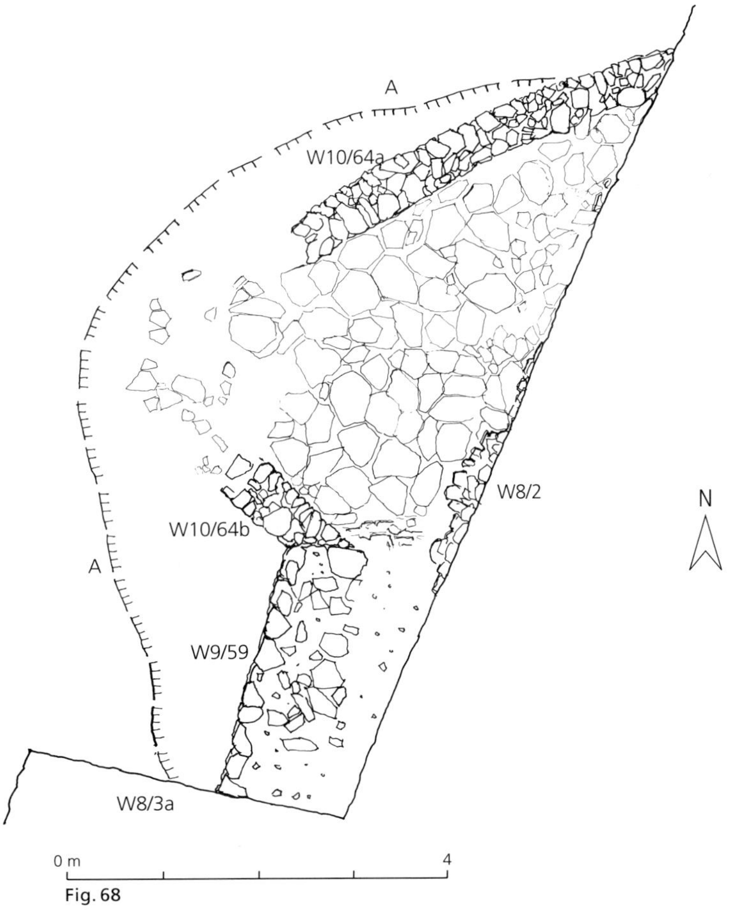

Fig. 68

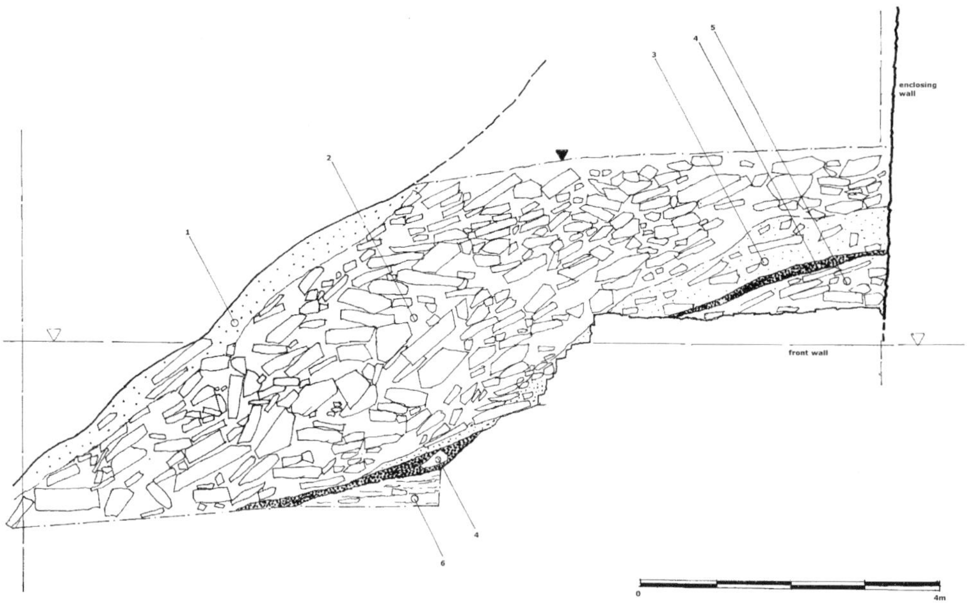

Fig. 69

1 Forest humus.
2 Secondary debris; clay, stones.
3 Primary debris; clay, a few stones.
4 Settlement sediment; solid, humus. Ceramics, animal bones.
5 Collapsed walls; stones, clay.
6 Natural clay.

The stratigraphy provided more information. On the slanting paving and on the crown of wall plinth W9/59, covered by the vast mass of debris, lay a distinct settlement layer, up to 40 cm in thickness. It consisted of blackish-gray, humous clay and contained a large number of finds, mainly animal bones and fragments of typologically diverse coarse ceramics (find complex Na/b.3). The settlement layer tapered off with the slope, where walls W10/64a and W10/64b as well as the stone paving terminated.

An interpretation of this remarkable feature is difficult in that the ascending enclosure wall W8/2 exhibited no significant characteristics and the room belonging to the western wing behind it (see 3.3.7.) has not been excavated. Nevertheless, there is no doubt that it concerns a waste disposal site, considering the unusually thick settlement layer with its strikingly high density of finds. The careful manner of construction featuring inclined paving and two funnel-shaped, converging enclosure walls, lead to the conjecture that the construction served the option of being able to wash waste heaps away with water from time to time, which could suggest its being the containment basin of a latrine system. In any case, the wall junctions and layer connections indicate that the whole construction did not exist from the beginning, but rather was inserted later into an already existing «open» disposal site and towards the end of the settlement period became covered by accrued waste.

Fig. 69 Drapham Dzong, layer profile NW–SE in the Na area. K.W.

Fig. 70 Sectors Na and Nb. Garbage and feces depot in front of the northwestern front. Skewed slab paving, bordered by walls W10/64a and W10/64b. Behind, enclosure wall W8/2. View towards southeast. W.M.

70

3.3.4b. Excavation Sector Nc

A section in the angle between tower wall W8/W3c and enclosure wall W9/57a was intended to clarify the stratigraphy of the foundation area of the wall course located there. First of all, it clearly showed that enclosure wall W9/57a abutted with a joint from the foundation footing upwards against tower wall W8/3c, i.e., that it was built later.

The foundations were embedded only 20–40 cm in the natural moraine clay. The foundation trench exhibited a correspondingly weak profile. At the foot of the tower wall W8/3c, built on the fall line of the mountain slope, it appeared that the foundation bed had been dug out in tiers.

A blackish-gray settlement deposit was revealed under the wall debris. Respectively it rested on the natural subsoil, which sloped down to the west, or on a thin, only patchily extant building horizon of white sand. The progression of the settlement layer was clearly distinguished by a blackish discoloration at the outside of tower wall W8/3c. Unfortunately, the settlement deposits in section Nc contained no ascertainable inclusions.

3.3.4c. Excavation Sector Nd

The section Nd was made in 2010 at the foot of enclosure wall W9/57a, just below the previously mentioned drainage canal, which belonged to room Gl. The expectation, that this canal would contain a deposit with significant inclusions, however, was not met.

Clearly distinguishable in excavation sector Nd was primary debris, approx. 0.8 m in thickness, which had been covered by great masses of secondary debris. It contained numerous fragments of clay plaster with red and black ornamental painting (find complex Nd.2). The grayish-black settlement deposit, which had already been observed in section Nc, also appeared directly under the primary debris in section Nd. At the lower edge it was accompanied by a building horizon, which ran along the wall as a band of white sand, 0.5 m in width. In the settlement layer there were few finds, except for small bone and ceramic fragments and a lead musket ball with a caliber of 10 mm (find complex Nd.3).

Respectively, under the settlement layer and building horizon, there were heterogeneous deposits divided into lenses. Together they formed a stratigraphic packet, 0.5 m in thickness, which was banked against the foundation footing of enclosure wall W9/57a. A foundation trench was not apparent. In excavation sector Nd the wall seems to have been built directly on the natural moraine debris lying on the surface and consisted of clay and erratic boulders.

No traces of building scaffolding, e.g., in the form of post positions, have been exposed in any of the three excavation sectors in zone N.

3.3.5. Northeastern Front (Excavation Sectors Ee, Td, Ud)

The walls of the northeastern front extend along the edge of the site terrain over the debris slope, which drops steeply towards the plateau of the northern bailey. Before the start of the excavation, only incoherent building remains were identifiable. However, both corner towers (W8/1a–d and W8/15a–d) as well as fragments of the Utse (W9/41d, W9/39 and W9/40) were clearly visible albeit only after the removal of the lush vegetation. Between the towers and the Utse, no connecting walls could be distinguished.

3.3.5a. Middle Segment (Excavation Sector Td)

The entire slope was covered with enormous masses of debris, which appeared to stem mostly from the Utse. Therefore, it was foreseeable that the exposure work in this excavation segment would involve major earthmoving. Shortly, i.e., already after the removal of the Utse's uppermost debris layers as the first parts of its wall emerged, further, more difficult problems became evident. Namely, it was clear that the northeastern front wall of the Utse (W9/41a) had not only been heavily dismantled and the stones carried away, but also beyond this, that it was in a state of advanced deterioration that

71

Fig. 71 Northeastern front of main fortress with heavily deteriorated northeastern section of the Utse, its eastern corner temporarily conserved. In the front (left), wall W9/49 with gate opening. View towards southwest. W.M.

Fig. 72 Stratigraphic profile in sector Ee. Above, partially already removed wall debris. Below, as dark band, settlement deposit on natural clay. In the background, wall W9/60 with shooting opening. View towards southwest. W.M.

extended down to the foundation area. (This observation was also made in the adjacent excavation sector Ud.) For safety reasons—not only the imminent danger for workers, but also because of the risk that the entire, completely unstable masses of debris and pieces of masonry would fall and collapse—it was necessary to forego an archeologically satisfying exposure of the walls in the middle of the excavation sector Td. Instead we had to be content with venturing forward in the area of the wall debris from the southeast (excavation sector Ud) and southwest (excavation sector Ee) to the corners of the Utse and to leave the exterior course of Utse wall W9/41a—or rather, what was left of it—undisturbed under a protective, supportive debris mantle. Allowing a safety distance of approx. 5 m, a terrace was leveled in the debris at the height of the upper excavation level of sector Ud, which interconnected excavation sectos Ud and Ee. We stabilized the truncated mound of debris with a dry layered wall 1.5–2 m in height. No archaeologically relevant information could be observed in the debris layers that had been removed.

3.3.5b. Western Segment (North Ta Dzong, Excavation Sector Ee)

The most important discovery in excavation sector Ee was evidence of wall W9/60, which interconnected the northern corner tower E (North Ta Dzong, W8/1a–d) with the Utse (W9/41a–d). Butt joints indicated that the wall course was built later between the two towers. The mouth of an embrasure or (arrow) slit revealed that a floor level must still have been lying in the debris to the southwest of the wall (see 3.3.9b.).

72

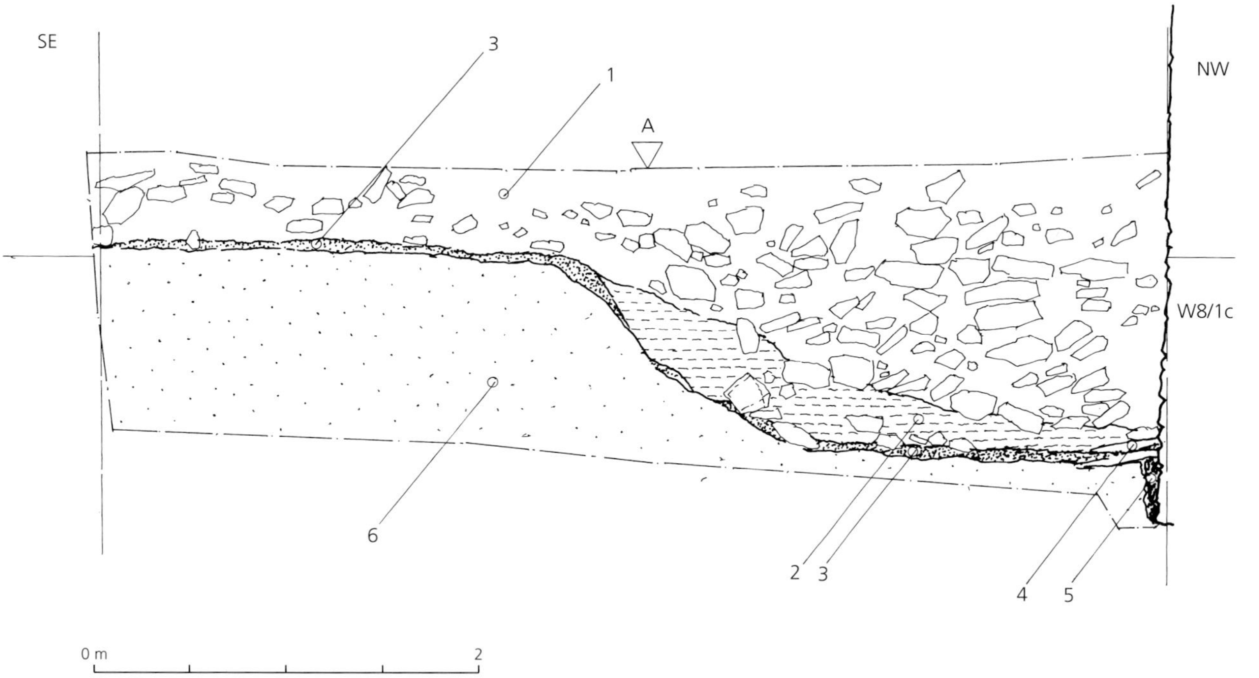

Fig. 73

Fig. 73 Stratigraphic profile in sector Ee.
A Removal level 2009.
1 Wall debris.
2 Brown clay.
3 Settlement deposit. Bone and ceramic particles. Two ^{14}C-samples: approx. 1520 and 1590 p. Chr. n.
4 Upper and lower construction horizon. Clay, white quartz sand.
5 Filled-in foundation trench of wall W8/1c.
6 Natural subsoil. Sandy clay. ^{14}C-Sample: approx. 40,000 a. Chr. n.
W.M.

In the angle between the southeastern wall of the corner tower (W8/1d) and connecting wall W9/60, there were some illuminating stratigraphic relationships. Under the upper parts of the wall debris, which was interspersed with humus and in places was up to 4 m in thickness, a depression or hollow, 3 m in width and 1 m in depth, appeared running parallel to tower wall W8/1d. It was partly filled with yellow clay without finds and partly with primary debris. At the bottom of the depression, as elsewhere under the wall debris, there was a blackish-gray, loamy settlement layer, 2–15 cm in thickness. It contained scattered particles of charred wood as well as small fragments of coarse ceramics. The layer was nestled against tower wall W8/1d, where it was accompanied by a lens band, which was up to 40 cm in width and composed of white, granular material.

The settlement layer rested on massive clay filling, which was deposited against tower wall W8/1d and through inclusions (charred wood particles, bone fragments) revealed its anthropogenic origins. Apparently, this was a manmade clay fill, which had been introduced onto the natural subsoil—which also consisted of clay—to protect the wall foundations.

From the stratgraphic profile of excavation sector Ee, plant remnants could be retrieved from the loamy, natural moraine debris, whose radiocarbon dating indicated an age of approx. 38,000 ± 300 years. This proves that the natural subsoil of the fortress hill had been deposited during the last Ice Age.

3.3.5c. Eastern Segment (Excavation Sector Ud)

In the eastern segment of the northeastern front, some masonry emerged, which, except for minor differences, mirrored that of the western segment axial-symmetrically. A connecting wall (W9/49) spanned between the eastern corner of the Utse (W9/41a–b) and the eastern corner tower (East Ta Dzong, W8/15b). Accordingly, the northeastern face of the main fortress formed a closed wall front, which had been presumed before the excavation began, but not yet proven.

Like wall W9/60 in the western segment, wall W9/49 was also built with butt joints against the two towers, which indicates it was erected after the towers. In the wall there was a door opening, whose threshold height corresponded to the walkway level of the adjacent southwestern room (excavation sectors Ua/Ue). To the southeast, there was a well-preserved embrasure or (arrow) slit next to the door (see 3.3.10b.).

The interior of the eastern corner tower (W8/15a–d) was not excavated. However, the contours of the building had to be exposed in the area of the upper debris layers in order to complete the overall ground plan (see 3.3.10a.).

Also, in the eastern segment of the northeastern front, the lower stratigraphic sequence was buried under a massive debris mantle. This reached up as high as the crown of the Utse (W9/41b) and subsided conically or fan-shaped onto the wall remnants of the eastern corner tower (W8/15a–d), of which, at the start of the excavation, only a few of its stone layers had protruded above the ground. The deposits of the primary and secondary debris covered a distinctly formed settlement layer. This consisted of blackish-gray clay. Its thickness at the northwestern edge of the excavation area at the foot of the Utse was only 5–10 cm. The settlement layer subsided to the southeast and in the angle between walls W8/15b and W9/49 filled a hollow, 50–80 cm in depth, which contained an extraordinarily amount of find material (find complex Ud.3), primarily animal bones and fragments of coarse pottery as well as pieces of metal. This hollow, that was so rich in finds, covered a total area of 2.5 × 4 m.

Close to the wall and extending under the settlement layer, there was a strip, approximately 30–50 cm in width, of thick lenses of white sand, 5–10 cm in thickness. Apparently, the lenses marked the building horizon. Together with the settlement layer, the lenses lay directly on the natural subsoil, which consisted of compact, yellow clay. Small, heterogeneous, backfilled disturbed pockets, 20 cm in depth, 15 cm in diameter, with a distance of approximately 80 cm from walls W9/49 and W9/41, could be interpreted as evidence of scaffolding.

Along these two walls, a foundation trench was clearly discernible in planum and in profile, which had been dug in the natural clay. At the foot of the Utse, the foundation pit measured 30–40 cm in width at the upper horizon. Along connecting wall W9/49, where its depth was 1.5 m as calculated from the building horizon, the pit was even 80–90 cm in width. Sloping steeply, it extended down to the level of the foundation footing.

The feature in sectors Ud and Ee permits important conclusions regarding the building process, not only on the basis of the traces of the scaffolding. The white material, which marks the building horizon, suggests that large areas of the outer walls had once been painted white. Furthermore, it is apparent that wherever the stability of the natural subsoil could not be trusted, the foundations were either set in deep trenches or stabilized by with massive clay lateral fill.

In light of find layer Ud.3, there is no doubt that a waste disposal trench once existed in the angle between walls W8/15b and W9/49. Puzzling, however, is the function of the door in wall W9/49. Considered alone, one interpretation as a connective opening to the northern bailey would have seemed obvious. Outside the gate, however, there was no evidence of a staircase or pathway. Lying with the threshold 0.6–1.0 m above the settlement deposit Ud.3, the door would have led nowhere. The possibility remains open, that in closing the door by walling it up (W9/47, see 3.3.10b.), a conceivable, probably wood staircase construction was so thoroughly dismantled, that absolutely no traces remained.

3.3.6. Southwestern Building Development (Zone L)

At the start of the 2008 excavation, there were no architectural remains in the southwestern segment of the main fortress, except for a few traces of the enclosure wall (W9/35a–b). Starting at the crown of the wall of the small tower (W8/10a and W8/10c), the terrain sloped steeply to the west and southwest, and the surface structure remained hidden under dense undergrowth. A probe or test trench already performed in 2008 at the southwestern foot of the small tower, where excavation sector Lf was to be marked out in 2010, led to the conclusion that enormous masses of debris must be piled up in entire zone L. The removal—which was carried out during the excavation campaigns of 2009 and 2010—called for proceeding step-by-step. Notwithstand-

74

Fig. 74 View towards northeast onto excavation zone L. In foreground, sector Sa and stepped ramp W9/36. W.M.

ing the steepness of the terrain and the looseness of the debris layers, there was significant danger of a landslide. To appease this risk, at the site workers built a small Chorten (stupa or ceremonial altar) to Lu, goddess of stones, caves, rocks and the earth.

From under the debris, various wall courses and walkway levels were exposed, whose existence had not been known prior to the excavation. Towards the exterior, the area of zone L was enclosed by right-angled enclosure wall W9/35a–b (see 3.3.1c.). The wall started in the north at the southwestern corner of older enclosure wall W9/57a–b, which was separated by a clearly pronounced butt joint. Zone L ended to the east at the small tower (W8/10b–c, see 3.3.3.) and at the large erratic boulder, which loomed in front of the southeastern corner of the tower.

The courses of the walls, which partitioned zone L respectively into areas and rooms of various sizes, divided the steeply falling terrain into two tiers. The upper tier, situated in the eastern part of zone L (excavation sectors Lc, Ld), was originally bounded on the sloping side by an angled course of wall (W9/58a–b). With joints, this abutted the older enclosure wall W9/57b, ran parallel to the northwestern wall of small tower W8/10b, and after 13 m, turned to continue at an almost right angle to the southeast. After about 8 m, the wall course terminated, presumably having once ended at the southern tip of the erratic boulder.

At the western-oriented corner of this wall (W9/57a–b), there were two walls abutting with joints, which, together with the corner part of enclosure wall W9/35a–b, formed a nearly square ground plan (excavation sector/room Lb). With interior dimensions of about 4×4 m, it maybe originated from a small tower. In any case, it must have served as an entry building, because in the southern wall (W9/35b), there was a door opening, which was accessible from the staircase ramp W9/36 (excavation sector Sc) via a wood balcony (see 3.3.1c.). The threshold of the door, which was 1.2 m in width, was slightly above the elevation of the walkway level in the interior of building Lb. A further door appeared in the opposite wall W9/61a. With a width of 1.0 m, it led at ground level into the adjacent, elongated room of sector La, whose northern narrow side was formed by old enclosure wall W9/57b. The jambs of both doors exhibited horizontal holes with vertically aligned rectangular cross sections, which had served to se-

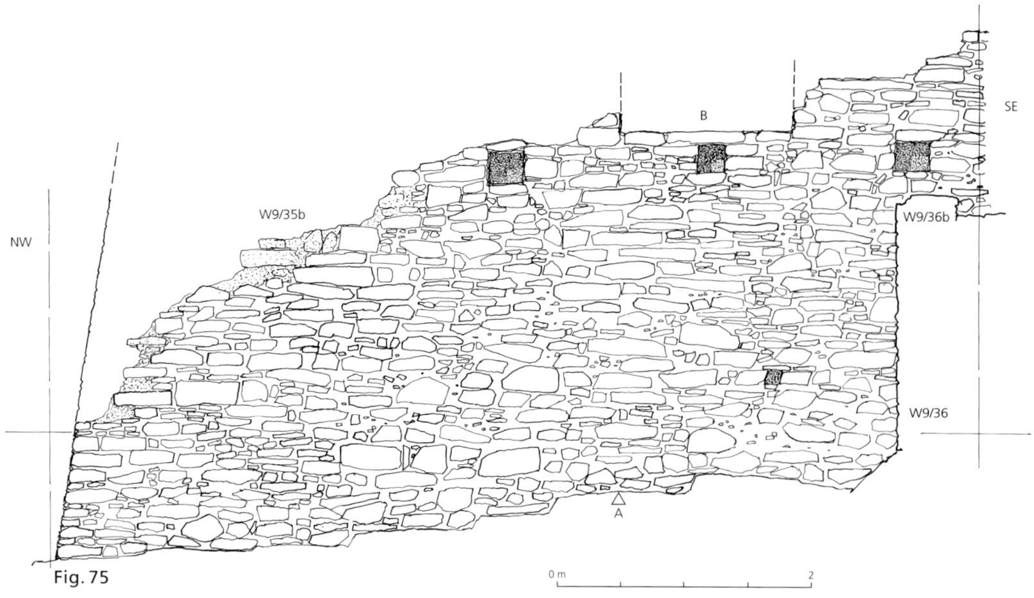

Fig. 75

cure the wood doorframe. Steep wooden stairs very likely could have led from the low-lying walkway level of the two rooms La and Lb to the higher adjacent terrace to the east (Lc, Ld, Le) and to the upper floors, whereby no traces of these stairs could an longer be detected.

On the upper terrace in the eastern part of zone L, an isolated wall course (W9/62) arose, approximately 2.8 m in length, which adjoined the narrow side of the small tower (W8/10b) at a right angle. Its function remains uncertain. Countering the seemingly plausible explanation that it might have indicated a supporting column or buttress, is the presence of the joint, 10 cm in width, whose front side divides the tower wall from the alignment, so it could not have had any supportive effect, unless the entire wall had become detached at a later time—e.g., on account of the foundation sinking—from the tower wall.

With the dismantling of the wall debris in zone L, the southwestern front of old enclosure wall W9/57b has also been unveiled. In excavation sector Lc, their course displayed an opening, 1.5 m in width, which had been subsequently walled up. The two butt joints reached a different height, and the stone layers of the walled up area merged with the masonry above the butt joints. Apparently, this wall gap was one of those openings, which had served during construction as a passage for transporting materials and was walled up once it was no longer needed (see 5.2.1).

The previously mentioned eastern corner of room Lb was striking because of the unconventional way in which it had been constructed, in that the northeastern and southeastern walls of the small building (W9/61a–b) abutted from outside against the edge of the corner bond of wall W9/58a–b. This feature provided unambiguous evi-

Fig. 75 Zone Sa. Exterior view of enclosure wall W9/35b. A: Upper edge of the artificially stepped, natural construction site soil. B: Door embouchure. D.O.

Fig. 76 Zone L with walls W9/61a and W9/61b. Above (right), small tower; behind (left), end wall W9/57b built in Phase 1. View towards northeast. W.M.

76

Fig. 77 Stratigraphic profile in sector Lb.
1 Forest humus.
2 Wall debris.
3 Settlement layer.
4 Clay infill.
D.O.

dence of the entire wall structure having been constructed in two phases. The historical sequence of building could be gleaned not only from the wall courses and their butt joints, but also from decisive information arising from the stratigraphy of zone L.

These stratigraphic relationships, however, did not prove to be undisturbed. Since northwestern enclosure wall W9/35a had been dismantled and carried away down to 0.5 m above the walkway level of the adjacent rooms La and Lb, the layers lying above had lost their grip and extensive areas had slid down. However, wall courses W9/58a and W9/61b in the interior of zone L had exercised a certain supportive effect for their eastern part (excavation sectors Lc, Ld, Le), so that the stratigraphy in this area was able to remain intact.

Under the wall debris, up to 4 m in height—primary and secondary debris could not be kept apart from each other—, a vast spread of slab paving appeared. It stretched over the entire eastern section of zone L, i.e., over sectors Lc, Ld, Le, and Lf. A blanketing settlement deposit was not to be detected on this slab level; only isolated, find-free lenses made of humous, blackish-gray clay, 1–2 cm in thickness, could be observed in the recesses of the bumpy, uneven slab floor. To the east, the paving was bounded by the large erratic boulder; to the west, by walls W9/58a and W9/61b. However, their wall crowns rose just to 0.8 m below the level of the paving. The upper infill and settlement layers in the western part of zone L had respectively slid down or eroded away, so no firm conclusions can be drawn regarding the western boundary of the slab paving.

The slab floor did not rest on the natural ground subsoil, but rather on heterogeneous infill earth, which, with a thickness of 0.8 m covered the crown of wall course W9/58b. At the lower part of the infill, nestled against the exterior side of wall W9/61b, there was a burnt lens about 1.5 m in diameter and up to 15 cm in thickness, likely the remains of an earthen, non-masonry fireplace, which was probably created during the construction, i.e., infilling work.

Under the debris in the western part of zone L in excavation sectors La and Lb, a walkway level was found, in so far as this was still *in situ*, that lay almost 15 cm below the threshold level of the two doors in walls W9/35b and W9/61. It consisted of compactly trodden clay, which was lightly interspersed with pebbles. Spread over the walkway level was a thin, settlement layer of blackish-gray clay, only 2–5 cm in thickness. It contained some artifacts and some integrated burnt lenses, which consisted of blackish, charred wood substance that had stained the clay floor or screed red in places. The traces of fire in the eastern corner of room Lb, accompanied by laid stones, originated from a simple hearth at ground level.

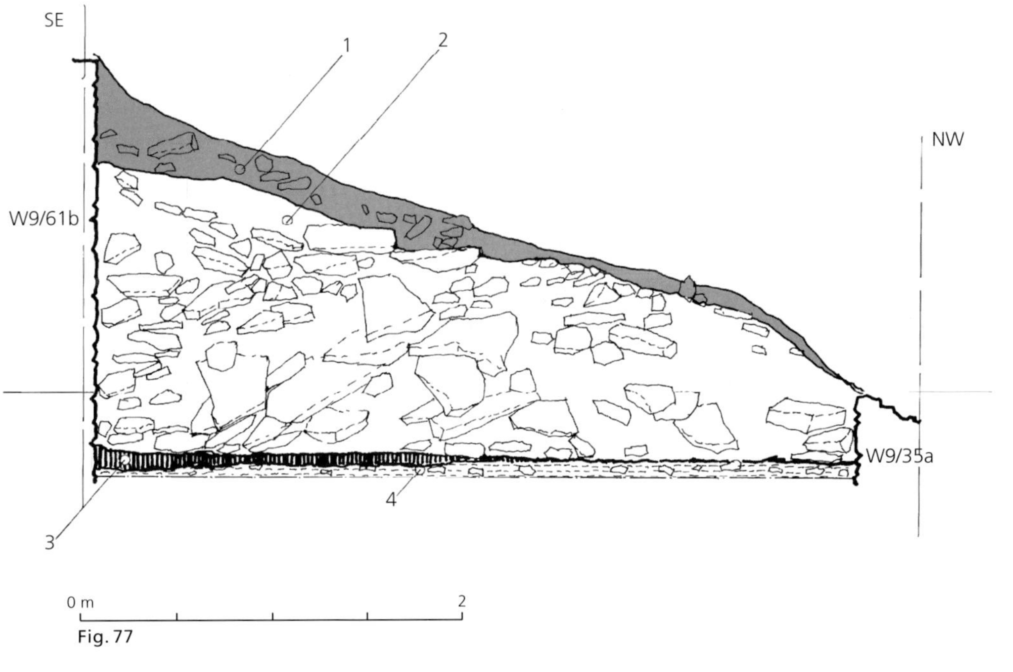

Fig. 77

The masonry with its butt joints and the stratigraphic relationships allow the building sequence in zone L to be broadly interpreted: In Phase 1 the wall courses are built, which delimit zone L to the north and east, i.e., enclosure wall W9/57b and walls of small tower W8/10c–d. Whether the isolated wall W9/62 originated from Phase 1 or is to be built only later remains unclear. In any case, wall angle W9/58a–b is also to be attributed to Phase 1. Originally, it may have served as a support for the steeply declining clay slope at the western and southwestern sides of the small tower.

With the erection of enclosure wall W9/35a–b, Phase 2 entails the extension of the main fortress to the south (see 5.2.2.). Integrating wall corner W9/58a–b, an almost square building (excavation sector Lb) emerges in the angle of the enclosure wall. This is connected by a door in wall W9/35 and a wooden arcade with the staircase ramp W9/36 (excavation sector Sc). A further door leads through wall W9/61 at ground level into adjacent room La to the north. The older wall course W9/58a serves as its interior, i.e., eastern boundary.

The ground floor of the two rooms La and Lb to the west actually rests on heaped infill deposited against enclosure wall W9/35a–b, but at a floor level lower than the eastern part of zone L, which is covered by a slab floor. For this paving, the existing floor level is elevated by 0.8–2.0 m, whereby the crown of wall W9/58b, which had become superfluous and was dismantled, vanishes into the mounded fill. Thereby, in the eastern part of zone L, an open, slab-paved courtyard is created, whose level corresponds to the walkway horizon of the adjacent sector Zb to the east (see 3.3.11a.).

Lacking significant masonry findings and informative artifacts, the function of the two unequally sized rooms La and Lb cannot be clearly determined. However, based on the two doorways in excavation sector Lb, it may be concluded that the ground floor of the corner building served as a passageway space. It seems that the squads had resided here—at least temporarily—in order to maintain a small fire in the eastern corner.

3.3.7. Western Wing and Western Flanking Tower (Shab Khor/West Drasha and West Ta Dzong)

Even before the beginning of the excavation in 2008, various wall remnants, sticking out of the debris at the western longitudinal side of the main fortress, were recognizable and apparently originated from an elongated complex with multiple buildings. During the process of the exposure work from 2008 to 2010, a large building tract, 50 m in length and 14 m in width, was detected, which consisted of at least five juxtaposed rooms, a projecting loggia (gallery corridor) on the courtyard side, and a flanking tower protruding from the enclosure wall. Only three parts were more closely examined archeologically: one at the northern end (excavation sectors Kb and Kd); one in the middle segment (excavation sectors Fa to Fe); and one in the southern area (excavation sectors Fd, Gc, Gd and Gl). In the unexposed parts in between, the wall connections and exact course of the wall could be comprehended and documented by means of surface abrasions. Soon after beginning to excavate, butt joints indicated that the entire tract must have been built in the course of difference stages of construction. The exact interrelationships of the history of construction, however, could only be initially surveyed after completion of the exposure work.

On account of the masses of debris that covered the entire compound of the western wing, at first it wasn't possible to estimate how deep in the ground the walls actually went, since they were just barely visible at the surface. Eventually, it turned out that the rooms filled with wall debris were distributed over three floors, with the whole tract extending skewed over the natural substrate, which steeply sank in steps from the northeast to the southwest. The western wing, however, was so positioned that its courtyard-side front—with the projecting loggia (gallery corridor) West Ta Zee—kept horizontal to a certain degree, namely at roughly the same level as the Doche, while the enclosure wall W8/2 respectively W9/57a (see 3.3.4.), which bounded the tract on

Fig. 78 Zone K, northern section of western wing. In front of wall W8/6c, small slab plastered courtyard of sector Ka. View towards southwest. W.M.

Fig. 79 Sector Ka with slab paving. Left, northern end of western tract (sector Kb with wall W8/6c). View towards northwest. W.M.

the slope side, sank with the foundations towards the southwest by approx. 7 m. This meant that in the northern section (excavation sectors Kb and Kc), the walkway level of the ground floor lay at the spot height of the loggia (gallery corridor), while further south, in excavation sectors F and G, it came to rest two stories below the loggia.

Enclosure walls W8/2 and respectively W9/57a did not run in a straight course, like their counterpart W9/43 at the southern side, but rather made a slight kink several times, which is particularly evident in the area of West Ta Dzong. The reasons for this striking change of direction is mentioned elsewhere (see 5.1.2.).

3.3.7a. Northern Segment (Excavation Sectors Kb and Kd)

With the removal of the surface debris from the southwestern corner of Utse, the northern end of the western wing (Shab Khor/West Drasha)—rather unexpectedly—emerged. A room was truncated out [through two intersecting structures] resulting in an interior measuring 4.5 m in width, Oriented towards the northeast, the foremost wall of the wing (W8/5c) bordered on a small, paved courtyard (excavation sector Ka, see 3.3.9b.) and was interlocked with enclosure wall W8/2. The foremost wall bent at a right angle at its eastern end and continued as longitudinal wall W8/5b in a southwesterly direction to excavation sector F (see 3.3.7b.). In 2008, only the northern third of the truncated-out interior space (excavation sector Kb) could be examined. In 2009, the whole room was successfully exposed up to transverse wall W8/5d (excavation sector Kd).

78

79

This southwestern transverse wall W8/5d was interlocked with enclosure wall W8/2 and courtyard-side longitudinal wall W8/5b. However, it didn't have any openings; as a consequence, there was no direct connection between room Kb/Kd and the adjacent southwestern—not excavated—part of the western wing. The middle of the courtyard-side longitudinal wall, 1.1 m in thickness, featured a door, 1.5 m in width, with a carefully joined threshold out of slabs. To the left and right of the door, in the wall crown there were still small parts preserved of two window openings, each 0.8 m in width. These were not embrasures or (arrow) slits, because the reveals pierced the wall crossways through their entire thickness. In the enclosure wall (W8/2), opposite the door at floor-level height, there was a small residue of an opening, 0.6 m in width, of unknown function.

Fig. 80 Excavation zone K. Northern section of the western wing. W.M.

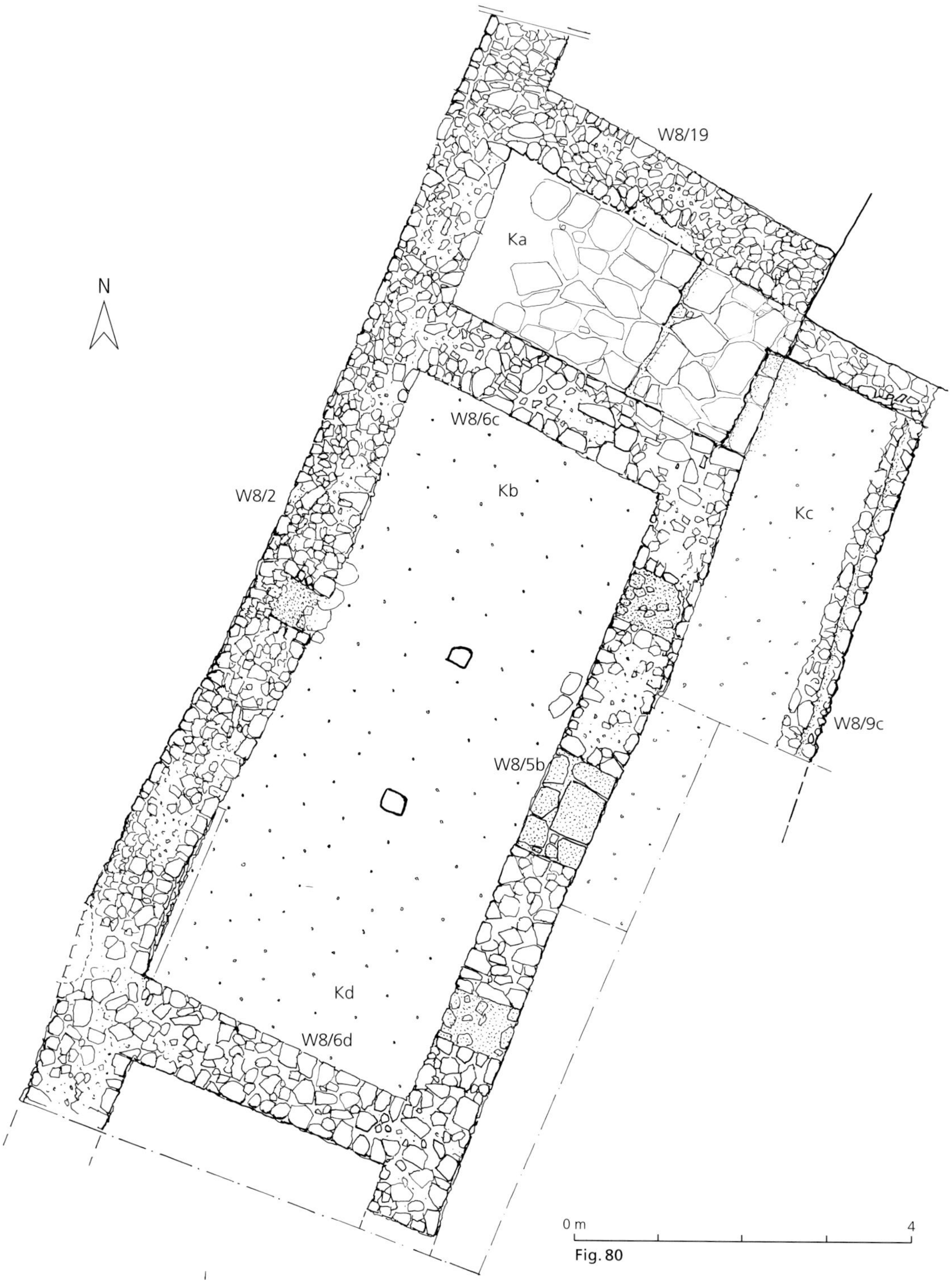

Fig. 80

Fig. 81 Section SE–NW through the main castle in zone F. W.M.

Measuring from the walkway level, the inner walls of the room (W8/5b, 5c, 5d) were even 1 to 1.4 m in height, while the enclosure wall on the northwestern longitudinal side towered above the ground surface by only 0.3 to 0.6 m. The wall crowns were covered by humous forest soil, partly also by wall debris. This filled the whole room all the way down to the floor, which consisted of a clay floor or screed. This was interspersed with densely scattered, round gravel, 2–4 cm in diameter. There was no settlement layer resting on this clay screed, but rather—quasi as lowest horizon of the primary debris—a heterogeneous, brown-gray clay layer, 5–20 cm in thickness, which, besides small round gravel, also contained animal bones, pottery, and charred wood particles (find complex Kb/d.3.). Apparently, the layer entailed the collapse of a floor with settlement garbage from an upper story.

Two stone slabs belong to this feature, which were embedded in the clay screed of the ground floor and still found *in situ*. Lying on the longitudinal axis of the room, they had apparently served as the basis for two wooden columns, which supported the floor of the upper level.

The door, inset into longitudinal wall W8/5b, led out into the loggia (gallery corridor) (West Ta Zee), which was built in front of the western wing along its entire length and whose northern end abutted the Utse (see 3.3.2a.). One reveal, only exposed superficially, in the southern continuation of longitudinal wall W8/5b, belonged to a door, through which the non-excavated room south of transverse wall W8/5d could be entered from the loggia.

3.3.7b. Middle Segment (Excavation Sectors Fa, Fb, Fc, Fe, Ff)

The section, 2 m in width, made in 2008 straight through the middle part of the main fortress (excavation zone F) encountered—in the western part—different wall courses, which belonged to the western wing and to the protruding flanking tower. In several places the section was enlarged, so that the exposed walls, as well as the stratigraphic features, could be fully captured and documented in planum.

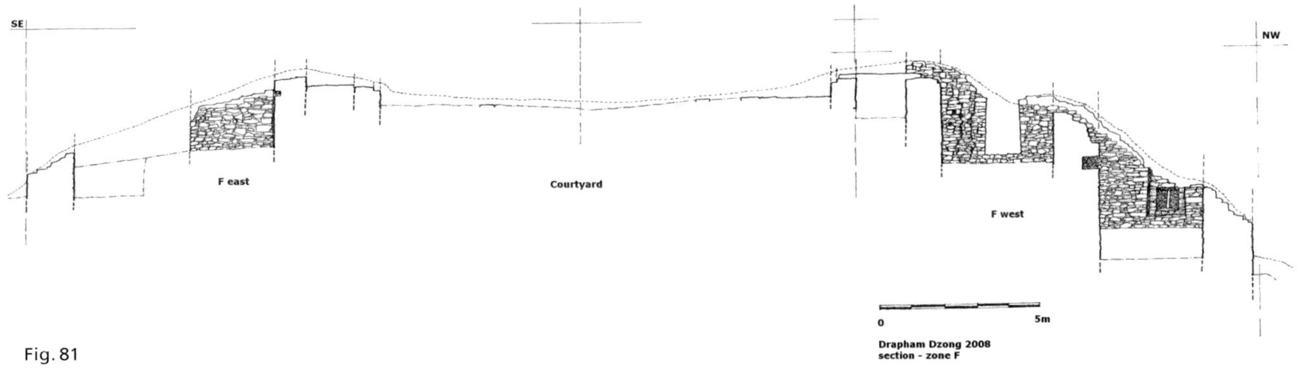

Fig. 81

No enlargement of the section seemed compelling in the middle portion in the vicinity of the Doche. Here, lying above the walkway horizon, which consisted of leveled clay, there was only forest humus and slight amounts of debris interspersed with humus, which at the middle axis of the interior courtyard measured merely a total of 30 cm in thickness and contained no signs of a settlement deposit. Accordingly, more extensive exposure in the vicinity of the Doche seemed to be superfluous.

Already in zones K and G, exposed remnants of the courtyard-side loggia (gallery corridor) (excavation sectors Fa and Fe) were puzzling. *In situ*, a portion of approx. 6 m^2 of the clay screed interspersed with gravel had been preserved. The clay screed, approx. 15 cm in thickness, rested in sector Fa on a compact encasement constructed with yellow clay. Both layers, the screed with the gravel and the encasement, covered the plinth

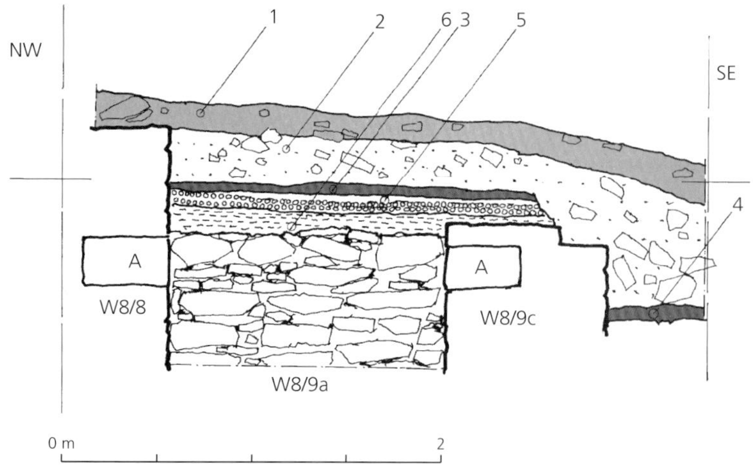

Fig. 82

Fig. 82 Stratigraphic profile in sector Fe (Loggia, western wing).
A Putholes.
1 Forest humus.
2 Wall debris.
3 and 4 Settlement deposits, humus.
5 Clay floor/screed with encasement out of pebbles.
6 Infill, yellow clay.
W.M.

Fig. 83 Sectors Ff and Fa. Middle section of western tract. In foreground to the left, slab paving of interior courtyard with stairs to loggia, wall W8/9c. View towards southwest. W.M.

wall of the loggia (gallery corridor) (W8/9c) to the edge of the rebate of the horizontal beams, on which the wooden columns of the loggia had been placed. On top of the clay screed, there was a thin, settlement layer—with no finds—consisting of humous, blackish-brown clay. Measuring 10 cm in thickness, this layer probably consisted not only of humus-producing settlement garbage, but rather—according to the color—was also from the decomposed remains of the wooded parts used in constructing the loggia.

At the courtyard side, plinth wall W8/9c was accompanied by a carefully jointed slab pavement, approx. 2.5 m in width (excavation sector Ff). Its border towards the interior of the courtyard proceeded in an unevenly frayed manner. At the northern edge of excavation sector Ff, a three-step staircase appeared in the profile of the wall, which led up from the Doche to a walkway level approx. 0.7 m higher than the loggia. The steps were executed using stone slabs. Fitted exactly into the middle step was a charred wooden board. This supported the assumption that stair steps at Drapham Dzong were at least partially reinforced with wooden planks. In any case, there were no traces of wear on the step slabs, and, in addition, the slabs were so thin (5–6 cm) that with frequent traffic, they would have soon become detached from the clay fitting.

The wall courses, which were revealed in the western part of excavation zone F, initially created a somewhat confusing impression, mainly because of the various butt joints that revealed an eventful sequence of construction, and because of the stratigraphy, which was distributed on three stories, one on top of the other. In zone F, the

83

under-construction of the loggia displayed a striking change. In the northern part (excavation sector Fa), a clay screed and encasement rested on a heterogeneous infill, which extended down into the foundation area of walls W8/9c and W8/5b (see below). Towards the south, this infill ended at transverse wall W8/9a. This was interlocked with the plinth wall, but abutted wall corner W8/5b–c with a joint. A hollow space began south of the transverse wall under the walkway level of the loggia (gallery corridor), over which spanned a frame of joists that had supported the clay screed of the loggia. The beam holes were still clearly recognizable on both sides, i.e., in walls W8/9c and W8/5c, insofar as the height of the wall structure had been preserved. The once hollow space—whose function remained unexplained—was filled with heterogeneous wall debris (see 3.3.7c.).

Adjacent to the loggia, in ground plan the middle section of the western wing formed almost a square shape, the outer length of the sides measuring approx. 11 m. The wall thickness varied between 1.1 and 1.6 m. A transverse wall (W8/4) divided the room into two large, approximately equal halves (excavation sectors Fb and Fc). This transverse wall followed the extension of enclosure walls W8/2 respectively W9/57, which ran north–south, adjacent to the building; inscribed in the course, however, was a notable kink, which can be explained by subsequent corrections of the overall ground plan (see 5.1.2.).

The interior of the trapezoidal walled-in area, consisting of rooms Fb and Fc, has not been fully excavated. By means of surface abrasions, however, the exact course of each wall could be comprehended and documented. Although the four exterior walls were interlocked, they received—due to the chronological staggering of the excavation—different designations. In the eastern half, where the building volume was integrated into the western wing, the walls were identified as W8/5a, W8/5b, and W8/5c. For the surrounding wall of the western part, which projected approx. 4.5 m from the course of enclosure wall W8/2, respectively W9/57a, the designations W8/3a, W8/3b, and W8/3c were assigned.

Following the topography of the slope of the debris, the crowns of the preserved wall courses steeply decline from the northeast to the southwest. The individual wall courses, partly still up to 5 m in height, enabled—once freed from debris—three stories to be detected, which were staggered following the slope.

With the progressive exposure of the wall courses, a number of openings were displayed in different states of preservation. From the loggia (gallery corridor) (excavation sector Fa), a door led at ground level to the first upper floor of room Fb. The southern reveal, aligned flush with wall W8/5c, had been preserved, as well as a piece of the threshold, which consisted of the clay screed of the loggia that extended into the door opening. The width of this door could no longer be determined.

The walkway level on the ground floor of room Fb was approx. 2.7 m lower than the clay screed of the loggia (gallery corridor). At the height of the flooring, there were two doors. One was installed in the middle of wall W8/5c. It led into the adjacent southern room Fd, which was subsequently erected. Its reveals, located up to a height of 1.7 m above the threshold, were still preserved and were oriented opposite each other, an inclination characteristic of wall openings at Drapham Dzong.

The second door opening, only still tangible at the height of the threshold, was detected in the middle of partitioning wall W8/4. It connected the ground floor of room Fb with the first upper floor of room Fc. Its ground floor, located approx. 2.5 m lower, was equipped on each of all three sides, which faced towards the outside, with a shooting embrasure or (arrow) slit. The embrasure or slit in northern wall W8/3a, only visible at the outer shell (see 3.3.4a.), aimed in a flanking manner along enclosure wall W8/2 towards the north. The embrasure or slit in the western longitudinal wall W8/3b was only distinguishable by small residues. It opened out onto the slope. The most well-preserved embrasure or (arrow) slit was the one in southern wall W8/3c. It was oriented

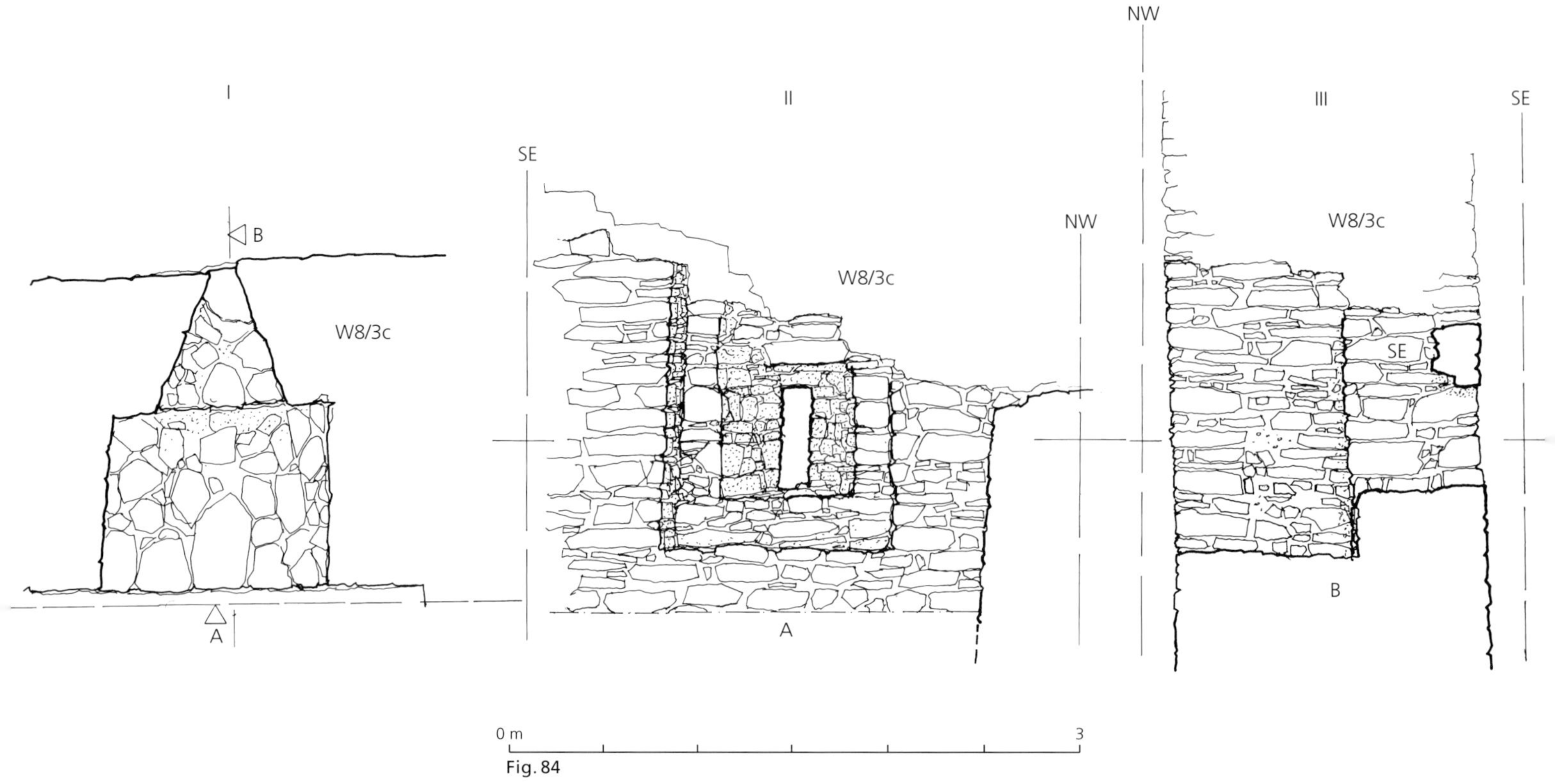

Fig. 84

towards the south and intended for flanking fire along enclosure wall W9/57a. It consisted—as presumably did the other two embrasures or slits—of a rectangular chamber, whose wooden covering was gone, and a conically narrowed shooting hatch with an orifice of approx. 60 cm in height and nearly 10 cm in width. The covering out of stone slabs had been preserved *in situ*.

In addition to doors and windows, further kinds of openings, which did not go all the way through, could be observed in the masonry. A series of holes with a rectangular cross section, embedded in wall W8/8, had held the load-bearing beams of the ceiling between the ground floor and first upper story of room Fc. Another series of beam holes was located in wall W8/4, which had belonged to the ceiling construction between the ground floor and first upper floor of room Fc. Smaller slots, with a rectangular cross section of 10 to 15 cm in length of the sides and a depth of 30 to 40 cm, had served to either hold scaffolding poles or lodge sacred objects.

The vertical articulation of the mass of building Fb/Fc into three still discernable volumes can be distinguished accordingly by the beam holes for the ceiling construction, by the thresholds of the connecting doors, and by the walkway levels of the re-

Fig. 84 Sector Fc. Western tower, shooting opening in wall W8/3c.
I Ground plan,
II Interior view,
III Longitudinal section
G.B.

Fig. 85 Sector Fc, interior of western tower. Embrasure (arrow slit) in wall W8/3c. View towards southeast. W.M.

85

Fig. 86 Middle section of western tract. Southern exterior wall of western tower (wall W8/3c) with shooting opening. View towards northwest. W.M.

spective ground floors. What the remains of the structure revealed was confirmed and complemented by the stratigraphy.

The upper layers, which consisted of approx. 20–30 cm in thickness of forest humus and loose secondary debris measuring up to 2 m in thickness, rendered little information of value. At most, to be mentioned are two stone base plates for wooden columns from the debris of room Fb. Both disclosed careful stone carving craftmanship, one was circular in form with a diameter of approx. 15 cm, the other was square in shape. Where the plates had been used, could no longer be determined, but considering the high quality of their execution, they must have belonged to a construction intended for representative display.

The primary debris in rooms Fb and Fc, up to 1.1 m in thickness, consisted mainly of compact clay. It contained lenses of small, round gravel and individual layers of humus, dark clay with anthropogenic inclusions (pottery, animal bones, find complex Fb.3). Apparently, this was sedimentation that resulted through the collapse of upper levels.

In room Fb, this primary debris—with its settlement deposits resulting through the collapse of upper stories direct on the walkway horizon—lay a manmade-leveled, yellow clay probably of natural origins. Material had been spread by the collapse up to the threshold of the door in wall W8/5c, where a humous lens with artifacts could be detected. In room Fc under the primary debris, this [spread of material] merged into a dark gray, loamy layer measuring 0.5 m in thickness, which probably had gradually accumulated as sedimentation of disposed garbage containing animal bones and pottery fragments (find complex Fb.3). Both in this layer, as well as in the primary debris, a loose scattering of charred wood remnants and burnt lenses appeared. A continuous, surface-covering burnt layer, however, could not be observed.

Important clues concerning the progression of construction were provided by the stratigraphic investigations in the foundation area of the individual wall courses. In excavation sector Fa, it was revealed that the plinth wall of the loggia (W8/9c) was placed with the foundation footing at a depth of 0.8 m below the clay screed on the surface of the natural moraine substrate. In contrast, for the longitudinal wall of the western wing (W8/5b), the moraine clay was steeply dug out, so that the bottom edge of the foundation came to lie on the level of walkway horizon Fb. The empty space between parallel walls W8/9c and W8/5b—as previously mentioned—was filled in with heterogeneous clay. A building horizon of white chalk particles was found approx. 20 cm below the clay screed.

86

87

Fig. 87 Middle section of western tract, sector Fc (in the front) and Fb. In between, wall W8/4. View towards southeast. W.M.

According to this feature, initially the lower levels of wall W8/5b were raised up to about the level of the inner courtyard, then the foundation trench that had been driven into the slope was backfilled, and a new, elevated building horizon was executed from the upper parts. Only afterwards was wall W8/5b continued to the loggia, whereby its plinth wall with the foundation footing came to rest directly on the natural surface of the moraine clay.

Constructing the foundation of partition wall W8/4 appears to have been executed following the same principle as was employed for wall W8/5b, since the outer, i.e., westward-oriented, lower edge of the foundation was placed directly on the natural, artisan-worked moraine clay. Its leveled surface formed the underlay not only for the construction horizon, preserved as white sand lens, but also for the first walkway level of room Fc, which—as already has been mentioned—was to gradually increase by 0.5 m in height through ongoing sedimentation of disposed waste.

The question arises, as to how the upper floors of the building might be imagined. A definite answer cannot be provided. Offering a quasi-minimal solution, it can be assumed, in terms of the structure, that there were three stories, so that from the courtyard side, the building appeared to be a single story. However, this solution cannot be

Fig. 88 Sector Fd. Wall W8/8 with putlog holes for ceiling over (not excavated) sub-story. View towards southeast. W.M.

satisfying, because according to the findings in excavation sector Kb/Kd, the courtyard side of the façade of the western wing in the northern section entailed at least two floor levels, which is why it's also to be assumed for the middle segment, that a further story had risen above the documented ground floor of room Fb, respectively above the three stories of room Fc. The possibility that still a further story had been raised out of the course of the enclosure wall's protruding room Fc is not to be ruled out, which would underscore its tower-like impression.

The shooting openings in the projecting part of the building are evidence of its integration in the defensive apparatus of the upper fortress.

Further reflections about the usage of the space remain speculative, even if the finding of two base plates for wooden columns might be interpreted as an indication of a representation function, which, however, cannot be more closely specified.

3.3.7c. Southern Segment (Excavation Sectors Fd, Ga, Gb, Ge, Gl)

The southeastern corner of the western wing was already truncated in 2008, when the small tower (South Ta Dzong) was investigated. At that time it was discovered that end wall W9/227b abutted at the northeastern corner of the small tower (W9/10b) with a joint. After the removal of the upper debris layers that covered the entire southern section, the main features of its ground plan were exposed. The walls of two rooms, whose narrow sides aligned next to each other (excavation sectors Gc and Fd), which the loggia (gallery corridor) (excavation sector Gb) was built in front of opposite the Doche.

Only a relatively small sector measuring 2×6 m in room Gc was exposed in the southern segment of the western wing. A portion of the loggia remained untouched, and in room Fd, as well as in the northern part of room Gc, it seemed sufficient to remove the secondary debris down to the ground level of a floor marked by putlog holes that was located below the loggia level. On the one hand, this restraint in removing the debris seemed advisable and justified considering the sparseness of finds and features in the fully excavated part of room Gl, and, on the other hand, on account of the poor condition of the exposed masonry, which remained most protected by the accompanying debris.

In the southern segment there were not any butt joints to be observed within the wall courses of the western wing. Therefore, it might be possible to assign the two rooms Fd and Gc, together with the loggia, to one and the same phase of construction, even if, based on certain features (see below) in the case of the interior finishings of room Fd, a subsequent change of the building plan must be assumed. However, the entire complex of the southern section adjoined the small tower as well as the building vol-

88

ume of the middle segment (rooms Fb and Fc, see 3.3.7b.) with continuous butt joints, indicating that it must have been built in the process of a more recent construction phase.

The courtyard-side longitudinal wall of the southern part of the western wing (W8/8) began at the northern front side in sector Kb with butt joint at wall W8/5c and at the southern end reached end wall W9/57b, where it dovetailed with it at a right angle. Running parallel at a distance of 1.6 m, the plinth wall of the loggia (W8/9c) was also dovetailed with wall course W9/57b. Between the angle of walls W8/9c–W9/57b and the small tower, there was a gap of approx. 0.6 m in width, analogous to the convergence of the small tower and the eastern wing (see 3.3.11d.). This anomaly of building technology probably stems from the aim to give the inner courtyard (Doche) as equal a width as possible along its entire length.

The construction of the exposed portion of the loggia in excavation sector Gb corresponded to the feature in excavation sectors Fa and respectively Fe. On the outer edge of the crown of wall W8/9c, the rebate for accommodating the foundation beams for the wooden columns was preserved. At the interior side of the loggia, the shells of wall courses W8/8 and W8/9c were eroded down to more than 0.5 m below its walkway level, so it was not possible to assess, whether the no longer existent clay screed in Gb had rested on supporting beams, as in excavation sector Fe, or had rested on an infill, as in excavation sector Fa. The heterogeneous, loamy material, which filled the room between the two wall courses W8/9c and W8/8, supported both interpretative options. This infill was only removed to a depth of 1.5 m below the preserved wall crowns. Small fragments of polychrome painted clay plaster alluded to the representative character of the building.

In wall W8/8 there was a rebate of a horizontal opening, slightly inclined towards the west, whose function remained unclear. At this level, it could not have belonged to a window, and, according to the width (0.6 m), it could also not have originated from a door. Two similar, but completely preserved openings appeared in wall courses W9/57a and W9/57b. Their base was located at the height of the walkway level of room Gl, and they could have served for the disposal of wastewater.

There was no doorway observed in the inner shell of the southern boundary wall W9/57b. On the other hand, in the outer shell (see 3.3.6.), an opening measuring 1.5 m in width, appeared, which had been subsequently walled up and which was similar to the feature in wall W9/38 east of the small tower (see 3.3.11d.). This entailed a hole in the wall, which was kept open during construction and pouring or chute work to facilitate material transport, and then walled shut when no longer needed.

Adjoining wall W8/5c to the south, the ground plan of room Fd defined a rectangle with interior dimensions measuring approx. 11 × 4.5 m. On the southern narrow side, there was a course of a transverse wall (W8/7), which dovetailed at its western end with enclosure wall W9/57a and to the east with the longitudinal wall W8/8. Room Fd was exposed only down to the level of an intermediate floor, which corresponded with the threshold level of the connecting door in wall W8/5c. In the southern transverse wall W8/8, no passageway to the adjacent room Gc was observed.

The level of the intermediate floor mentioned above in room Fd could be read by a series of putlog holes, which penetrated the western, i.e., inner shell of the courtyard side of longitudinal wall W8/8. Measuring an average of 0.3 m in height and width, they extended into the wall at different depths ranging from between 0.4–1.1 m. The varying depth of the holes was attributed to the unequal length of the beams, which apparently had been inserted into the wall as it was being built up.

On the opposite longitudinal side of the room Fd, the corresponding putlog holes were missing. In the southern part of the room, the wall was already eroded down below the level of the intermediate floor. To the north at wall W8/5c and respectively at pieces of abutting segments of W8/3c, the wall crown overtopped the spot height of the frame of joists by 0.5 to 1.2 m. But here as well, the corresponding putlog holes were missing in the wall shell. Instead, a bulwark (W9/5c) measuring 0.4 m in width appeared, which was adjoined with a longitudinal joint on the inside of enclosure wall W9/5a and displayed notches for accommodating the supporting beams.

This feature made it apparent that in erecting enclosure wall W9/57a, the height of the intermediate story had not yet been determined. The level was only fixed by notching the putlog holes during construction of longitudinal wall W8/8 on the courtyard side. Therefore, a facing had to be built in front of the already completed—or, in any case, already higher reaching—wall W9/57a, which had to accommodate the western end of the supporting beams. Apparently, they did not dare to subsequently hone beam holes in the finished shell of the wall.

In total, fifteen beams supported the intermediate floor of room Fd. As could be read by the notches in wall W8/8, the distances from beam to beam ranged from 0.4 to 0.7 m. Located at the same height and in the same arrangement, the frame of joists continued in room Gc, but here only thirteen beams holes could be confirmed, since this most southern part of the western wing measuring 9 m in length was slightly shorter than room Fd. In room Gc, as enclosure wall W9/57a was heavily eroded—its crown lay approx. 1.5 m underneath the intermediate floor—, there were no more traces preserved of the anchoring of the supporting beams on the west side of the room. Evidence of the frontal facing did not emerge on the inside of the enclosure wall.

The intermediate floor of room W8/8, readable from the putlog holes in wall W8/8, was about 3 m above the walkway level of the ground floor. This could be soundly identified in the southern part of the room, which was dug down to the settlement horizon. Under the voluminous masses of debris, which filled the room, lay a heterogeneous, brownish clay layer measuring 0.3 to 1 m in thickness. This could well have been primary debris, as it contained much rotted wood substance, which seemed to stem from interior finishings and roof structure. Under this deposit, there was a thin layer of blackish clay, only 2–3 cm in thickness. It contained occasional anthropogenic inclusions (animal bones, small fragments of pottery) as well as charred wood particles. This weakly distinguished settlement layer lay directly on the walkway horizon, which was formed at the surface by loamy-sandy infill. As displayed by the probe or test trench Nd at the outer footing of enclosure wall W9/57a (see 3.3.4c), the natural substrate stood approx. 2 to 3 m lower, which is why a manmade lateral fill had to be brought into the interior of the room. Thereby, a horizontal walkway level was created in room Gc, and—presumably—analogously also in room Fd.

The purpose that had been served by the floors arranged on top of each other in rooms Gc and Fd could not be determined due to lack of significant building construction features and small finds. The drainage openings mounted at the height of the walkway level in wall courses W9/7a and W9/57b did not permit any unequivocal determination of the function of room Gc.

As already suggested, the western wing was built in two phases. First, the northern segment was executed together with the middle tower building. In a next phase, the loggia and both rooms of the southern segment were completed. It seems, however, that the basic architectural concept, the transversally positioned tower with the two symmetrically adjacent southern and northern segments, had been planned from the beginning, so that decisions about certain details—marking out the wall courses or partitioning of the stories—were only made in the process of the ongoing construction work.

The question about connections between rooms and stories with each other could only be partly answered. Presumably every room possessed a door, which opened at the ground level into the loggia. Three of these were ascertained. At the ground level the northern room (Kb/Kd) had no direct connection with the southern adjacent foursided structure, not even so much as a passageway between rooms Gc and Fd. The latter, however was connected by a door with the tower building (room Fb). Finally, there was a door between the ground floor of room Fb and the first upper story of room Fc.

No traces have been preserved of the vertical connections. In the no longer existing upper stories there may have been narrow, steep stairs leading into the loggia. Any further reflections concerning the placement of doors and stairs remain speculative.

3.3.8. Eastern Wing (Shab Khor/East Drasha and East Ta Zee)

On the eastern—to be more precise, southeastern—longitudinal side of the inner courtyard (Doche), even before the beginning of excavation, an expansive building complex was evident, which seemed to extend from the Utse in the north to the small tower in the south. Debris ramparts indicated the approximate outline of the tract, especially in the middle area, where, beyond these, few wall traces led to any conclusion as to former transverse partitioning. At the edge of the fortress plateau, positioned precariously above the steep slope, which declines towards the southeast, some parts of the wall revealed the course of an enclosure wall (W9/43).

Complete exposure of the tract, which had an area of approximately 11 × 45 m and was covered by substantial masses of debris, was out of the question due to limitations of time and personnel. It was imperative to establish the northern and southern perimeters of the building, the main characteristics of the ground plan arrangement, and the stratigraphic proportions. Particular attention was paid to the southern section, where the inner door system was presumed to be located. Except for on these segments (excavation sectors Go and Gp, see 3.3.11.), the excavations remained limited to the exposure of a middle piece (excavation sectors Fg, Fh, Fi) and the northern front side (excavation sector Uc) as well as a few surface scrapings to verify the wall connections.

The overall ground plan of the wing (Shab Kor/Drasha) strongly resembled that of the western wing on the opposite side of the Doche, but displayed a few obvious differences (see 3.3.7.). Respectively, the interior partitioning of the two tracts did not correspond, and there was no flanking tower at the front of the eastern wing, as found in its counterpart at the western side of the Doche.

At the beginning of excavation, due to the masses of debris, i.e., the entire compound of the eastern wing was covered over, which made it impossible to realize that the natural substrate—analogous to the western wing—sloped down in steps from northeast to southwest. As gradually became clear during the process of the exposure work, the consequence of these differences in grade was that in the northern segment (excavation sector Uc), the walkway horizon of the ground floor corresponded approximately to the spot height of the Doche, while the middle and southern segment (excavation sectors Fh, Fi, Go) lay one-story-height lower. The borderline between the two different ground levels was not ascertained. It must have run along a transverse wall (W8/13) in the non-excavated piece of the tract between excavation sectors Uc and Fh.

Making the interpretation of the feature difficult was the fact that the fringe zone of the main fortress, where the eastern wing extended, had suffered from particularly heavy erosion of the terrain, so that entire parcels of strata—also since enclosure wall W9/43 was eroded quite far down—had been washed away. Whether the severe damage to the enclosure wall is attributable to natural decay or deliberate destruction will be discussed further later.

With the exception of a small trapezoidal, walled-in structure W8/20, which adjoined the longitudinal wall of the eastern wing opposite the courtyard side through butt joints (see 3.3.8b.), all the wall courses of the eastern tract were dovetailed with each other and thereby belonged to one and the same building phase.

Fig. 89 Sector Ub. Northern corner of eastern wing. On outer walls W9/44b and W9/46, remains of clay plaster coating. Marked in gray: red coloring. D.O.

3.3.8a. Northern Segment (Excavation Sector Uc)

At the beginning of excavation in 2008, the narrow side of the eastern wing, which is oriented towards the northeast, was completely hidden under wall debris and was only uncovered in 2009 during the process of exposure work at the eastern side of the Utse (see also 3.3.2a.).

The northeastern end wall of the tract (W9/44a) was dovetailed at the eastern end of long enclosure wall W9/43 and at the western end turned at a right angle into wall course W9/44b, which concluded the eastern wing along its entire length on the courtyard side. (The identification label W9/44a applies only to excavation sector Uc. Further south, in excavation zones F and G, the wall course is labeled W9/32.)

On walls W9/44a and W9/44b, there was clay plaster, approx. 3–4 cm in thickness, adhering on the exterior side of the wall, upon which substantial remnants of surface-covering, brownish-red paint had survived that, according to the materials analysis, mainly consisted of ocher. The loggia (East Ta Zee), projecting on the courtyard side of the eastern wing, was extended over wall corner W9/44a–b to the foot of the Utse (see 3.3.2a.).

In the northern section of the eastern wing an interior area of approx. 6.7 × 2.5 m could be exposed. Thereby, a wall niche measuring 0.45 m in width and 1.9 m in length was revealed in wall W9/44a. The bottom lay 0.5 m above the walkway horizon. The upper end had been lost through the disintegration of the wall.

The eastern end of the interior space in excavation sector Uc, enclosure wall W9/43, displayed a particularly advanced stage of ruin. Severely sloping from inside outwards, the wall crown only reached up to just 0.4 m under the walkway level of the interior space. Accordingly, the eastern segment of the floor abutting on the enclosure wall was on the verge of dissolving.

The upper layers seemed to be also disturbed as a secondary consequence, because apparently parts of the sloping wall debris deposit had slid down through erosion over the deep coursing crown of enclosure wall W9/43. As far as it was still intact, the stratigraphy in the interior space of excavation sector Uc displayed the familiar sequence from top to bottom with humous-rich forest soil, loose secondary debris, and more compact clay-rich primary debris. A settlement deposit was barely to be distinguished. Under primary debris, there was a layer of humous, gray-black clay, 1–2 cm in thickness and without finds. There were no burnt traces.

Fig. 89

90

Fig. 90 Sector Uc with northern section of eastern wing. In background, the Utse. View towards northwest. W.M.

Fig. 91 Sectors Fh and Fi. Middle section of eastern tract. Trapezoidal walled-in structure W8/20; in front, interior wall W8/21. In background, the Utse. View towards north. W.M.

A clay screed, 10–15 cm in thickness, formed the walkway horizon, which—as far as could be observed under its damaged edge at the eastern side—rested directly on the artificially leveled moraine substrate. The clay screed was densely interspersed with small, round gravel stones, 2–4 cm in diameter. The same gravel also appeared in looser, but more frequent succession in the clay of the primary debris, which supported the conclusion of the existence of at least one upper floor.

The spot height of the floor in the interior space of excavation sector Uc corresponded approximately to the level of the projecting loggia corridor and the adjacent northern section of the Doche. Accordingly, the room might have been accessible at ground level through a door executed in the non-excavated segment of longitudinal wall W9/44b.

3.3.8b. Middle Segment (Excavation Sectors Fg, Fh, Fi)

At the beginning of the excavations in 2008, a long section, approx. 2 m in width, was made across the compound of the main fortress in a northwest-southeast direction, which was intended to provide the first insights into the proportions of the layers under the forest substrate. In the eastern segment, through the test trench, several wall courses were recorded, which then in 2008, prompted an extension of the study area to a square measuring approx. 11 × 11 m (excavation sectors Fg, Fh and Fi).

At the eastern edge of the Doche (excavation sector Fg), a wall course appeared, which in hindsight proved to be a piece of the plinth wall for the loggia (W9/33). This

91

Fig. 92 Zone F west. W.M.

Fig. 93 Sectors Fh and Fi. Middle section of eastern tract. Courtyard-side wall W9/32, next to trapezoidal walled-in structure W8/20. View towards south. W.M.

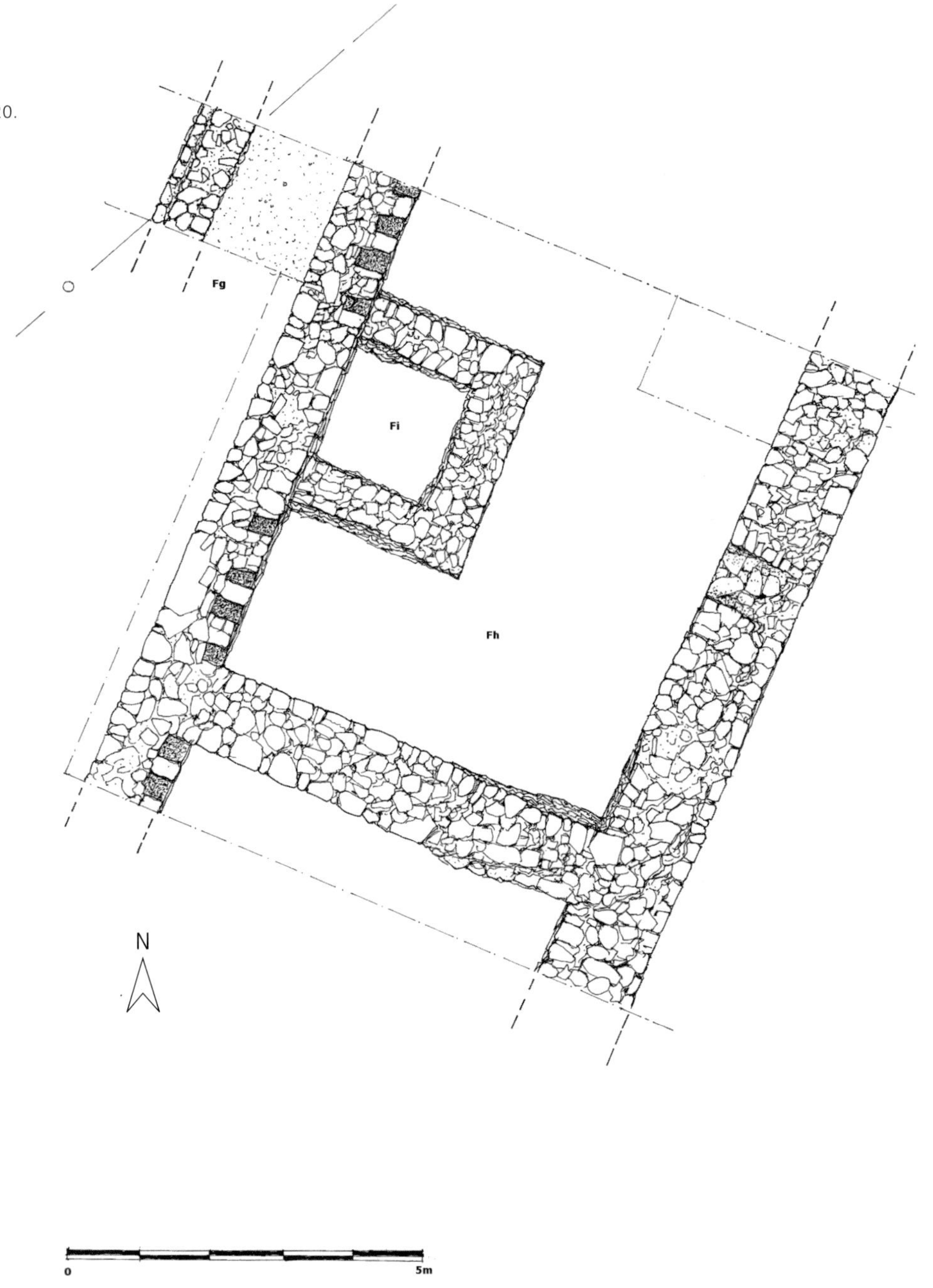

Fig. 92

wall course formed the stony underlay for the wooden columns of the loggia, approx. 1.5 m in width, which was built projecting at the front of the eastern wing along its entire length on the courtyard side. In the wall crown the rebate for the foundation beams, which had carried the columns, was still clearly recognizable. The surface of the clay screed, which formed the walkway horizon of the loggia, lay approx. 0.6 m higher than the level of the Doche, whose spot height could be read clearly on the basis of some irregularly laid stone slabs. Incidentally, located on this walkway level at the lower horizon of the wall debris, there was a fragment of a plinth disk, which had served as an underlay for a wooden column at a not identified spot.

Densely interspersed with small, round gravel stones, the clay screed of the loggia corridor lay on a loamy, heterogeneous infill, with which the height difference between the natural moraine substrate and the walkway level had been evened out.

The longitudinal wall of the eastern wing (W9/32), 1.2 m in thickness and running behind the loggia, had been preserved only up to the height of the clay screed in the loggia. In the crown, however, there was a strikingly large stone slab measuring 1.2 m

93

in length, which is presumably to be interpreted as a threshold of a door, through which the interior of the eastern wing could have been entered from the loggia.

Barely 0.5 m south of this presumed threshold slab and branching off at a right angle with dovetailing, there was a transversal wall (W8/21), 1.1 m in thickness, which sank down to enclosure wall W9/43. Although the merger of these two wall courses was greatly disturbed by roots, their dovetailing could still be clearly distinguished. As already observed further north in excavation sector Uc, enclosure wall W9/43 was eroded quite far down. Its crown lay approx. 2.5 m below the destruction horizon of parallel inner wall W9/32.

As a consequence, excavation sector Fh encompassed a room, which occupied the entire width of the eastern wing, and to the southwest was separated by a transverse wall (W8/21) from an adjacent room with the same width, but of unknown length. Possibly this entailed the same room that had been partially truncated by excavation sector Go (see 3.3.11b.). Indications of a connecting door in wall W8/21 leading to the south have not emerged. The northeastern perimeter of room Fh remained hidden under the debris that was not removed.

A small, almost square walled-in four-sided structure (W8/20a–c), whose exterior perimeter measured approx. 2.8 × 2.8 m, leaned inwardly on wall course W9/32. With a wall thickness of approx. 0.6 m, the building was separated from wall W9/32 by butt joints. The fact that the trapezoidal, walled-in structure was only built later was not only apparent from the two butt joints, but also from a series of putlog holes, which had been inserted into the inside of wall W9/32 and had been partially obscured by the adjacent walled-in four-sided structure W8/20. Apparently, the intermediary floor, which the beams embedded in these holes had supported, was subsequently changed to make room for the small walled-in four-sided structure W8/20. However, this had replaced an older, construction, presumably made out of wood, because the sequence of putlog holes in the interior of walled-in four-sided structure W8/20 showed an interruption. The inside of the walled-in four-sided structure (excavation sector Fi) was filled with heterogeneous debris, which did not support making any conclusions about the function. In the adjacent room to the southwest, the series of putlog holes continued at the same level, suggesting, as a consequence, that this room must also have contained an intermediary ceiling.

The putlog holes were positioned at a height that corresponded with the level of the clay screed in the loggia and presumed door threshold in wall W9/32. As a consequence, there must have been a further floor located below this level in room Fh. This conclusion was also correlated by traces of an opening that had been preserved in the heavily eroded crown of enclosure wall W9/43, which, with a width of 0.8 m, could be interpreted only as the remnants of a window.

The stratigraphic features in rooms Fh and Fi remained obscure. In the clay parcels of debris deposits, there were many small, round gravel stones, which must have originated from the floors of stories located higher up. However, neither a walkway horizon nor a settlement deposit was distinguishable anywhere below the level of the putlog holes, neither in profile nor in planum. Despite an exploratory shaft up to 3.5 m under the spot height of the frame of joists, a floor for the deeper lying room could not be detected. The clay screed in the loggia and the frame of joists mounted at the same height thereby constituted the only clearly tangible walkway horizon.

The window opening in the enclosure wall disproves the hypothesis that the story underneath the frame of joists is to be considered as only an unused hollow space. On the other hand, not to be ruled out, is the possibility that the clay and stone masses that filled the interior of the room concern an applied infill, similar to the material that was exposed in room Go (see 3.3.11b.).

Explaining the function of the small, subsequently built walled-in four-sided structure W8/20a–c proved to be impossible. Based on the dimensions, an initially plausible-

94

Fig. 94 Northern exterior corner of the Utse, wall W9/41a. Clearly visible outward-sloping masonry in a state of disintegration. View towards southeast. W.M.

Fig. 95 Sector Ea, interior of northern tower. View towards northwest. W.M.

seeming interpretation as a collection tank for drinking water had to be rejected as untenable, since there were no traces of a sealant having been used in the weak wall structure. Any water filled into the structure would have immediately seeped away. Because of the lack of small finds in excavation sectors Fh and Fi, which might have provided possible clues, the entire features in the middle segment of the eastern wing had to remain functionally non-interpreted.

3.3.9. Northwestern Annex and North Ta Dzong (Excavation Sectors Ea, Ka, Kb, Tf)

The wall remnants located to the northwest of the Utse, which were visible before the beginning of excavation, permitted the outlines of a rectangular tower (North Ta Dzong) to be recognized. Due to the voluminous masses of debris stemming from the Utse, most of the masonry was covered, and its integration into the overall ground plan was no longer distinguishable. In particular, what remained unclear was how North Ta Dzong was interrelated architectonically with the Utse. The exposure work began in 2008 inside North Ta Dzong (excavation sector Ea), where the wall remnants sticking out from the debris conveyed the most indications. Likewise in 2008, a small, flagged courtyard between the western corner of the Utse and enclosure wall W8/2 (excavation sector Kb) emerged, while the talus cone between the Utse and North Ta Dzong (excavation sector Tf) was first removed in 2010, albeit only down to the height of the crown of enclosure wall W8/2.

Among the most important discoveries in this excavation compound was verification of wall W9/60, which directly connected North Ta Dzong with the Utse (see 3.3.5.). Through the removal of the talus cone in excavation sector Tf, the northwestern wall of the Utse (W9/41d) lost its support and had to be secured by oblique wooden poles.

3.3.9a. North Ta Dzong (Excavation Sector Ea)

The exposure work inside of North Ta Dzong in 2008 was part of the first archaeological interventions at the excavation site. Respectively, there was great uncertainty as to which stratigraphic and constructive features might likely surface, and especially, at what depth a walkway level would appear. As the crown of the four-sided, walled-in structure of the tower (W8/1a—1c), coursing almost horizontally, lay under a compact, humous cover, 10–20 cm in thickness and consolidated by roots, which provided an excellent means of protection against weathering, complete removal of the covering was foregone, and the wall surface was only partially exposed, especially in the area of the window openings (see below).

The footprint of the tower formed a rectangle with a clearance of 4.5 × 7.4 m. The wall thickness varied between 1.4 m at the southeastern wall (W8/1d) and 1.7 m on the

95

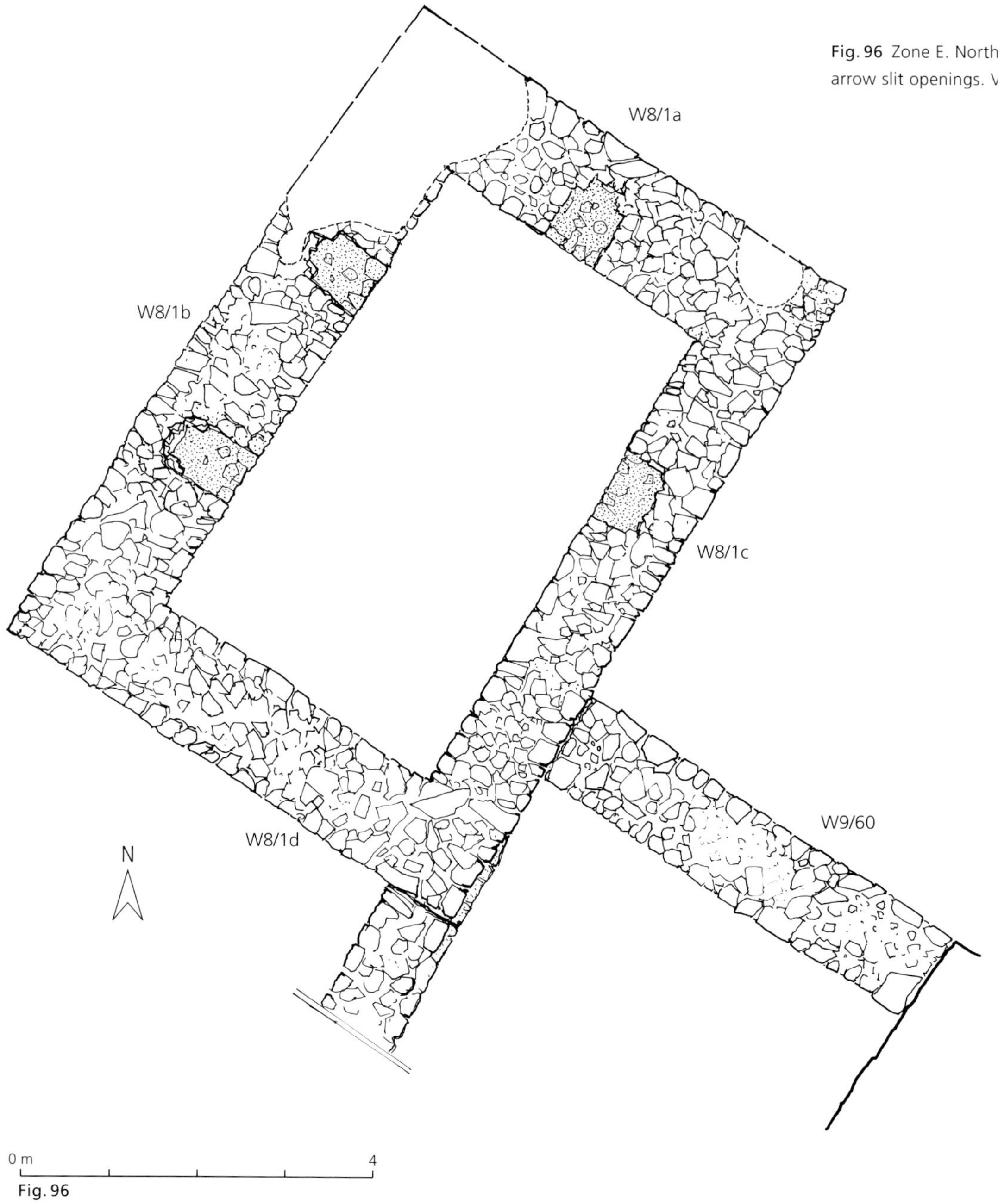

Fig. 96

Fig. 96 Zone E. Northern tower with collapsed arrow slit openings. V.W., G.W.

remaining sides. The outer wall shell showed a slight inclination of six degrees. After the exposure of the connection walls, it was apparent that North Ta Dzong jutted out for 4.3 m on the northwestern side and 4.7 m on the northern side from the course of the respective enclosure walls (W8/2 and W9/60), whereby it could be identified as a flanking corner tower.

At the beginning of the excavation, where the wall crowns of the tower showed noticeable sinking, in the process of the exposure work, window openings appeared. Except for a few remnants, their wooden lintels had so completely decomposed in the rebates at the sides over the jambs that the wall structure lying above it had collapsed, which had caused the aforementioned sinking. In total, there were five window openings, one each in the southeastern, northeastern, and southwestern walls plus two in the northwestern wall. Their construction corresponded to a typology also observed elsewhere in the main fortress (see 3.3.2., 3.3.7., 3.3.10.). This concerned embrasures or (arrow) slits consisting of a rectangular chamber, approx. 1.4 m in height, covered with wood beams, and a narrow, conically tapered mouth covered with stone slabs. In wall W8/1 there was one with a horizontal, rectangular contour (*Maulscharte*, horizontal embrasure), in other embrasures, a vertical slit, slightly widened towards the bottom.

Fig. 97 Collapsed lintel of shaft opening in wall W8/1c of northern tower (sector Ea). View towards northeast. W.M.

Fig. 98 Zone E. Shooting opening in northern tower, wall W8/1c. Collapsed lintel. Transverse-rectangular shooting hatch. G.B.

97

The question of the location of the entrance to the tower remained unanswered. It had to be positioned in the southeastern corner, where the masonry—exposed only at the surface—, however, contained no evidence of a doorway. In the wall crown not only was any rebate indicating a reveal missing, but there was also no telltale sinking that might have suggested the location of an opening lying deeper below. Moreover, the distance between wall course W9/60, abutting from outside, and the inner corner of tower W8/1c–d was only 0.8 m, which would hardly have been enough for a doorway. The conjecture that the entrance to the tower had been installed higher than the current height of the wall crown seems plausible.

The inner shells of the walls of the tower exhibited a variety of rectangular holes, approx. 0.4 m deep, with a square cross section and a side length measuring 10–15 cm. They were too numerous and positioned too close together to be able to be interpreted as scaffolding lever holes. Small round gravel stones were deposited in individual holes, which suggested that the openings were intended to accommodate objects having religious significance.

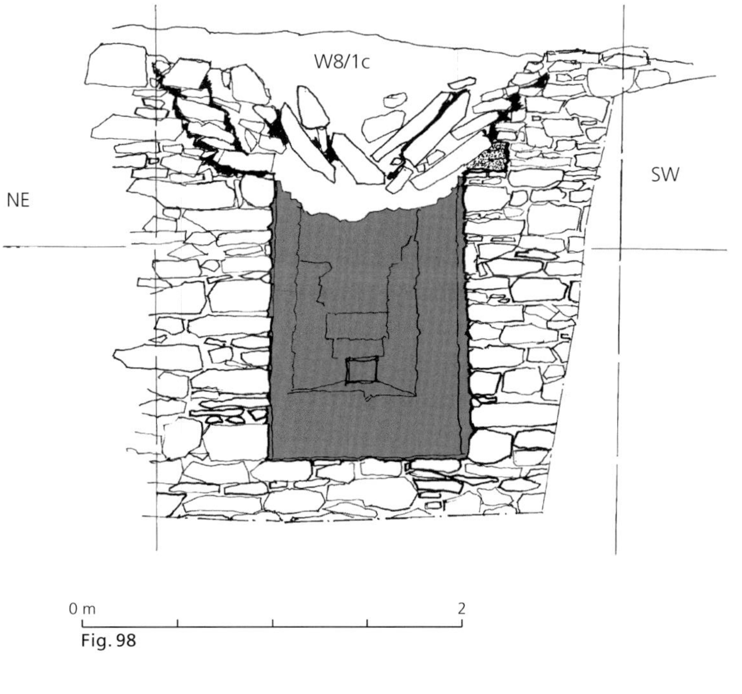

Fig. 98

Fig. 99 North-western tower in the corner zone E, wall W1a with arrow loop. G.B.

Fig. 99

Few indicators were provided by the stratigraphy in the interior of the tower. From the level of the windowsills up to the wall crown, the entire room was filled with debris consisting of clay and stones. A clearly identifiable walkway level did not appear. Approx. 0.5 m below the windowsills in the northeastern and southeastern walls, there was a thin burnt layer that tapered off towards the middle of the room. In the burnt layer traces of several beams were outlined, apparently the remains of a collapsed wood ceiling.

Beginning under the burnt layer was an infill composed of clay and a few stones, which had probably formed the artificially built underlay for a floor, from where the five balistraria or arrow loops beyond could be accessed.

3.3.9b. Northwestern Annex (Excavation Sectors Ka, Kb, Tf)

After the removal of debris masses totaling approx. 2 m in height from in between the western corner of the Utse (W9/41c and W9/41d) and enclosure wall W8/2, a slab paving emerged (excavation sector Ka), which occupied a rectangle measuring approx. 4.5×2.2 m. At the southwestern longitudinal side, it bordered on the end wall of the western wing (W8/5c); at the northeastern side, on a wall course W8/19, which extended between the Utse and enclosure wall W8/2. Dovetailed with the latter, the wall course touched the corner of the Utse with a distinct butt joint.

Paved with slabs, sector Kb was accessible from the Doche, respectively from the loggia of the western wing along its entire width via two steps executed with stone slabs. A settlement deposit was neither visible on the surface of the slab paving nor on the steps. The slab paving led to the conclusion that sector Ka had not been covered or roofed, but rather had formed a small, open courtyard.

A walled room (excavation sector Tf) bordered this courtyard to the northeast, which in plan defined a slightly shifted trapezoid with internal dimensions measuring 9×6.1 m, respectively, 5.5 m. Its northwestern longitudinal side was bounded by enclosure wall W8/2, respectively wall W8/1d of North Ta Dzong, which were dovetailed with each other. To the southeast, the room abutted the Utse (W9/41d), to the northeast, against wall W9/60, which stretched with butt joints between North Ta Dzong and the northern corner of the Utse. On the southwestern narrow side, the aforementioned wall course W8/19 completed the room. The doorway must have been located in this wall, through which room Tf could have been entered from the small courtyard Ka. Since its crown, however, was heavily eroded, in places down to below the slab level of sector Ka, there was nothing preserved of the door, not even the threshold sill.

The wall debris on excavation sector Tf was only removed to a spot height of approx. 0.5 m below the crown of enclosure walls W8/2 and W9/60. Underneath this level, however, there must have been still another entire story, as proven by the two deep-seated embrasure or (arrow) slit openings in the outer wall shells of wall courses W8/2 and W9/60. Accordingly, the presumed entrance in wall W8/19 would therefore have led from the paved courtyard of sector Kb into the first upper story of annex room Tf.

The crown of wall courses W8/2 and W8/1d pointed to the inner edge of a horizontal rebate, approx. 15 cm in width, whose interpretation remains open. The lack of a counterpart at the opposite outer wall of the Utse discourages a reading as support for a wood construction.

Since annex room Tf has only been exposed at the surface, further statements, namely about finishings and stratigraphy, are not possible. Nonetheless, the balistraria or arrow loops in the outer walls prove that the room was integrated in the defense system of the main fortress.

3.3.10. Northeastern Annex and East Ta Dzong (Excavation Sectors Ua, Ub, Ue)

At the time of the 2007 reconnaissance expedition, a literally impenetrable situation prevailed east of the Utse. Thick bushes and tall trees prohibited a view of the structure of the site terrain and allowed only occasional detection of traces of walls. The removal of vegetation, already started in 2007 and completed in 2008, brought few new insights. There were some buildings remnants, which seemed to stem from a corner tower (East Ta Dzong) and an enclosure wall (W9/43). But the southeastern outer wall of the Utse (W9/41b) could not be distinguished; accordingly, there were also no visible traces of an architectonic link between the Utse and East Ta Dzong. The entire complex—later assigned to excavation zone U—was covered by a steep heap of rubble,

100

Fig. 100 Zone U, Northeastern Annex, Overview. View towards northeast. W.M.

whose thickness was initially not known, which extended from the summit of the Utse, where the hermit had built his hut (see 3.3.2d.), dropping down to the barely discernable enclosed walled structure of East Ta Dzong. Also these tower remnants appeared to be stuck in meter-high masses of rubble.

Given the imposing amounts of debris, only a broadly defined sector excavation was considered feasible. The work began in 2009 and was completed in 2010. It encompassed the compound between the Utse and corner tower W8/15a–d and enclosure wall W9/42. The corner tower itself remained largely untouched. After successful documentation of the still visible wall traces, its inner sector served as a depot for the accrued wall masonry blocks from the wall debris of zone U.

In ground plan, the wall courses that emerged in the process of the exposure work revealed an approximate mirror image of the feature on the northwestern side of the Utse (see 3.3.9.), however, important details distinguished these courses in the two sectors from each other.

As on the other excavation sectors, in zone U most of the wall courses soon appeared from under the humous cover of the forest floor. Apparently, the walls had gradually collapsed, until the growing coat of debris had reached the height of the wall crown and had thereby prevented further collapse. The consideration of traces of destruction by humans is addressed elsewhere (see 5.2.3.).

3.3.10a. Eastern Corner Tower (East Ta Dzong)

Of the eastern corner tower (W8/15a–d), only the outlines of the exterior as well as parts of the entrance in the southwestern corner (excavation sector Ue) were exposed. With a clearance of 4.8×7.6 m and a wall thickness of 1.4–1.7 m, the dimensions of the outlines corresponded in ground plan exactly with the rectangular measurements of North Ta Dzong (see 3.3.5b.).

Enclosure walls W9/49 and W9/43 (see 3.3.10b.) adjoined the tower with distinct butt joints. Accordingly, the tower was initially executed as a standalone structure, until it was integrated in the overall complex during a later phase of construction. The entrance, a door opening measuring 1.3 m in width in wall W8/15b, led from the ground floor annex room of excavation sector Ue into the interior of the tower, whereby the southern jamb was aligned flush with the inner shell of the southern tower wall W8/15c. The lowness of the position of the two openings or arrow loops (balistraria) of the embrasure or (arrow) slits, which appeared at the outer face of the northwestern and northeastern walls (W8/15b and W8/15), indicated that there must have been a further story under the threshold sill level of the entrance. Both openings were rectangular horizontal embrasures or loopholes. The embrasures presumably executed on the eastern and southern sides of the tower (W8/15c and W8/15d) have not been excavated.

While no certain statements about the original height of East Ta Dzong are possible, estimating on the basis of the amount of debris inside, however, it may have surmounted the abutting enclosure walls by the height of at least one story.

3.3.10b. Northeastern Annex (Excavation Sectors Ua and Ue)

At the southeastern narrow side of the Utse, there was an adjoining trapezoidal walled structure, approximately 8.9 m in interior length and 5.4–6.5 m in width. Besides Utse wall W9/41b and southwestern corner of East Ta Dzong (W8/15b), it was enclosed to the northeast by end wall W9/49, to the southeast by the northernmost section of enclosure wall W9/43, and to the southwest by the partition wall or bulkhead W9/45. The wall courses showed butt and dovetail joints, which made the construction sequence in zone U clearly visible. End wall W9/49 was spanned with butt joints between the northeastern corner of the Utse and East Ta Dzong. Enclosure wall W9/43 adjoined the southwestern corner of East Ta Dzong, being slightly recessed or set back with a

Fig. 101 Zone Ua. Interior view of enclosure wall W9/43 with two shooting openings. A.S.

butt joint, but dovetailed with partition or bulkhead wall W9/45, which in turn adjoined the southeastern corner of the Utse with a butt joint. In the masonry of zone U, three stages of construction could be distinguished: First, the Utse was built, then came East Ta Dzong, and in the third stage, the enclosure and connecting walls W9/49, W9/43, W9/45 were executed.

Apart from the entrance in East Ta Dzong (see 3.3.10a.), further and different kinds of openings appeared in these wall courses. In the middle of the Utse wall, a well-preserved embrasure with a vertical slit emerged. (Its interior, a niche with wooden lintels, however, had completely collapsed, see 3.3.2d.). The other door and window openings were still preserved up to the rebates of the wood lintels, which were located at the height of the horizontally worn-down wall crowns.

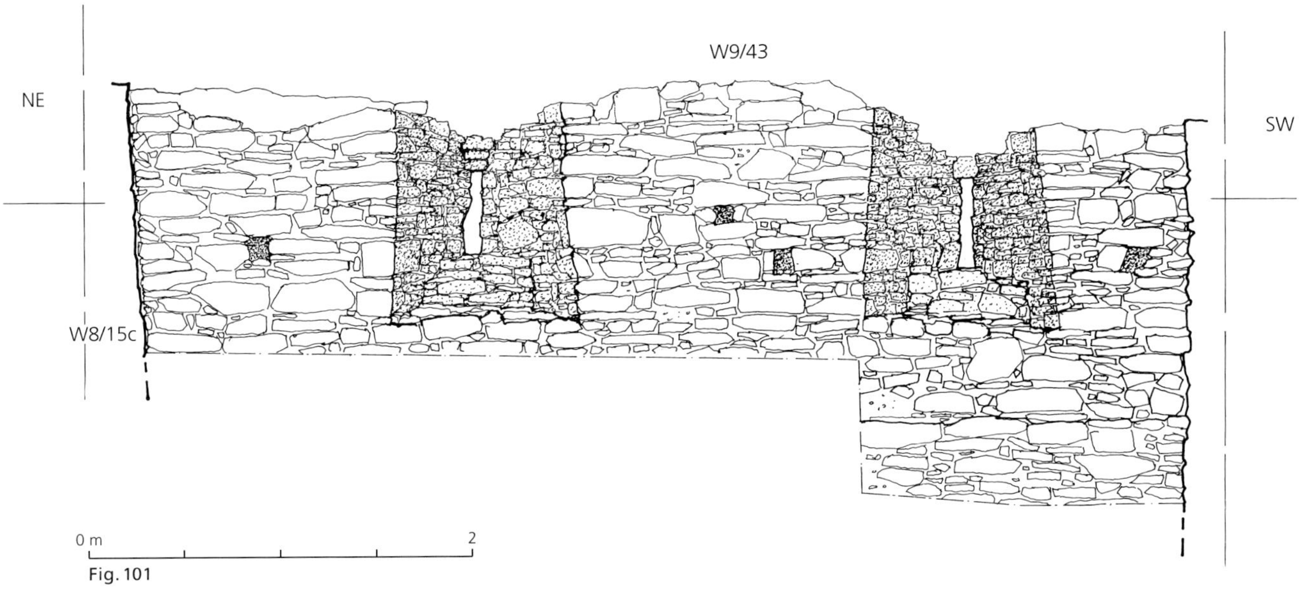

Fig. 101

Wall W9/45, which defined the annex to the southwest, i.e., towards the corridor (sector Uc), contained a door opening, 1.6 m in width and slightly shifted from the middle. The upper parts were heavily damaged, because a thick rootstock had disturbed the wall course exactly at this location. There was no paving of the threshold sill of the passage at the ground, but rather a walkway level on the manmade-leveled natural substrate. This was located at the same height as the floor of the interior (excavation sector Ua), but approx. 20 cm lower than the level of the adjacent corridor to the south (excavation sector Ub, see 3.3.10c.).

The end wall on the northeastern narrow side of the annex (W9/49) was pierced by two openings: a door and an embrasure or (arrow) slit. The latter appeared to be in relatively good condition, apart from the missing wooden beams of the lintel, whose notches still existed over the reveals. The embrasure consisted of a rectangular chamber, 0.8 m in width and 0.7 m in depth, as well as a conical slit or balistraria, which was sheltered above by stone slabs. These were partially still existent *in situ*.

The door opening, executed 1.2 m west of the embrasure, was in bad condition, but after being completely exposed, it was evident that most of the stone slabs, which had formed the threshold sill paving, had been ripped out. The reveals were also damaged, but still permitted recognition of the horizontal notches for the wooden cladding. As the doorway gradually emerged during the process of removing the debris, it was evident that the door opening was walled up with single-skin masonry and was positioned flush with the outside alignment (W9/47). Towards the interior of the annex room, the structure of the walled up construction blended smoothly into the debris that filled the room.

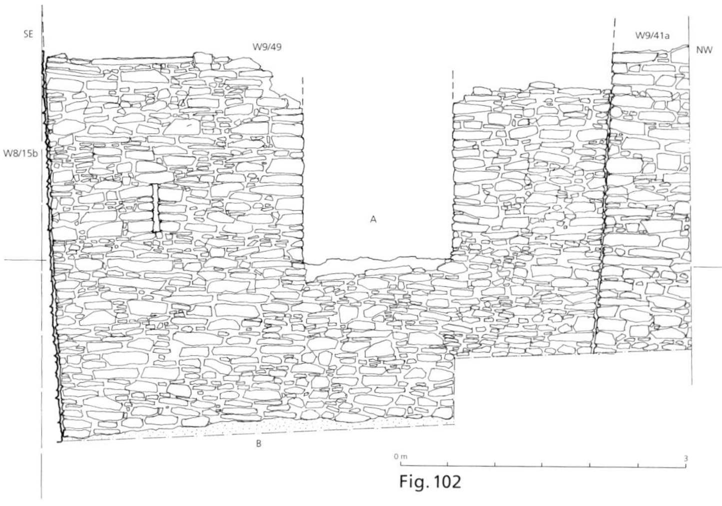

Fig. 102

Fig. 102 Sector Ud. Exterior view of enclosure wall W9/49. A: Gate opening (walled-up W9/47 dismantled), B: natural subsoil. D.O.

Fig. 103 Sector Ue. Shooting opening in wall W9/49. Near the scale, notch for the wooden lintel. W.M.

Two balistraria or arrow loops, with a distance of 1.5 m between them, appeared in the 3.5-m-long piece of enclosure wall W9/43, which bounded the annex room on the southeastern side. This entailed simple embrasures, tapered conically towards the outside with vertical slit openings over a tier raised 25 cm on the horizontal bench. The slits were 10 cm in width and 50 cm in height. Approx. 50 cm below the embrasure bench at the inside of the wall, there was a rebate approx. 30 cm in width. This belonged perhaps to a wooden platform, from where the embrasures could be used.

Leaning against the foot of Utse wall W9/41b, there was a square wall plinth, with a side length of approx. 0.8 meters (W9/48). It was positioned just below the abovementioned embrasure opening. The plinth could hardly have been any higher; otherwise, it would have blocked the embrasure opening. Perhaps it had served as a base for a prayer wheel.

Stratigraphically, the interior of the annex room yielded few conclusive features. In the wall debris, occasional charred wood fragments appeared, which originated from the Utse. The lower layers of debris, 2–3 m in thickness, contained higher proportions of clay than the upper layers, in which there was rather a predomination of loosely wedged wall masonry pieces. The single-skin, walled up doorway on the northeastern side (W9/47) was combined with the loamy, lower debris sedimentation layers.

Under the debris, a burnt layer, 5–10 cm in thickness, could be identified that consisted of amorphous, gray ash lenses, reddened clay, and black micro-particles of charred wood substance. There were no definable artifacts preserved in the layer, just as there were none in the subsequent underlying, only very weakly defined settlement sedimentation out of blackish clay. The manmade-leveled surface of the natural moraine substrate formed the walkway horizon, which was discolored black and red by the burnt and settlement sedimentation that had collected on top of it. No floor covering, neither a clay screed nor stone slab construction, could be ascertained in the annex room. In contrast, there was a depot of rounded pebble stones found at the footing of the Utse wall (W9/41d) along its entire length. Piled up against the Utse wall, directly over the walkway horizon, and in a mass measuring 1.2 m in width and 0.7 m in height, the seemingly carefully selected stones had a rounded, ball-like form with a diameter of approx. 8–12 cm. Individual specimens were stained with ocher. The function and significance of these stone depots—one smaller, but also of the same kind also appeared in excavation sector Sb (see 3.3.1b.) will to be addressed elsewhere.

The absence of a slab floor could indicate that the annex room Ua/Ue was roofed or covered. Considering the height of the upper window opening in the southeastern wall of the Utse, however, it is to be assumed that the annex building included only a ground story.

103

3.3.10c. Corridor (Excavation Sector Ub)

Similar in ground plan to the small courtyard in excavation sector Ka (see 3.3.9b.), yet differing from it in certain details, a narrow, rectangular room adjoined the northeastern annex to the south, respectively the southwest. The room was enclosed by the partition or bulkhead wall W9/45, by the northeastern narrow side of the eastern wing (W9/44a), and a segment of enclosure wall W9/43. All of these wall courses were dovetailed with each other, i.e., belonged to one and the same stage of construction.

Towards the northwest, the room opened to the northernmost segment of the loggia that is positioned in front of the east wing. The open passage between walls W9/45 and W9/44a was narrowed by a column (W9/46) with a resulting expanse of 2.4 m. This was rested against the northwestern corner of the east wing with a butt joint.

In enclosure wall W9/43, remains of an embrasure or (arrow) slit were still visible. In terms of type, here they corresponded with the two best preserved loopholes in excavation sector Ua, but featured—in heavily damaged condition—a slightly oblique orientation of the breakthrough.

Under the debris that filled the entire room up to above the preserved wall crowns, there was a weakly defined settlement layer of blackish clay permeated with thin burnt lenses. There were no small finds. The settlement layer had discolored the walkway horizon—which it covered—alternately dark gray and reddish gray. It consisted mostly of the manmade-leveled, natural substrate, but contained paving with loosely laid stone slabs. Before the entrance to the annex room in wall W9/45, a slab pavement extended over a triangular area measuring approx. 2 m^2, which formed a step in front of the door to its lower lying passage.

The difference in level between the clay-gravel ground of the loggia and the walkway horizon lying approx. 25 cm lower than the corridor was bridged by a step constructed out of stone slabs, which was spanned between the partition wall or bulkhead W9/45 and column W9/46.

The balistraria or arrow loop in wall W9/43 proves that the corridor was integrated together with the annex building and East Ta Dzong in the defensive apparatus of the main fortress. The room provided the ground-level connection between the Doche and annex building as well as the eastern corner tower. Whether the narrow space, approx. 2.5 m in width and 6 m in length, was covered or roofed, could not be determined with certainty. The scant burnt remains did not yield a conclusive image. Possibly the room was designed as an open, narrow courtyard, which, however, was equipped with a small roof at the inner face of enclosure wall W9/43, which would have protected the standing position behind the balistraria or arrow loop from rain.

3.3.11. Inner Gateway (Excavation Sectors Go, Gp, Za, Zb)

The features processed in 2008 and 2009 in Zone L and in the area of the small tower (excavation sectors Gb, Gc) suggested that access from the outer gateway in zone S to the inner courtyard (Doche) was to be found under the voluminous masses of debris that were piled east of the small tower. Except for some stone layers of presumed enclosure wall W9/37a, any remains of walls were not recognizable in this southeastern segment of the main fortress. Then in 2010, it turned out that massive amounts of debris—900 to 1,000 m^3—had to be removed before the expected gateway with its wall courses, gate openings, and walkway levels was finally exposed.

In the process of removing the debris, a massive erratic block with multiple fractures also appeared, which protruded out of the moraine clay in front of the southern corner of the small tower. The boulder was imbedded at an inclined angle in the clay substrate and appeared to have largely kept its natural form. Only on the northern side did the inclined surface feature an artisan-hewn, horizontal rung, 15 cm in width and 80 cm in length, presumably a support for the scaffolding at the outer side of small tower.

104

Fig. 104 Sectors Za and Zb. Forecourt of gate building Go. In foreground, wall W10/63 with stair steps. View towards northeast. W.M.

Fig. 105 Section through gateway, sector Gp. A: Frame of joists above corridor (^{14}C-Dating: approx. 1475 p. Chr. n.), B: Reconstructed route of stairs to interior courtyard, C: Moraine boulder.

1 Forest humus.
2 Wall debris.
3 Clay and gravel level of loggia.
4 Infill in loggia.
G.W.

Fig. 106 Excavation 2010, top view, areas Go, Gp, Za, Zb. W.M., J.O., V.W.

As the massive debris was removed sector-by-sector, the southeastern-oriented enclosure wall of the main fortress also appeared, which made it possible to distinguish two phases of construction whose separation from one another was demarcated by a continuous butt joint. The northern section of wall W9/43 was conjoined with end wall W9/38 that branched out from the small tower (W8/10a–d). These two wall courses formed a right-angled corner abutting the southern section of enclosure wall W9/37, which extended beyond to the southeast over several rock heads, steadily following the slope until reaching the outer gate in sector Sd (see 3.3.1a.).

The features determined in the vicinity of the inner gateway are expected to be extremely informative for construing the circumstances of the history of the construction of the main fortress.

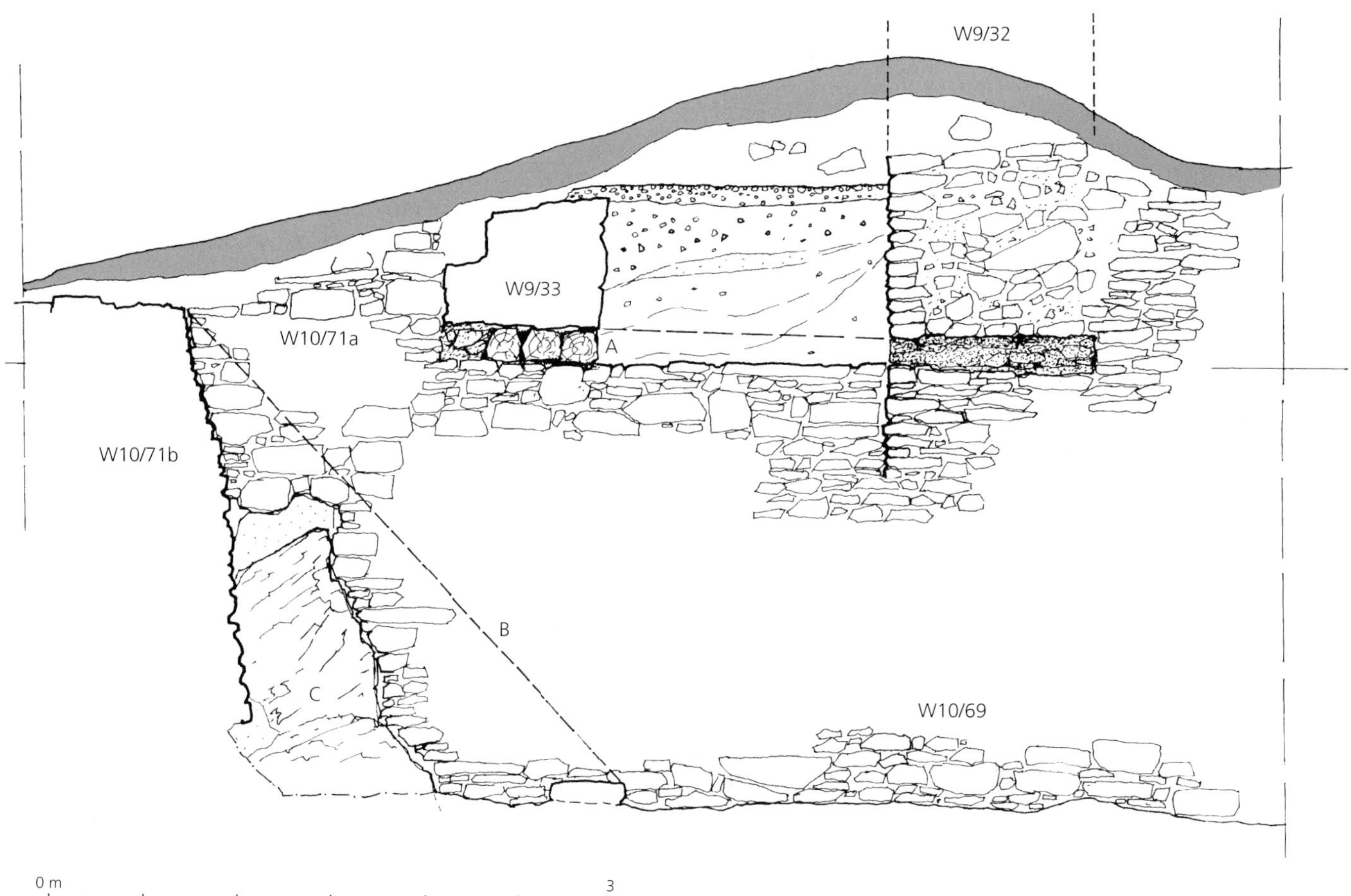

Fig. 105

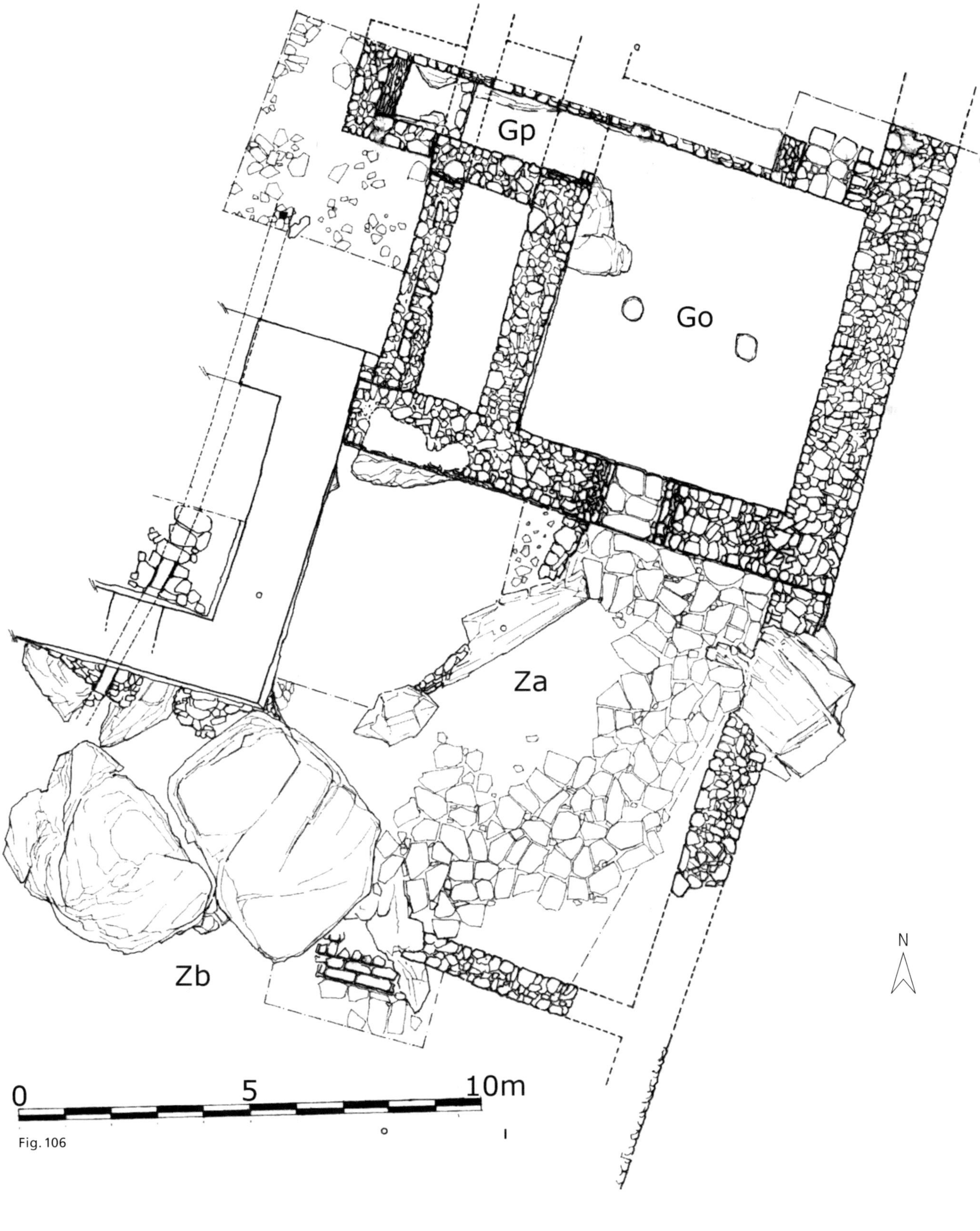

Fig. 106

3.3.11a. Forecourt (Excavation Sectors Za, Zb)

The erratic block in front of the southeastern corner of the small tower seemed to have channeled the tower's debris of the collapsed walls in two directions, i.e., to the southwest and to the east, so that only very little debris accumulated at the southern foot of the erratic block. Accordingly, the walkway level—which lay at the height of the uppermost stair tread determined in excavation sector Zc (see 3.3.1b.) and was executed as a slab paving—already appeared at a depth of 0.6 m. At this point, no distinctive stratigraphic anomalies were to be observed.

This slab level determined at the southern edge of excavation sector Zb—it was obviously the same as the paving identified in zone L (see 3.3.6.)—was defined to the north by the large erratic block and to the northeast by a wall course (W10/63), which extended at a right angle from the erratic boulder to enclosure wall W9/37a. The merger of these two walls was no longer detectable, since the entire manmade-deposited substrate had slid away at the presumed location.

A four-step set of stairs approx. 2 m in width led from the aforementioned slab level closely against the side of the erratic boulder to a delimiting, higher lying terrace (Za) to the north. The stair's slab paving—unfortunately, only traces of it being still recognizable—covered the crown of wall course W10/63, which thereby revealed it to be a simple terracing or retaining wall between two walkway levels of unequal heights, what also corresponded to the modest thickness of 0.7 m.

The above-mentioned upper slab paving in sector Za covered an area approx. 10 m in length (north-south direction) and 4.5–6 m in width. To the north, i.e., more precisely, to the northeast, it abutted against end wall W9/38; to the east, against enclosure wall W9/37a; and, to the west, against a step in the terrain approx. 1.5 m in height, which consisted of two smaller erratic blocks with short, single-faced retaining walls (W10/66 and W10/67) spanning between them. The northern of the two abutted with a joint against end wall W9/38.

Delimited by the small tower and end wall W9/38, a triangular terrace stretched from the upper rim of the edge of the terrain to the northwest. From under the wall debris on the elevated area opposite the slab paving and directly above the natural substrate of clay and rock heads, a weak settlement deposit consisting of humous, blackish clay emerged. Only measuring 1–2 cm in thickness, it contained only a few inclusions, among them a lead musket bullet. On the natural substrate along the southwestern wall of the small tower (W8/10d), a construction horizon of white sand, approx. 30 cm in width, was to be seen.

107

Fig. 107 Sector Za. Slab paving on forecourt of gate building. View towards southeast. W.M.

Fig. 108 Sector Go. Northern inner corner of gate building. Collapsed entrance to gateway GP. View towards northwest. W.M.

108

The slab paving to the east below the edge of the terrain was in very good condition. The surface, however, did not lie exactly on a horizontal plane, but evidenced noticeably uneven areas. These could be explained by differences in the composite structure or texture of the stratum underlying the slabs. In some places, the slab paving rested directly on stable bedrock, in others, on fill material that in the course of time had sunk by 5–10 cm. On the slab paving, no coherent settlement deposit was detected. Only in some cavities and in the joints between the slabs were traces found of humous, dark gray clay without inclusions.

The eastern rim of the slab paving followed an edge of the terrain, along which enclosure wall W9/37a proceeded. Here landslides had significantly disturbed the feature. Tilting towards the outside, the crown of wall W9/37a had survived only up to a height of 0.6–0.8 m underneath the slab level. Thereby, approximately parallel to the wall course, a profile section could be drawn, which registered the stratigraphy beneath the slab flooring. It turned out that heterogeneous material had been filled in between the heads of the erratic blocks protruding out of the natural clay as an underlying supporting stratum for the paved floor in order to achieve a flat surface. An older walkway horizon could not be detected under the paved surface, even though the fill material contained individual lenses of humous, blackish gray clay. However, deducing from the junction of the slab flooring with end wall W9/38, it appeared that the entire terrace in excavation sectors Za and Zb, together with wall courses W9/37a and W10/63 as well as the slab level, could have only been created at a later date. This conclusion is based on the fact that in wall W9/38 there was a walled-up door opening, whose threshold lay approx. 0.4 m lower than the slab flooring in excavation sector Za. Together with its underlying infill stratum, this slab flooring abutted the walling-up W10/70 of the door opening (see 3.3.11b.).

The feature detected in excavation sector Za provided conclusive proof that all the buildings in zones Z, L, and S must have originated from a secondary phase of construction.

3.3.11b. Gatehouse (Excavation Sector Go)

Already ascertained in 2009, but only completely exposed in 2010, wall W9/38 formed the southern, respectively the southwestern end of the eastern wing (see 3.3.8.), and, at the same time, the exterior front of a gatehouse, of whose existence no traces had been detected before the beginning of excavation. Under the wall debris, which in some places had reached a height of over 4 m, a trapezoidal, walled-in structure appeared that closed the eastern wing to the south and enclosed an internal space of approx. 6

Fig. 109 Sector Za. Wall W9/38 of gate building with walled-up gate entrance W10/70. Collapsed lintel. W.M.

Fig. 110 Sector Za. Entrance to gate building Go in wall W9/38. View towards northeast. W.M.

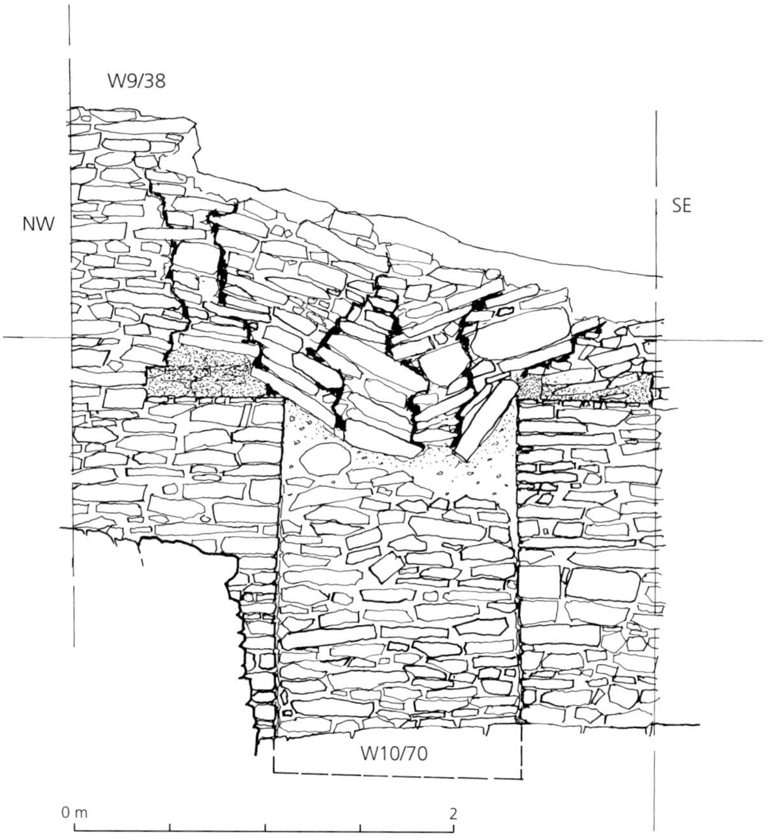

Fig. 109

by 7 m. Wall course W9/32 defined the room on the northwestern side; on the northeast, transverse wall W10/69. Coursing on the southeastern side was long enclosure wall W9/43, which was interlocked at a right angle with southwestern end wall W9/38.

Several openings were provided in these wall courses. The walled-up door in end wall W9/38 has already been mentioned. Measuring 1.3 m in width, it was carefully fitted with a threshold made of stone slabs. On both sides, the reveals up to the rebate of the wood lintel were preserved, which made it possible to determine the height of the opening (2 m). Although the supporting beams or lintels had disappeared, their rebates in the reveals, partially incised, were still easily discernable. The wall structure above the door opening, still approx. 1 m in height, indicated the characteristic deformation resulting after the loss of the supporting lintel. Only four horizontal putlog holes, each measuring 20 cm in depth, remained as evidence in the reveals of the former wood cladding of the door. On both sides there was one inserted directly under the door lintel and another halfway up the height of the reveal.

The walling up of the doorway (W10/70) posed an irritation. It extended from the threshold only up to approx. 0.5 m under the door lintel, and—what seemed especially strange—was only single-faced, i.e., executed flush with the exterior course. Towards the inside, i.e., towards the northeast, the wall structure merged without a clear dividing line into the debris that filled the interior of the walled-in trapezoidal structure in excavation sector Go.

Diagonally opposite the door in wall W9/38, another doorway appeared in wall W10/69. Measuring 1.1 m in width, it led into the adjacent northern room of the eastern wing. This has not been excavated. The door showed the same constructive features as its counterpart lying across from it in wall W9/38, except that the threshold protruded approx. 0.4 m out of the northern course of the wall. In addition to the doorway, a small stone plinth measuring approx. 30 by 30 cm appeared, which overtopped the level of the threshold by 20 cm.

110

Fig. 111 Sector Za. Southern end of gate building. Walled-up gate in wall W9/38. Collapsed lintel. View towards northwest. W.M.

111

Demarcating the third opening in the wall crown, there was a rebate of a window in the middle of the southeastern wall W9/43. Only the inner part with a clearance of 0.7 m had survived. The windowsill lay approx. 1.5 m above the walkway level.

The fourth wall opening was located in the northwestern corner of room Go. Executed in wall W9/32, it led into a narrow, tunnel-like passage that belonged to excavation sector Gp (see 3.3.11c.).

Stratigraphically, excavation sector Go yielded only vague indices. As already suggested, under the forest humus in the interior space, enormous masses of debris measuring up to 4 m in height had accumulated that covered all the wall crowns and extended down to the former walkway level. The bottommost layers, measuring 0.8–1.5 m in thickness, consisted of much clay, a few rather smaller stones as well as numerous small round gravel pebbles, partly concentrated together in lenses, what suggested the structure of primary debris. This deposit merged into the doorway of wall W9/38 into the single-faced, walled-up structure (W10/70).

Under the debris there was a thin settlement layer measuring only 1–4 cm in thickness. It consisted of blackish gray or red clay and contained only a few inclusions (find complex GO.4). The charred remains of an isolated beam or board could not be identified in terms of their constructive function. Along the northwestern-southeastern middle axis of the room, two round stone slabs had been fitted into the floor, which apparently had served as the underlying support for two wooden columns, similar to the features in room Kb/Kd (see 3.3.7.). Together with the small round gravel in the lower debris layers, this column construction can be construed as evidence for the existence of at least one upper story.

The natural substratum, upon which the thin settlement deposit rested, consisted of moraine clay and erratic blocks. The surface had apparently been worked and leveled so that its level corresponded with the threshold heights of the doors in walls W9/38 and W10/69. Only at the footing of wall W9/32, directly next to the opening to the gate tunnel in room Gp, did an erratic block remain, which measured 2 m in length, 1.4 m in width, and 0.6 m in height. Its artisan-flattened peak suggested the possibility of having been used as a landing.

3.3.11c. Gateway (Excavation Sector Gp)

As already mentioned in the previous section (see 3.3.11b.), an opening appeared in the northwestern corner of room Go, which penetrated transversely through wall course W9/32 with a width of 1.3 m. A fitted threshold was missing. Formed through leveling of the natural substratum, the walkway level of room Go extended at the same height into the opening. Above the sidewalls, notches for the wood lintels executed using planks had survived, whose height corresponded to that of the doors in walls W9/38 and W10/69. There were no indications of lateral wood cladding. Above the opening, the wall structure had collapsed on account of the loss of the wood covering.

The absence of a threshold and wooden paneling aroused doubts as to whether a door construction had been built in the opening of wall W9/32, even when there was no question about reading the opening as a passageway. Finally, the issue was resolved in 2010 by further exposure work in excavation sector Gp, which began to the northwest at wall course W9/32 and included the eastern rim of the Doche compound. Bit-by-bit, the following features were revealed: with a width measuring 1.3 m, the passageway in wall W9/32 flowed into a ground-level corridor, which was defined on both sides by connecting walls W10/71a and W10/71c. The corridor ended after 4 m at head wall W10/71b with a steep inclination. The rear, i.e., northwestern part of the corridor was wrought into the natural, compact rock-like moraine substratum. Approx. 2 m in front of head wall W10/71b, a transverse-running stone arrangement appeared on the ground. Connecting W10/71a and W10/71c were interlocked in the lower layers of the wall with the reveal construction of wall W9/32. A butt joint was first to be distinguished in the upper parts.

Understanding these constructional structures was made difficult by the fact that approx. 2 m northwest of wall W9/32, a parallel-running wall course W9/33 emerged, which was built in front of the eastern wing and whose foundation footing extended across the corridor. This was the under construction for the row of columns of the loggia (gallery corridor), which had accompanied the eastern wing along its entire length (see 3.3.8. and 3.3.11d.). Across the corridor, its foundation footing rested on a joist or set of wooden beams, which were positioned at the same level as the wood sup-

Fig. 112 Gateway, sector Gp, isometric oblique view. J.O.

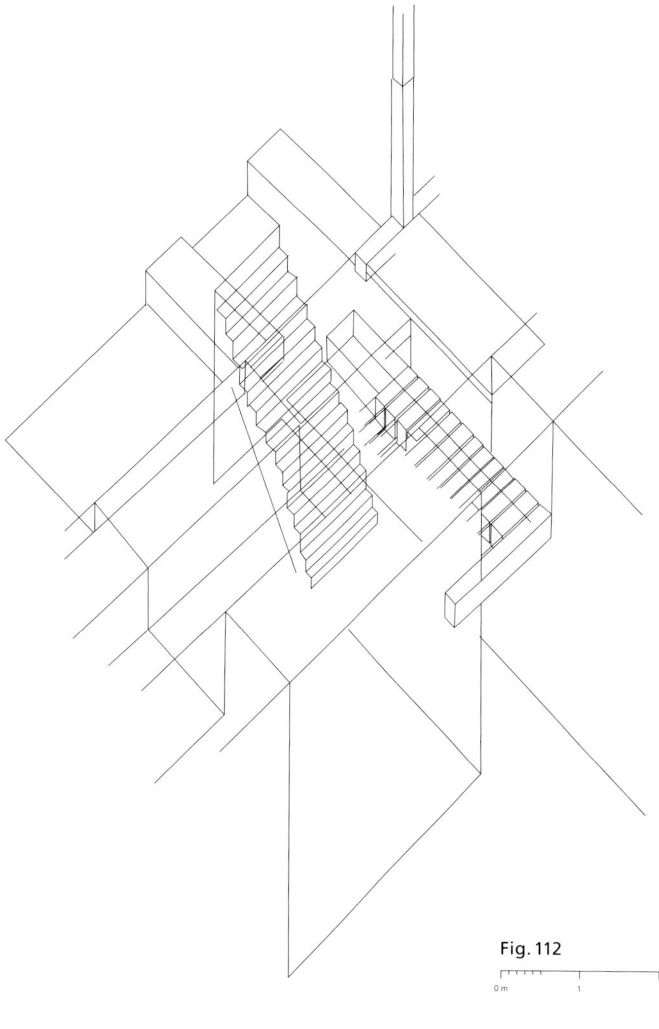

Fig. 112

Fig. 113 Sector Gp. Gateway in initial, partially exposed state. In the front, *in situ* cypress wood support beams of corridor covering. View towards northwest. W.M.

Fig. 114 Stratigraphic profile in interior of gateway Gp. Below, coarse debris; above, collapsed clay infill. Above hollow space, very fragrant cypress support beams. Covering of debris has already been removed. View towards northwest. W.M.

113

port or lintel in wall W9/32. Such wooden beams covered the connecting walls between parallel wall courses W9/32 and W9/33 and the loggia (gallery corridor), because the connecting walls extended between these wall courses only up to the height of the covering of beams, where they had carried the load of the filled-in material under the clay-gravel floor of the loggia. Accordingly, beginning with the opening in wall W9/32, the corridor formed a kind of tunnel, which, being covered by beams, provided a throughway under wall W9/33 and the infill material of the loggia (see 3.3.11d.). In the northwestern section, between wall W9/32 and head wall W10/71b, there was an exit [for climbing out] that led via a very steep wooden staircase from the level of the tunnel corridor, respectively of room Go, up to the walkway horizon of the Doche, whose level could be determined on the basis of some installed floor slabs.

114

From the set of beams covering the tunnel corridor, what had survived was predominately only the notches in the masonry, respectively the bearing supports on the crown of walls W10/71a and W1/71c. Only under wall course W9/32, where voids had formed at the surface of the debris that filled up the corridor, were there two beams that had survived intact. They consist of cypress wood and still exude a strong fragrance.

The debris layers in the interior of the corridor could be clearly distinguished into two categories. In the upper layers, one appeared that was segmented in lenses and comprised of heterogeneous clay with only a few wall stones, but much small round gravel. It probably resulted through the collapsed infill material of the loggia. The lower layers were mainly composed of course blockish wall debris. Over the manmade-leveled walkway horizon made out of natural moraine debris, there was a settlement deposit up to 10 cm in thickness consisting of blackish clay without inclusions, which had darkly discolored the surface of the walkway horizon.

3.3.11d. Southern End of the Loggia (Gallery Corridor) (Gi)

In order to fully comprehend the ground plan of the Small Tower at its eastern corner, in 2009 a limited test trench or probe was executed in the sector, i.e., in excavation sectors Gi and Gk, the latter having been merged into sector Go in 2010. The probe not only led to the exposure of tower corner W8/10a–d, but also the detection of several, previously unknown wall courses, which closely conjoined the tower.

End wall W9/38 appeared at first, which abutted with joints against the masonry of the tower. Branching out from this wall course to the northeast and with a span between them of approx. 2 m, were two parallel-running walls (W9/32 and W9/33), which apparently belonged to the elongated eastern wing and demarcated its southern segment on the courtyard side (see 3.3.8.).

115

Fig. 115 Sector Gi. Subsequently walled-up construction opening in wall W9/38. Front right, wall W9/33 of loggia. View towards southwest. W.M.

Fig. 116 Zone G. Interior view of the end wall W9/38. A: Subsequently walled-up construction opening. A.S.

Wall course W9/32 turned out to be the under construction for the row of columns of the loggia (gallery corridor), which was built in front of the entire eastern wing. The rebate for bearing the horizontal beam, upon which the vertical columns had rested, was still easily discernible.

The probe or test trench Gi was executed down to the natural substratum. It turned out that the truncated wall courses W9/38, W9/32, and W9/33 were positioned on the surface of the natural moraine ground, without a foundation trench, and then raised. Bit-by-bit, the space in between had been filled up to the level of the inner courtyard or respectively the walkway horizon of the loggia. Heterogeneous, loamy material was used as infill. On the surface of the natural substratum, a thin, blackish walkway stratum was to be observed.

In the exposed masonry of excavation sector Gi, certain irregularities appeared that called for special attention. Approx. 1 m away from the small tower in wall W9/38, a subsequently walled-up opening was discernible. Its reveals, readable at the butt joints, already began at the foundation footing and continued up to the crown, which, however, had been greatly disturbed by rootage. The width of the opening measured 1.2 m. Another butt joint emerged in wall W9/32, which revealed that its southernmost portion, which—also with butt joints—conjoined wall W9/38 and involved a stretch 2.2 m in length that had been subsequently built, beginning with a higher foundation footing located to the northern adjacent section of wall W9/32. Through a change of color and structure, the infilling of the hollow space between walls W9/32 and W9/33 indicated that the southernmost two linear meters had been introduced later than the infill material deposited to the north.

Initially, this feature was quite puzzling. The following explanation is plausible: During the building process, which consisted of wall masonry and infill, one gap was left open in each of the two walls W9/38 and W9/32 in order, on the level of the natural substratum—identical with the building horizon—, to keep an angled opening free, which should make the transport of construction and fill material into the interior of the main fortress easier (see also 5.2.1.). As soon as this temporary passageway was no longer needed, first the gap in wall W9/38 was closed, then infilling of the remaining hollow space between the walls was started, and finally wall W9/32 was completed by setting up the missing section with joints against the part of the wall that had already been completed.

The feature in excavation sector Gi clearly demonstrated that enormous quantities of infill material were transported into the interior of the main fortress, upon whose surface the respective walkway horizons were laid.

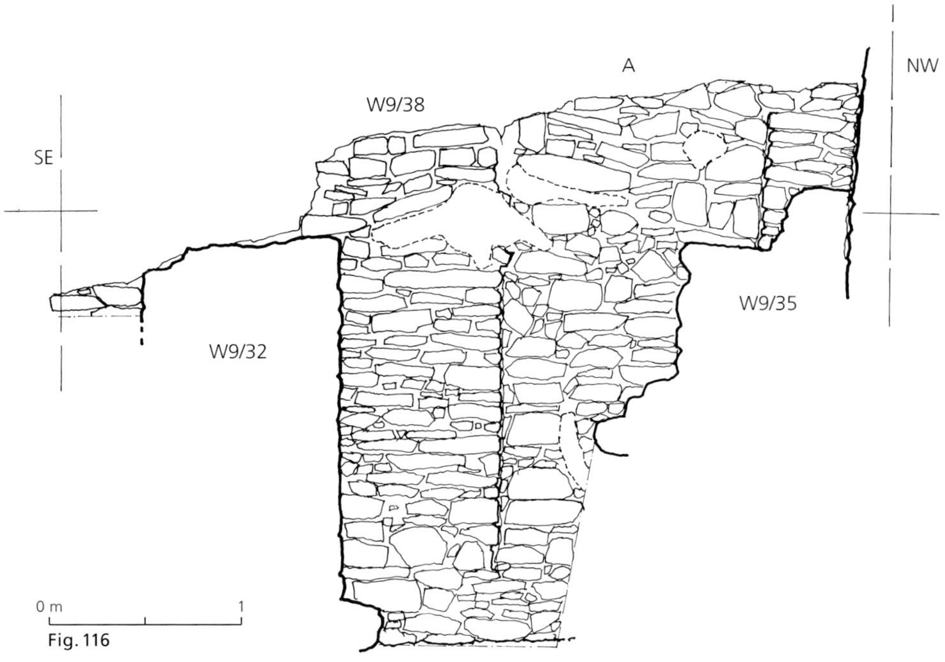

Fig. 116

3.3.11e. History of the Construction Process Sequence in the Area of the Interior Gate Compound

Concerning the history of construction the interpretation of the features under the debris masses east of the Small Tower is complicated by the fact that as a whole the stratigraphy in the individual excavation sectors delivered few useable clues.

The small tower (South Ta Dzong) is regarded as the oldest building. The subsequently erected wall W9/38 is connected with a butt joint at the small tower's eastern corner, which together with dovetail-jointed walls W9/33, W9/43, and W10/69, encloses the square-shaped room Go. This forms the core element of the inner gate complex and at the same time the southern end of the eastern wing (see 3.3.8.). The doorway in wall W9/38 and the gate tunnel—located in excavation sector Gp, equipped with a wooden staircase, and leading out from room Go to the higher-lying Doche—mark the procedure of the gateway. Accordingly, the entire complex, including the courtyard-side loggia included in Gp and Gi, belongs to a single stage of construction, which is to be considered as occurring after the erection of the small tower. The two walled-up openings in walls W9/38 and W9/32 constitute an exception, which were closed only later, probably towards the end of Phase 1.

Nothing is known about the ascent, which in Phase 1 must have led from the plateau of the southern bailey beyond to the gate in wall W9/38.

What is known for sure is that in Phase 2, the gateway in wall W9/38 was single-facedly walled up, and, to the south of this wall course, a slab floor was laid on top of a filled-in level that was raised in height. However, what remains completely unclear is how in Phase 2, i.e., after the closure of the gateway (wall section W10/70), the interior of the main fortress was entered from this slab paving. Due to the lack of features, all conjectures remain speculative. There are also unresolved questions concerning the procedure of events in the history of the construction in rooms Go and Gp during Phase 2. Because the gateway in wall W9/38 towards the outside is walled up only on one side (W10/70), and as this walling-up merges towards the inside into the debris filling up room Go, it seems as if in Phase 2 the entire ground floor of room Go together with the gate tunnel (excavation sector Gp) were abandoned and filled up. An upper walkway horizon from Phase 2 that would be expected over such an infill, did not manifest stratigraphically.

The problem of the re-designing in Phase 2, which is to be conceived in association with landfills, also occurred in other excavation sectors (see 3.3.6. and 3.3.9.). Therefore, conclusive remarks will be subsequently discussed along with the assessment of the constructive development of the entire complex (see 5.2.1. and 5.2.2.).

3.3.12. Connection of the Stairway to the Southern Bailey (Excavation Sector Ba)
Unfortunately, lack of time and personnel did not allow for extensive excavations to be carried out in the southern bailey. For this reason the investigations on the southern corner of the bailey complex remained limited, where the bailey's enclosure wall abutted with the stairway leading to the valley settlement (excavation sector Ba).

After removal of the dense vegetation, scant wall remnants appeared on the surface, which seemed to belong, on the one hand—as expected—, to the southeastern enclosure wall of the southern bailey, and, on the other, to the descending stairway steeply sloping to the southeast. The visible wall crowns were penetrated by rootage and were accordingly in poor condition. Although at the southern side of the bailey plateau, a terrain edge showed the approximate course of the enclosure wall, masonry was no longer discernible.

As a whole, the exposed excavation sector Ba, encompassing an expanse of approx. 40 m^2, yielded a meager—not to say, disappointing—feature, in as much as there was no sign of a walkway horizon or of stairsteps, as had been detected in 2007 in a lower-lying section of the stairway through a small test excavation. Emerging immediately under the forest floor and a humus-penetrated, shifted or re-located debris layer measuring 0.5 to 1.0 m in thickness, appeared the natural ground, which sloped steeply down towards the southeast. This natural substratum consisted of sandy clay, out of which protruded individual boulder heads. The foundations of the detected wall courses had been dug into the clay. The foundation footing followed stepwise the slope of the natural surface. Along the wall courses, heterogeneously in-filled foundation pits up to 0.5 m in depth could be traced. In contrast, building horizons could not be discerned, and there were no remnants of a settlement deposit.

Fig. 117 Zone B. Interior view of wall W10/73.
A Loophole,
B Door embouchure.
W.M.

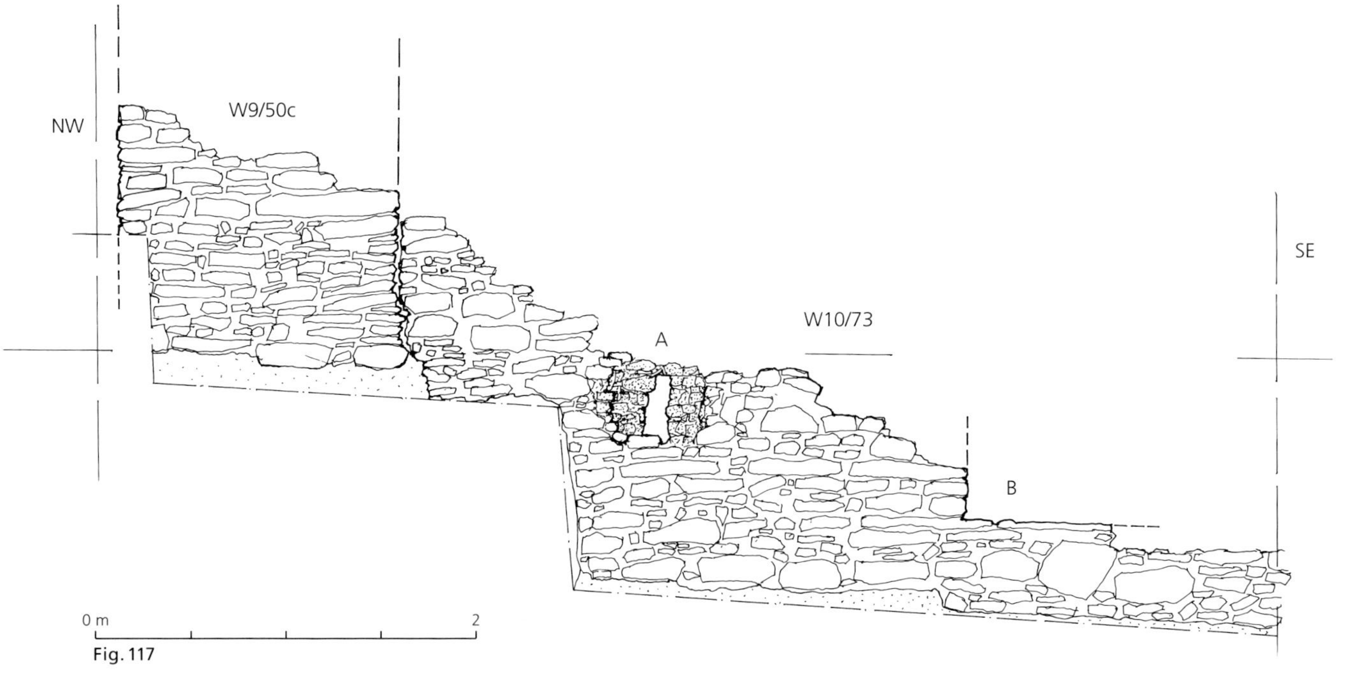

Fig. 117

Fig. 118 Zone B. Southern bailey and upper end of stairway.
A Arrow slit,
B Door embouchure.
W.M.

The exposed wall courses—including the foundation area—were still a maximum of 1.3 m high, and the upper parts were in an advanced state of disintegration. Nevertheless, it was still possible to make some important observations. Thereby, it was evident that the southwestern connecting wall of the stairway merged, without a joint and without changing direction, into the enclosure wall of the southern bailey. In contrast, the northeastern connecting wall abutted against the head of the southeastern enclosure wall at an obtuse angle, namely with an obvious butt joint and a foundation footing inserted approx. 1 m. deeper.

Despite the high degree of destruction, two important details in the northeastern connecting wall could be observed and documented. In the crown of the northern connecting wall, the rebate of a simple conical embrasure or (arrow) slit tapered towards the outside appeared at a distance of 1 m from the southeastern enclosure wall, and 1 m further down, the remnants of a doorway could be detected. Still preserved were parts of the reveal towards the mountainside and parts of the threshold made out of slabs. This gave an idea of the probable height of walkway horizon and respectively that of the stair level.

In the transition area between the bailey complex and stairway, no evidence of a closable doorway has emerged. The absence of a settlement deposit makes it understandable that no artifacts have been detected on the entire excavation sector Ba.

Despite its barrenness, the feature in excavation sector Ba permitted some insightful conclusions. First, it can be said that the erection of the bailey and stairway was carried out analogously with the buildings of the main fortress in individual stages and construction phases. The relatively shallow depth of the foundation and rather weak walls of no more than 1 m in thickness indicate a low height. The question of whether the stairway was covered or not remains open. The modest volume of the wall debris speaks in any case against a vaulting of the passageway.

The evidence of an embrasure or (arrow) slit oriented towards the steep slope to the east and a doorway seems important. The latter could be addressed as postern (back door or gate) and interpreted as evidence for the concept of active defense.

Fig. 118

4. Finds and Probes

4.1. Overview

Small finds were distributed very unevenly within the individual excavation zones and sectors. Apart from a few single pieces from the debris layers, the artifacts appeared in the settlement sedimentations that mainly were given layer numbers 3 or 4. The most important find complexes—with the exception of the collapsed layers in the small tower (hearth, find complex Gm.4) and in the western flanking tower (find complex Fb.3)—showed up at the periphery of the main fortress, more precisely, outside of the enclosure walls: find complex Ud3 in the corner angle between wall W9/49 and the eastern flanking tower (East Ta Dzong), find complex Na/b.3 outside western enclosure wall W8/2, and find complex Sa.3 in the corner angle between southern enclosure wall W9/36 and stepped ramp W9/36. All other excavation sites contained only a very modest amount of finds in their settlement layers, although some with very special individual pieces, such as, e.g., find complex Te/g.3. Here in very thin layers covering the slabs level, there were musket bullets and porcelain fragments, which have seldom been found elsewhere.

Fig. 119 Fragmented coarse ceramics in location of find. Sector Gm, collapsed hearth in small tower. W.M.

119

The small find material consists of unequal distributions of ceramics of variable quality, metal (predominantly iron), stone and animal bones. In terms of the material, one remarkable single piece is a brass arm bangle (La.2.1).

What should also not fail to be mentioned are types of material that are not substantiated in the collection of finds. That fact that there are no easily deteriorating substances such as leather or textile, or that only very little wood substance has survived, is not surprising considering the conservation conditions provided by the soil on Drapham Dzong. However, glass is also missing, even though it is a very resistant type of material. As well, among the metal finds, which as a whole were not very abundant, there were no objects containing gold or silver additives. Moreover, it is exceptional that no coins have appeared at Drapham Dzong. There is also hardly any worked bone substance existing in the collection of finds.

Allegedly over the course of time local inhabitants were said to have repeatedly harvested iron objects from the steep slopes surrounding Drapham Dzong. However, this rumor could not be confirmed by asking around among the local residents, among both men and women. The situation was different in the case of a mountain slope northeast of the fortress hill, which was pointed out to our crew from Sangay by a local woman employed as part of the project. The densely overgrown terrain was extensively littered with iron slag pieces. Several slag probes were collected for material analysis, as similar pieces had appeared at the main fortress, making a comparative study mandatory. Together with probes of other materials (stone, clay, wood, and plant remains), these pieces were salvaged for conducting various laboratory analyses.[12]

The stone, clay and wood probes not only came from the settlement sedimentations, but also from primary and burnt debris as well as various infill and leveled-off layers. For the purpose of comparison, rock and clay probes were also gathered from the area surrounding Drapham Dzong. A range of remnants from living plants will round out the comprehensive collection of probes of all kinds.

4.2. Material Categories and Group Types

4.2.1. Coarse Pottery

Fragments of coarse pottery make up the bulk of the artifacts that appeared on Drapham Dzong. With few exceptions, the sherds are from bellied pots. These were used for cooking, as evidenced by the soot crusts occurring extensively on the exterior. The sherds are characterized throughout by a copious, mica-rich tempering.[13] The grain size measures up to 2 mm. The composition of the tempering as a whole corresponds to the structure of the sand in the riverbed of the Chamkhar and its tributaries. The mica,

12 D. Oppler, R. Soulignac and V. Semeels, *Entdeckung einer metallurgischen Industrie am Fusse des Hochhimalyas* (Hochwald, 2013).

13 Mineralogical study of the mica tempering conducted by S. Graeser, Institute of Mineralogy and Petrology, University of Basel.

however, could stem from a small stone quarry located close to the fortified valley settlement. The possibility that the pots were manufactured in the Bumthang Valley, however, cannot be ruled out, even though none of the present-day inhabitants can recall the existence of any former pottery workshops. [14]

Concerning the color of the shards—blackish-grey to brownish-red—it can be concluded that they resulted through reduction as well as oxidation firing. The average thickness of the walls ranges from 4–12 mm. For the most part the ware was hand-formed on a wheel, then finished, i.e., smoothed. In the entire inventory of ceramic finds there are no fragments of horizontal bottoms or of angled foot-wall junctions. Therefore, it is possible to assume, that all pots had convex-shaped undersides, which also permits conclusions to be drawn about the type of hearths that were used (see 5.3.1).

With an average orifice diameter of 20–30 cm and a reconstructed height of 22–27 cm, the pots from Drapham Dzong are clearly larger than the medieval, unglazed cooking pots of Europe, even if ones of this particular shape—bellied wall, everted or flared rim—appear very similar. Decor applied to the pot shoulder is not at all common. Rounded strap handles, which are attached to the orifice, are occasionally found. These don't appear to belong to a particular vessel category, but in each case may have been affixed in pairs.

The rim and neck profiles can be divided typologically into six groups, with group A itself consisting of seven sub-categories. In terms of stratigraphy the individual groups, i.e., types cannot be distinguished from each other. The collection of coarse ceramic finds extends throughout the entire settlement period, considering that more exact dating would not be possible. Thereby, the coarse pottery can be arranged typologically as follows:

Group A
Curved, everted rim above a short, thickened neck. Most common, variant-rich profile type.

Type A1
Curved, everted rim, rounded orifice. Neck only slightly thickened.

Type A2
Curved, everted rim, Neck considerably thickened, interior with pronounced edge.

Type A3
Curved, everted rim, interior grooved. Rounded orifice. Neck slightly thickened.

Type A4
Steep, slightly bent funnel rim, rounded-up orifice. Short neck.

Type A5
Slightly curved, thickened funnel rim, rounded-up obliquely beveled towards exterior. Thickened neck, interior with bevel.

Type A6
Short, outwardly turned, thickened rim, merging directly in shoulder.

Type A7
Horizontal, outwardly turned rim, beveled round-off. Short neck.

Group B
Cylindrical neck, orifice with outwardly-turned lip. Only one type.

Group C
Inverted rim, rounded orifice, no neck, merging directly in shoulder. Only one type.

---

14 Traditional pots, still preserved in Bumthang households. E. and B. Fischer, «Clay pots in Bumthang dzongkhak (Central Bhutan),» *SLSA Annual Report* 2008.

Fig. 120 Coarse ceramic, Table of Types.
A1–G: Main types of Profile Edge.
H: Reconstructed cooking pot, Type A2.

Group D
Rounded steep rim, sitting directly on shoulder. Interior grooved. Only one type.

Group E
Rounded rim, turned outward horizontally. No neck, sitting directly on shoulder. Only one type.

Group F
Rim horizontally thickened. No neck, sitting directly on shoulder. This partly with horizontal notched decor. Only one type.

Group G
Rounded funnel rim, no neck sitting directly on the cylindrical. Slightly bellied wall. Only one type.

Special Shapes
Considering the material of the coarse ceramic finds as a whole, a few pieces fall outside of the shape parameters of the A–G group types. On the one hand, the exceptions include a single specimen of a hand-shaped incense stick holder (Ud.3.53), and, on the other hand, fragments of two thick-walled melting crucibles, which have traces of exposure to intense heat (Nc/d.3.1–6) on the interior.[15]

The individual profile groups are distributed remarkably unevenly over the site (see Table). In view of the total numbers, caution must be exerted with respect to any statistical evaluation. Yet it cannot be overlooked that profile groups A1–A2 make up by far most of the material, that group E appears only in complex Ud.3, or that groups B and C show up only in complexes Sa.3 and Fb.3. Moreover, groups A1–A7 are strongly represented in complexes Gm.4 and Ud.3, but they appear only sporadically in complex Sa.3, which is otherwise rich in finds. One could surmise that the individual waste depots served various fire pits and hearths. Further conclusions, however, would be purely speculative. Likewise, given the scarcity of the overall comparative material gathered to date, it would be premature to date group B and C types first to the late 17th century, simply because the documented finds stem from a settlement layer which was not deposited until first in Phase 2.

Table

Profile type			*Find complex*			
	Sa.3	Gm.4	Fb.3	Kb/d.3	Ud.3	Na/b.3
A1	1	9	1	1	10	3
A2	2	6	2	–	8	–
A3	1	6	1	–	9	2
A4	–	–	–	–	2	1
A5	–	1	–	–	6	–
A6	4	3	1	1	4	–
A7	–	–	–	–	3	1
B	6	–	6	–	–	–
C	5	–	5	–	–	1
D	–	–	–	–	1	–
E	–	–	–	–	6	–
F	–	1	–	–	1	1
G	–	–	–	–	–	1

15 Analysis of the residue in the crucible fragments by A. Burkardt, Institute of Destruction-Free Analysis and Archaeometry IfZAA.

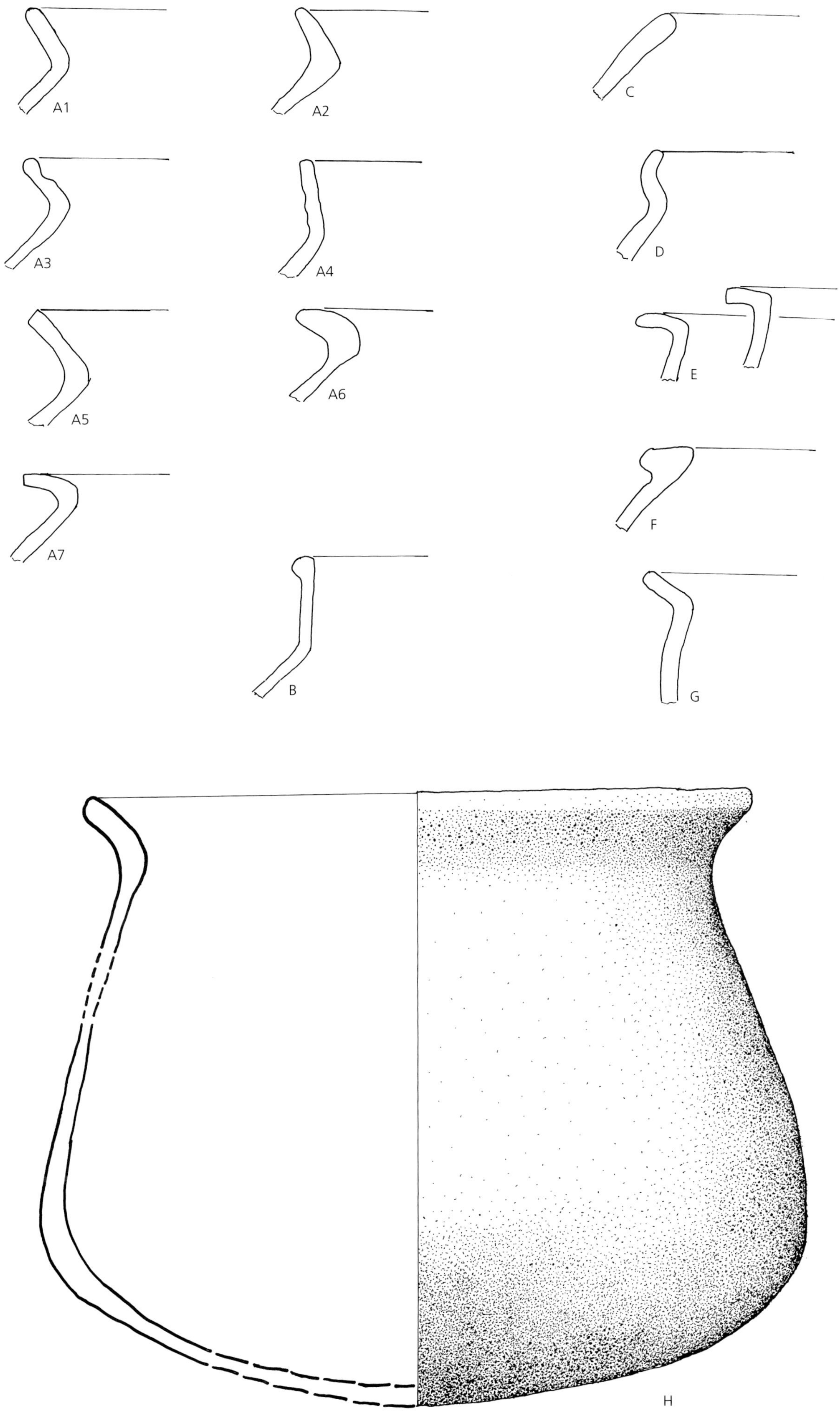

Fig. 120

4.2.2. Fine Ceramics

Apart from porcelain fragments and broken pieces of imitation porcelain, which will be treated as a separate finds group (see 4.2.3.), there are very few documented examples of fine ceramics. These originate from find complex Na/b.3, and, except for a few fragments too tiny to be included in the catalog, comprise two rim profiles from small, wheel-turned bowls with an orifice diameter of 11 and 17 cm respectively. The sherds consist of brick-red fired, fine, and sparingly tempered clay. The remarkably meager number of pieces concentrated in a single find location does not permit any compelling conclusions concerning the original function. One may assume that the majority of vessels of this particular shape and size were fashioned out of wood, which would shift them to the context of eating and drinking utensils.

4.2.3. Porcelain and Imitation Porcelain

Of great cultural historical interest, the fragments of porcelain crockery which have been unearthed not only attest to a higher standard of living, but also—though admittedly, not clearly in quantifiable terms—to trade relations with China (see 5.3.3.). Most of the pieces stem from the paved courtyard in front of the Utse (excavation sectors Te and Tg), while on the remaining compound only isolated specimens have occurred. Broken pieces of imitation porcelain (see below) were found exclusively in excavation sectors Te/Tg.

The condition of all the material is heavily disintegrated or crushed. The largest individual fragments have a diameter of barely 5 cm. There are hardly any pass sherds. Nonetheless, it is evident that only one single vessel category exists, the bellied bowl or cup with a foot rim and an orifice diameter—as far as can be determined—of approximately 13–15 cm. The fragments reveal that the entire porcelain complex had a rather uniform profile. The wall thickness, measuring 2 cm below the orifice, varies from 2–4 mm, in the foot area, 5–7 mm. With respect to the rim profiles, two similar types can be observed. Type 1 shows a simple, rounded steep rim extending from the wall; Type 2 shows a rounded rim, approximately 8–10 mm, below the orifice slightly shifted towards the outside.

On either the interior or exterior (occasionally on both), most of the porcelain fragments have a dark blue decor, with exceptional fragments sometimes being brown. With the fragments without decor—most, very small—it remains uncertain whether they stem from an entirely white vessel or an unpainted part of some otherwise decorated vessel. One group (Te/g.9–15) is distinguished by an interior, non-tinted, flat mold-pressed relief decor, which features a rosette pattern.

Spectral analysis of the porcelain—which, as is generally known, entails the raw materials kaolin and feldspar—yielded variable high values for iron, cadmium, and cobalt in the area of the blue decor. The blue color of the decor is due to the high proportion of manganese.[16] With respect to the few specimens with brown decor, the color is due to high proportions of potassium and, above all, iron; manganese is completely absent.

Despite the heavy fragmentation, the porcelain decor can be classified stylistically in general terms. Related motifs can be identified on porcelain vessels of the Ming Period (beginning from the mid-16th century) and Quing/Kanxi Period (late 17th to early 18th centuries). The time frame associated with the porcelain finds also concurs with the natural sciences determination of the duration of the settlement. Unfortunately, concrete production sites cannot be interpreted from the small fragments.[17]

While the «genuine» porcelain stems with certainty from China, given the present state of research, the question of whether the imitation porcelain was produced within Bhutan or—quasi as cheap ware—imported from China remains unanswered. The fact that the finds are indeed imitations can be deduced from the identical vessel form, the bellied bowl or cup with foot rim. The imitation finds, however, are clearly distinguishable from the genuine wares in terms of material and workmanship. The sherds con-

[16] Analysis by A. Burkardt, IfZAA.

[17] Comparative material from Gunhild Avitabile and Stephan Graf von der Schulenburg, *Chinesisches Porzellan*. Frankfurt 1992.

sist of light-red fired clay and the quality corresponds to that of the few existing unearthed specimens of fine ceramics (see 4.2.2.). The wall thickness measures 2 cm; below the orifice, approximately 5–6 mm. The sherds are generally covered with a thickly spread, white glaze. Besides a considerable amount of iron, the glaze consists primarily of cadmium. In contrast to the genuine porcelain, the imitation fragments exhibit no painted ornamentation. For this reason, cobalt, the component characteristically used for blue decor, is also lacking as an ingredient of the glaze.

The utilization of fine ceramics, which imitate porcelain in both shape and color without attaining the same quality, indicates that Chinese porcelain was highly coveted at Drapham Dzong, however, for whatever reasons, the demand for genuine imported wares could not be fully met.

4.2.4. Metal

As a whole, it is remarkable that the excavations at Drapham Dzong have yielded only few metal finds; for the time being, there is no conclusive explanation, even though some speculations about this phenomenon can be made. The argument that most of the finds occurred in waste depots, and that metal objects were thrown away hesitantly on account of their high material value, is hardly convincing considering the proven link between the fortress operations and iron mining (see 4.1. and 5.3.3.). Such questions, as to how often and in how many functions, metal (particularly iron) was generally used, remain open. The virtual absence of nails, to mention just one example, which contrasts strongly with the downright wasteful use of nails of all sizes in medieval fortresses in the West, can only mean that at Drapham Dzong iron nails were used as an exception in wood construction and furniture fabrication. The scarcity of horseshoes and horseshoe nails is easy to explain, because horseshoeing was still unknown in Bhutan in the early modern age. It is tempting to explain the complete absence of valuable metal objects—e.g., cult or representational objects, weapons or precious vessels—by hypothesizing that at the latest in the course of the most likely violent dissolution of the fortress (see 5.2.3.), such objects would have been carted off or plundered.

In view of the rarity of metal objects, the individual specimens gain in significance, even if upon excavation the condition of the iron was highly precarious.

4.2.4a. Iron

All in all, the only meager number of iron objects found, can provide no clear insight into the entirety of the equipment out of iron that would have been utilized at Drapham Dzong. Certainly various tools with iron parts were used, e.g., knives, hoes, and hammers. With most of the pieces, at least to the extent that they are identifiable, the finds entail arrowheads, although they are in a more or less fragmented condition. Typologically, there are different shapes to be distinguished. Specimens with tangs as well as with collars are represented. To a certain extent, the latter resemble types still being used in cult rituals today, whereby, however, the knob affixed to the neck, i.e., between blade and collar, is missing. Such a knob also appears on the fitted ends of ritual flagpoles. Due to their advanced corrosion, the original shape of most specimens can only be recognized in x-rays. Overall, the following types can be distinguished:

Type A
Arrowhead with collar and long, slender blade featuring rhombic cross section.

Type B
Arrowhead with collar and lancet-like blade. Only one specimen.

Type C
Arrowhead with tang and long, slender blade featuring rhombic cross section.

Tiny iron rings with a diameter of approximately 12 mm may be regarded as pieces of chain mail. Further finds include two attachment plates with clamps for fixation to a wooden base, presumably elements belonging to a furniture piece. Finally, x-rays of a shapeless, rusted lump indicate that it contains the remains of a small, rectangular box, in which the remains of a locking mechanism are hidden inside. Apparently it is a fragmented padlock.

Also worth mentioning are clumps of iron slag pieces associated with the iron mine in the vicinity of Drapham Dzong (see 5.3.3.).

4.2.4b. Lead

The objects composed of lead are musket bullets or balls. Most of them were discovered lying on the slab pavement of the inner courtyard in front of the Utse (excavation sector Te/Tg). The bullets were cast in a two-part mold, as indicated by the still easily visible casting seam on several specimens. The caliber can be classified into three ranges by size:

1. 11.5–13.2 mm
2. 15.0–18.0 mm
3. 19.5–20.5 mm

It is not possible to determine the caliber of each of the specimens, which were deformed upon impact. The difference in caliber indicates with certainty that the musket balls were fired from different weapons. Since the caliber scope of the primitive, smooth barrels of the period is not precisely known, the total number of muskets used cannot be determined with any certainty.[18]

Analysis of the lead musket balls provided an informative feature, which is summarized by A. Burkhardt (IfZAA) in his ED-XRF analysis as follows:

> The bullets or balls from find complex Te/3 clearly evidence concentrations of Sb (antimony) and Ag (silver), which allude to the origins. These traces are important because lead is mostly extracted from galena, which, to a degree, however, is only a waste product of the silver smelting process. Moreover, the antimony—here with a lead concentration of more than 1 % Sb—indicates antimonite, which apparently was likewise used as ore for the silver smelting process and still appears in small concentrations in the extracted lead.[19]

Evidently the musket shooters obtained lead for their munitions, at least in part, from silver production sites. Admittedly, with this assessment nothing can be surmised about the exact source of the lead used in casting the musket balls. The discovery of several balls directly at the foot of the Utse wall permits the conclusion that the bullets were not fired from the Utse, but rather from the courtyard in the direction of the Utse. Why some musket balls remained intact and others were deformed cannot be answered without resorting to speculative conjectures.

4.2.4c. Brass

In addition to the not very numerous iron and lead objects, a further type of metal is represented in the inventory of finds from Drapham Dzong, a brass alloy. The only find, however, is evidenced by a single object, an arm bangle (La.2.1). According to ED-XRF analysis (A. Burkhardt, IfZAA), the alloy consists of 82–86 % copper, 3.8 % zinc and 3–6 % lead. Further, there are minimal amounts of tin (2 %) and arsenic residual content from the copper ore (0.2–0.5 %). This composition corresponds to Chinese coins of the Hong Zhi Period in the 16th century. Given the current rudimentary state of the research and lack of comparable finds, it is very uncertain whether the arm bangle, which is currently typologically unique, may be regarded as a product of China.

Fig. 121 Arm bangle made of brass (Cat. No. La. 2.1). Strands with engraved decor. S.S.

121

Fig. 122 Basis slabs for wooded columns, found in wall debris. W.M.

4.2.5. Stone and Bone

Compared to the objects out of metal, utilitarian objects fashioned from natural stone or animal bones are only weakly represented in the collection of finds. Not considering the bones shattered by slaughter, cooking and eating, altogether only two pieces of worked bone were found. Their fragmentary condition precludes more exact identification. One specimen (Ud.3.56) is the sawed-off end of a horn cone; the other (Ti.6.3) is the fragment of a ring cut from a tubular bone.

The yields of stone artifacts are somewhat more abundant. However, valuable types of materials such as jade, quartz crystal, or precious stones are not contained in the collection of finds. As well, there is no soapstone, which was known in India, China, and Afghanistan. The complete inventory of stone derives from moraine sedimentation and the Chamkhar riverbed, i.e., all stones had been gathered in close proximity of the surroundings of Drapham Dzong. Accordingly, the individual pieces indicate different types of stone.[20]

Not all of the artifacts out of stone can be identified in terms of function. There are two broken pieces from millstones (Ea.2.1 and Ua.2.4), which were unearthed in the wall rubble, and as fragments had apparently been once built into the masonry work. The same applies to two stone slabs distinguished by several, artificially made cavities. Their function, however, is not clear. One of the specimens (Tc.2.1)—judging by the dimensions of both holes—may have been a double butter lamp. No definite function can be assigned to the other specimen (Ub.2.2), a fragment characterized by five smallish holes.

18 For more information concerning the emergence of firearms in Bhutan, see Aris, 1979, p. 289ff.

19 Analysis by A. Burkardt, IfZAA.

20 Mineralogical determination by S. Graeser, Institute of Mineralogy and Petrography, University of Basel.

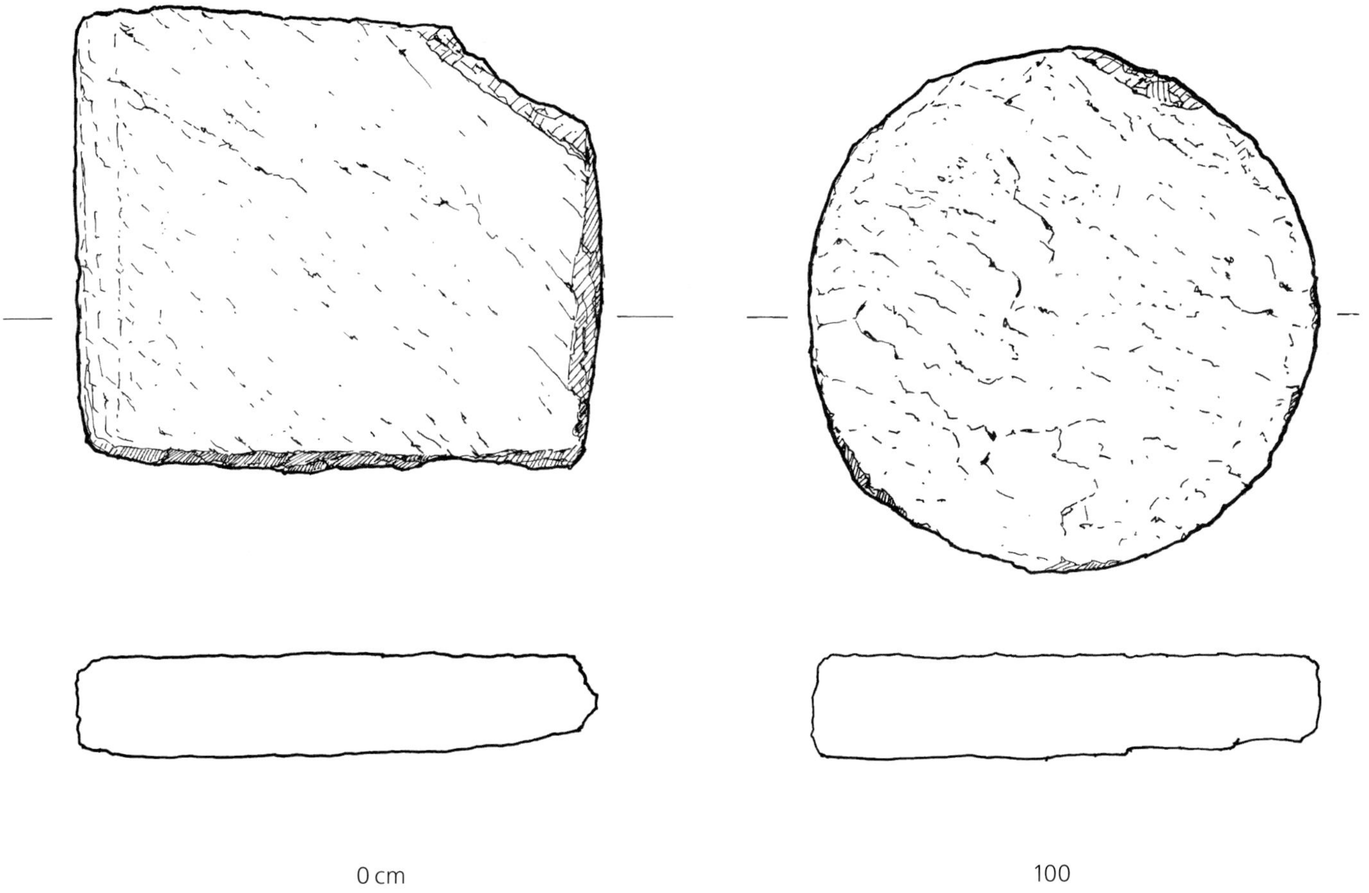

Fig. 122

It is possible, however, to determine with certainty the function of eight fist-sized specimens of river gravel, which are polished or ground smooth on one side and thereby recognizable as slick stones or smoothers. These were used to spread and smooth freshly applied clay plasterwork.

Difficulties were encountered in assessing the unworked round gravel stones, which were uncovered at the foot of the Utse in excavation sectors Ua and Ub as well as in sector Sb in the corner angle between walls W9/36 and W9/37b. The location of the finds suggests two deliberately laid depots. Entailing a total of more than 200 pieces, the majority were left *in situ*. One specimen (Ua.3.1), which had been tinted with ochre, was excavated for sampling purposes.[21] Based on size and weight, the gravel stones would have been suitable for throwing, yet the extraordinary location of both find places speaks rather for a sacred function. This also applies to a small ellipsoidal gravel stone featuring a smoothed or polished surface.

For the sake of completeness, the five meticulously crafted foundation slabs for wooden columns should also be mentioned. Two round ones were discovered *in situ* at the entrance to the small tower. The other three—two round and one square—were hoisted from the rubble in excavation zone F. Since the workpieces as building components do not qualify as transportable artifacts, they have not been included in the catalog of finds.

The conjecture that there were still more stone devices serving various functions at Drapham Dzong sounds plausible, but given the lack of actual evidence among the finds, this remains speculative.

21 Identification by A. Burkardt, IfZAA.

4.3. Catalog of Small Finds

4.3.1. Find Complex Sa.3

Find complex Sa.3 was derived from a settlement layer exposed at the southwestern front of the main fortress in the angle between enclosure wall W9/35 and staircase plinth W9/36 (see 3.3.1c.). It consisted of blackish-gray humous clay, measured 15–30 cm in depth, and tapered off towards the west and south. The layer rested directly on the artificially leveled natural ground and was covered by wall debris. The layer was nestled against wall courses W9/35 and W9/36, i.e., must have been deposited after their construction, namely, during Phase 2, what the inclusions date to the 17th and early 18th centuries.

Various animal bones formed *in situ* continuous parts of skeletons, which accordingly signified slaughter waste. This observation as well as the large number of coarse ceramic fragments are evidence that settlement deposit Sa.3 was a waste disposal site.

Coarse Ceramics

Sa.3.1a

Rim fragment of a pot. Accompanied by 6 wall fragments (Sa.3.1b–Sa.3.1g), found in a nest position, 2 join sherds. Hand-shaped, wheel-turned ware, reduction fired. Mica-rich, coarse-grained tempered. Curved, protruding rim, rounded mouth, short neck, slightly thickened. Exterior with soot residue.

Type Group A1. Finds Table 1.

Inv. No. Sa.3.32.

Sa.3.2–Sa.3.3

Rim fragments of pots (Sa.3.2 includes 5 join sherds; Sa.3.3, only 2). Wheel-turned ware, reduction fired. Mica-rich tempered. Curved, protruding rim. Neck strongly thickened with noticeably angled edge. Exterior with soot residue.

Type Group A2. Finds Table 1.

Inv. Nos. Sa.3.10, Sa.3.5.

Sa.3.4

Rim fragment of a pot. Wheel-turned ware, reduction fired. Mica-rich, fine tempered. Curved, protruding rim, rounded. Slightly grooved inside.

Type Group A3. Finds Table 1.

Inv. No. Sa.3.16.

Sa.3.5–Sa.3.8

Rim fragments of pots. Hand-shaped, wheel-turned ware, most reduction fired (Sa.3.8 oxidized). Mica-rich, partly coarse-grained tempered. Short, turned-outward rim, rounded. Without neck, sitting directly on shoulder. Sa.3.8 with steep wall. Exterior with soot residue.

Type Group A6. Finds Table 1.

Inv. Nos. Sa.3.9, Sa.3.3, Sa.3.4, Sa.3.2.

Sa.3.9–Sa.3.14

Rim fragments of pots. Wheel-turned ware, reduction fired. Mica-rich tempered. Cylindrical neck, partly grooved. Mouth with lip turned outwards.

Type Group B. Finds Table 1.

Inv. Nos. Sa.3.21, Sa.3.23, Sa.3.22, Sa.3.25, Sa.3.17, Sa.3.20.

Sa.3.15–Sa.3.19
Rim fragments of pots. Hand-shaped, wheel-turned ware, reduction fired. Mica-rich, partly coarse-grained tempered. Inverted rim. Mouth beveled towards the interior at an angle. Neck missing. Exterior with soot residue.
Type Group C. Finds Tables 1 and 2.
Inv. Nos. Sa.3.19, Sa.3.18, Sa.3.26, Sa.3.8, Sa.3.28.

Sa.3.20a–d
Wall fragment of pot with handle. Hand-shaped, wheel-turned ware, crafted with thick walls. Mica-rich, coarse-grained tempered. Wall with inverted edge and horizontal ornamental grooves. Saddle-shaped strap handle with two vertical grooves. Three wall fragments of same clay quality (Sa.20b–d), but no join sherds. Exterior with soot residue.
Finds Table 2.
Inv. No. Sa.3.9a–d.

*Sa.3.21–Sa.*3.22
Pot handle fragments. Hand-shaped ware, reduction fired. Mica-rich tempered. Saddle-shaped strap handles, each with two vertical decorative grooves.
Finds Table 2.
Inv. Nos. 3a.3.29a–b.

Sa.3.23
Fragment of a foot of a pot. Hand-shaped ware, oxidation fired. Mica-rich tempered. Rounded horizontal ridge at junction bend between belly and concave base. Exterior with soot residue. Rim profile group not determinable.
Finds Table 2.
Inv. No. Sa.3.36.

Sa.3.24
Game token, from a wall fragment of a pot, ground to an oval-round shape.
Finds Table 2.
Inv. No. Sa.3.30.

Not included in the catalog:
141 wall fragments of coarse ceramics, which cannot be identified more closely.

Iron
Sa.3.25
Arrowhead fragment, heavily corroded. Socket broken off, still recognizable at the neck. Point with lancet-shaped contour and rhombic cross-section.
Finds Table 13.
Inv. No. Sa.3.38.

Sa.3.26
Small iron ring, 13 mm diameter. Perhaps part of a chainmail mesh.
Finds Table 13.
Inv. No. Sa.3.39.

4.3.2. Find Complex Gm.4

The larger of the two find complexes that surfaced in the interior of the main fortress originated from the southeastern room of the small tower, South Ta Dzong (see 3.3.3.). In comparison to the waste disposal site, which had gradually accumulated outside the enclosure walls (find complexes Sa.3, Ud.3, Na/b.3), the layer, in which find complex Gm.4 objects were contained, was formed of burnt, humous collapse debris. This originated from an upper floor of the tower that during its destruction had fallen down onto a ground level, which was covered by a thin, find-free settlement layer. The composition—burnt humus, ash and stone slabs—indicated that the collapse layer was the residue of a cooking hearth, which had been situated in the middle of the room. The density of finds decreased as the layer tapered off in all directions, but it extended out from the core zone in sector Gm until reaching the adjacent excavation sectors Gd, Ge, and Gh. The many join sherds from bellied cooking pots, lying closely together in a nest-like fashion, indicated that most of the vessels were initially broken by the collapse of the building. As a whole, the find complex could have originated from the late phase of the complex (late 17th or early 18th century). Radiocarbon dating of the burnt collapse debris dates it to around 1700. It is noticeable that the majority of the ceramic fragments belong to profile group A, namely type A1, and in the whole find complex neither fine ceramics nor porcelain are represented.

Coarse Ceramics

Gm.4.1–Gm.4.2

Rim fragments of pots. (Gm.4.2 includes 2 join sherds.) Wheel-turned ware, oxidation fired. Mica-rich tempered. Curved, protruding funnel rim, rounded. Exterior with soot residue.

Type Group A1. Finds Table 2.

Inv. Nos. Gh.3.10, G3.2.

Gm.4.3–Gm.4.5

Rim fragments of pots. (Gm.4.3 and Gm.4.4 each consist of 2 join sherds.) Wheel-turned ware, reduction fired. Mica-rich, partly coarse tempered. Curved, protruding funnel rim, rounded and slightly thickened. Gm.4.5 includes 2 join sherds. Exterior with soot crust.

Type Group A1. Finds Table 2.

Inv. Nos. G8.3, Gh.3.4a–c.

Gm.4.6–Gm.4.7

Rim fragments of pots. Wheel-turned ware, reduction fired. Mica-rich tempered. Curved, protruding funnel rim, slightly thickened and obliquely beveled to the outside. Exterior with soot residue.

Type Group A1. Finds Table 2.

Inv. Nos. G6.9, G6.8.

Gm.4.8–Gm.4.9

Rim fragments of pots. (Gm.4.8 includes 5 join sherds.) Wheel-turned ware, made with thin walls, reduction fired. Short, curved, protruding funnel rim, rounded.

Type Group A1. Finds Table 2.

Inv. Nos. G8.2a–e, G3.6.

Gm.4.10–Gm.4.16

Rim fragments of pots. (Gm.4.14 includes 2 join sherds, Gm.4.15 includes 21 fragments, but only 2 join sherds, found in nest position.) Wheel-turned ware, mostly reduction fired, Gm.4.13 oxidation fired. Mica-rich tempered. Curved, protruding, thickened rim, rounded. Short neck, thickened with bent edge. Exterior with soot crust.

Type Group A2. Finds Table 3.

Inv. Nos. Gh.3.1, Gh.3.9, Gh.3.2, G6.5, G3.3, G6.2, G6.7.

Gm.4.17–Gm.4.21

Rim fragments of pots. (Gm.4.17 includes two join sherds.) Wheel-turned ware, reduction- and oxidation fired (Gm.4.18 and Gm.4.19). Mica-rich, rather fine tempered. Curved, protruding, rounded rim, grooved inside. Short neck, slightly thickened. Exterior partially with soot residue.

Type Group A3. Finds Table 3.

Inv. Nos. Gh.3.3, G6.10, Gh.3.17, G8.4, G6.6.

Gm.4.22

Rim fragment of a pot. Wheel-turned ware, oxidation fired. Mica-rich tempered. Curved, protruding, rim, edge beveled towards exterior. Thickened neck with distinct bent edge.

Type Group A5. Finds Table 3.

Inv. No. Gh.3.7a–c.

Not included in the catalog:

Two heavily damaged fragments from the same pot, Inv. Nos. Gh.3.7b–7c.

Gm.4.23–Gm.4.25

Rim fragments of pots. (Gm.4.25 includes 3 join sherds.) Wheel-turned ware, reduction fired. Mica-rich tempered. Rim flattened towards exterior, rounded, strongly thickened. Short neck. Exterior with soot residue.

Type Group A6. Finds Table 3.

Inv. Nos. Gn.3.5, G6.4, Gh.3.5.

Gm.4.26

Rim fragment of a pot. Wheel-turned ware, oxidation fired. Mica-rich tempered. Rim strongly thickened, bulging towards exterior and interior.

Type Group F. Finds Table 3.

Inv. No. Gh.3.13.

Iron

Gm.4.27

Slightly fragmented arrowhead. Point with rhombic cross-section, broken off from shank. Length: 52 mm.

Finds Table 13.

Inv. No. Gh.3.29.

4.3.3. Find Complex Fb.3

The objects, which surfaced in the middle section of the western wing (excavation sectors Fb, Fc, Fd), can be summarized in a single find complex Fb.4, although they do not all stem from just one single layer (see 3.3.7b.). In rooms Fc and Fb, although there was a thin settlement layer observable over the naturally leveled natural floor, it contained, however, only a few finds. Most of these objects were in a higher level, intermixed collapse debris layer, which formed a heterogeneous packet of grayish-black humus clay, of lenses with small pebbles and of yellowish clay, apparently stemming from the collapsed floors of upper stories. This deposit also stretched over the slab paving of the door in wall W8/5c/3c, which connected rooms Fb and Fd.

The find complex is characterized by the lack of metal objects; by the preponderance of coarse ceramics, largely belonging to profile groups A1 and A2; as well as by the frequent appearance of slick stones, which are only occasionally documented in the rest of the excavation sectors. Chronologically, the dating of find complex Fb.4 cannot be pinned down exactly. The collapsed settlement deposits stemming from the upper stories probably belong rather to the late period, what dating of the majority of the finds suggests as the late 17th or early 18th century.

Coarse Ceramics

Fb.3.1–Fb.3.2

Rim fragments of pots. Wheel-turned ware, reduction fired. Mica-rich tempered. Curved, protruding rim, mouth beveled towards exterior.

Type Group A1. Finds Table 4.

Inv. Nos. F5.8, F5.9.

Fb.3.3

Rim fragment of a pot. Wheel-turned ware, reduction fired. Mica-rich tempered. Curved, protruding rim, mouth beveled obliquely towards exterior.

Type Group A1. Finds Table 4.

Inv. No. F5.4.

Fb.3.4

Rim fragment of a pot. Wheel-turned ware, oxidation-brick-red fired. Mica-rich tempered. Curved, protruding rim, rounded mouth.

Type Group A1. Finds Table 4.

Inv. No. F3.3.

Fb.3.5–Fb.3.7

Rim fragments of pots. Wheel-turned ware, reduction fired. Mica-rich tempered, surface with glaze spatters. Curved protruding rim, rounded mouth.

Type Group A1. Finds Table 4.

Inv. Nos. F6.4, F6.5, F5.7.

Fb.3.8–Fb.3.9

Rim fragments of pots. Wheel-turned ware, oxidation fired. Mica-rich tempered. Curved protruding rim, thickened, short neck with sharp edge inside.

Type Group A2. Finds Table 4.

Inv. Nos. F5.3a, F5.3b.

Fb.3.10–Fb.3.12

Rim fragments of pots (Fb.3.10 includes 2 join sherds). Wheel-turned ware, reduction fired. Mica-rich tempered. Curved protruding rim, thickened, short neck with sharp edge inside.

Type Group A2. Finds Table 4.

Inv. Nos. F5.2, F3.2, F6.3.

Fb.3.13

Rim fragment of a pot. Wheel-turned ware, reduction fired. Mica-rich tempered. Curved protruding rim, grooved inside.

Type Group A3. Finds Table 4.

Inv. No. F6.2.

Fb.3.14

Rim fragment of a pot. Hand-shaped, wheel-turned ware, reduction fired. Mica-rich tempered. Surface glazed (colorless) on both sides. Short, turned-outward rim, mouth beveled tilting towards exterior.

Type Group A6. Finds Table 4.

Inv. No. F5.5.

Fb.3.15

Rim fragment of a pot (2 join sherds). Wheel-turned ware, reduction fired. Mica-rich tempered. Horizontal, outward-turned rim, rounded mouth.

Type Group A7. Finds Table 4.

Inv. No. F5.6.

Fb.3.16

Rim fragment of a pot. Hand-shaped, wheel-turned ware, thick-wall crafted. Mica-rich tempered. Thin, colorless glaze inside. Rounded rim, turned outward and beveled. Neck missing, vertical, cylindrical wall.

Type Group E. Finds Table 4.

Inv. No. F3.3.

Fb.3.17

Wall fragment of a pot, probably piece of bottom. Hand-shaped ware, oxidation-light-red fired. Secondary grinding to form a round edge. Apparently fragment of a game token.

Finds Table 4.

Inv. No. F6.11.

Stone

Fb.3.18–21

4 slick stones, fist-sized gravel, 18 and 19 smooth on one side, 20 and 21 ground on both sides. From the bed of the Chamkhar River.

Finds Table 10.

Inv. Nos. F6.1a-c, F4.2.

4.3.4. Find Complex Kb/d.3

Find complex Kb/d.3 originated from the interior of the long rectangular room K at the northern end of the western wing (see. 3.3.7a.). It was distributed across two sectors (Kb and Kd). The stratigraphy proceeded very simply. Under forest clay (K.1) and wall debris (K.2) there was a thin settlement deposit, respectively Kb.3 and Kd.3. This rested directly on the artificially laid clay/pebble floor in the interior of the room and consisted of compact, blackish-brown, humous clay. In the southern corner of the room, the thickness of the layer was a maximum of 15 cm, tapering off to approx. 1–2 cm towards the north and west. The layer contained a modest number of ceramic fragments, heavily splintered animal bones alongside a fragmented cow horn and badly decomposed bamboo remnants.

The sedimentation of layer Kb/d.3 likely occurred in the later occupation period, which is why the majority of the inclusions ought to be dated to the 17th and early 18th centuries.

Coarse Ceramics

Kb/d.3.1

21 belly fragments of a large pot, several join sherds, retrieved from a nest-like find. Wheel-turned ware, reduction-fired. Rich, coarse tempered, mainly of sharp-edged mica. Rounded transition from belly to the convex-shaped foot. Exterior with soot crust.

Matching all type groups A–G.

Finds Table 4.

Inv. No. Kb.3.1a-x.

Kb/d.3.2–Kb/d.3.5

4 rim fragments of pots. Wheel-turned ware, reduction-fired. Abundant, mica-rich tempered. Rounded, protruding rim. Soot remnants on surface.

Only mouth area preserved, probably type group A1. Not illustrated.

Inv. Nos. Kd.3.6a-d.

Kb/d.3.6

Rim fragment of a pot. Wheel-turned ware, reduction-fired. Mica-rich, coarse tempered. Short, rounded, protruding rim. Soot remnants on surface.

Type Group A6. Finds Table 4.

Inv. No. Kd.3.8.

Kb/d.3.7

Rim fragment of a pot. Hand-shaped, wheel-turned ware, oxidation-fired. Mica-rich tempered. Short, rounded, rim shifted outward, merges directly into shoulder. Interior with prominently kinked edge.

Type Group A6. Finds Table 4.

Inv. No. Kd.3.5.

Not included in the catalog:

27 belly, foot and neck fragments of pots, not further determinable, no particular features, Inv. Nos. Kd.3.1–4 and Kd.3.7–9 (collective number).

4.3.5. Find Complex Te/g.4

Over the slab paving in the inner courtyard (Doche) at the foot of the Utse, there was a disjointed, only weakly formed settlement layer, approx. 1–5 cm in thickness, of grayish-black, humus clay (see 3.3.2a.). It occurred on both excavation sectors Te and Tg, the two sectors in which the exposed compound was divided. Individual layer remains lay on the crown of bulwark walls W10/65a and W10/65b. Most pronounced were the settlement deposits in the joints between the individual slabs of the paving.

The find complex from this settlement layer was not very voluminous, but in terms of the composition differed strikingly from all of the other find complexes. Coarse ceramics were completely absent, only a few bone splinters of animal remains were present, however, 11 lead musket balls originated from area Tg.4, while especially in Te.4, small fragments of vessels made of porcelain and imitation porcelain appeared. The musket balls might belong to the end phase of the occupation, i.e., the period after 1700. Evidence for a precise dating of the fragments of porcelain and imitation porcelain is lacking, however, they are most likely to be attributed to the 17th century.

Porcelain and Imitation Porcelain

Te/g.3.1–Te/g.3.2

Rim fragments of small bowls. Genuine porcelain, ground color white with pale brown tint. Rounded rim, obliquely angled towards exterior, with brown stripes on both sides. The two pieces probably stem from the same vessel, but do not fit together.

Finds Table 11.

Inv. Nos. Te.3.11, Te.3.11a.

Te/g.3.3–Te/g.3.4

Rim fragments of small bowls. Genuine porcelain, ground color white with faint blue tint. Rounded, steep rim. As decor, on both sides double horizontal stripes in blue below the mouth and flat flower pattern in varying bright blue on the outside.

Finds Table 11.

Inv. Nos. Te.3.14, Te.3.12.

Te/g.3.5–Te/g.3.8

Rim fragment of small bowls. Genuine porcelain, ground color white with pale blue tint. Rounded, steep rim. As decor, on the inside, horizontal band in varying bright blue, divided in rhombuses with irregular loop pattern.

Finds Table 11 (only Nos. 5 and 8 illustrated).

Inv. Nos. Te.3.13a, Te.3.13b, Te.3.13c, Te.3.13d (2 join sherds).

Te/g.3.9–Te/g.3.15

Rim and wall fragments of small bowls. Genuine porcelain, ground color white with pale blue tint. Rounded, steep rim. As decor, on both sides below the rim, horizontal band in varying bright blue. Exterior wall with geometric arrangement of dots and flat rosettes in blue. Interior flat, mould-pressed, uncolored rosette decor.

Finds Table 11 (only Nos. 9 and 10 illustrated).

Inv. Nos. Te.3.16a, Te.3.15b, Te.3.16b, Te.3.15a, Te.3.15c, Te.3.16b, Te.3.15d.

Te/g.3.16–Te/g.3.18

Foot Fragments of small bowls. Genuine porcelain. Ground color white with pale blue tint. Rudiments of a foot rim still recognizable. As decor, concentric horizontal stripes on the exterior and irregular plant pattern (pine?) on the interior, or vice versa.

Finds Table 12 (Te/g.3.17 not illustrated).

Inv. Nos. Te.3.17a, Te.3.17b, Te.3.17c.

Fig. 123–125 Porcelain fragments from courtyard in front of the Utse (sectors Te/Tg). S.S.

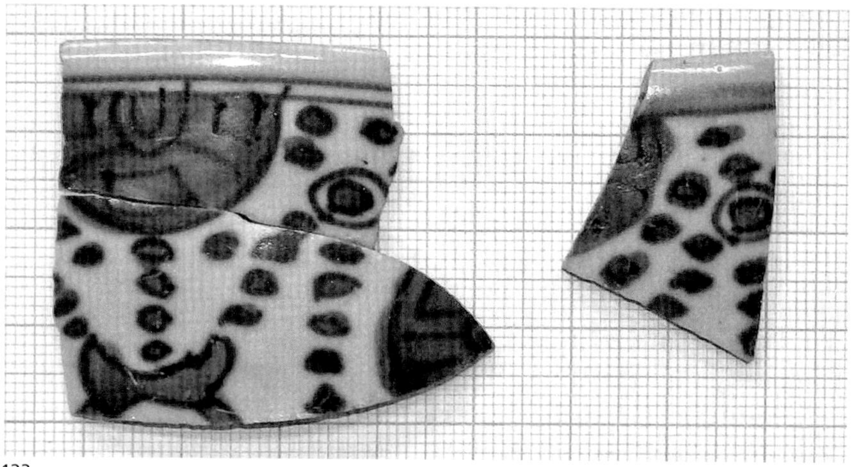

123

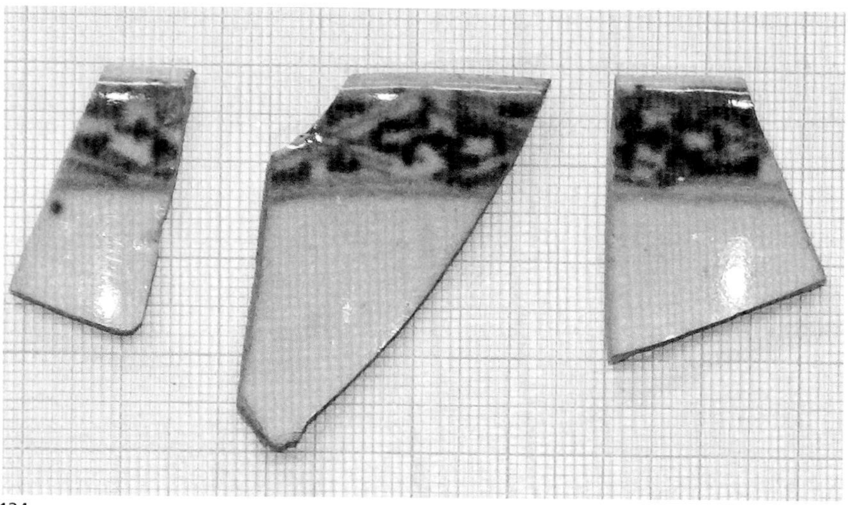

124

Te/g.3.19

Wall fragment of a small bowl. Genuine porcelain. Ground color white with pale blue tint. Dark blue flower pattern on the exterior.

Finds Table 11.

Inv. No. Te.3.18.

Te/g.3.20–Te/g.3.22

Rim fragments of small bowls. Imitation porcelain. Light, brick red, brownish sherds, white on both sides, pastose glaze. Rounded, steep rim.

Finds Table 12.

Inv. Nos. Tg.3.3a, Te.3.4a and b, Te.3.3.

Te/g.3.23–Te/g.3.24

Rim fragments of small bowls. Imitation porcelain. Light, brick red, brownish sherds, white on both sides, pastose glaze. Rounded rim, slightly bent towards exterior.

Finds Table 12.

Inv. Nos. Te.3.5a-b, Te.3.2.

Te/g.3.25

Fragment of a foot of a small bowl. Imitation porcelain. Light, brick red, brownish sherds, white on both sides, pastose glaze. Rudiments of a strong, perpendicular foot rim.

Finds Table 12.

Inv. Nr. Te.3.9.

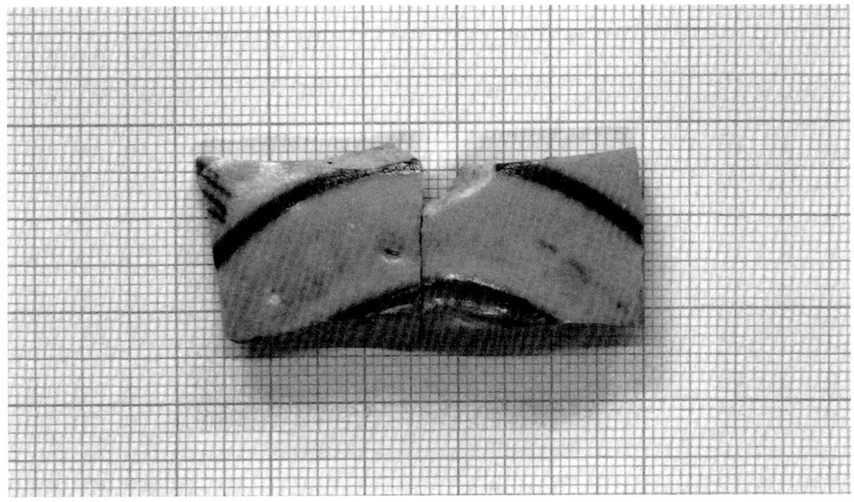

125

Not included in catalog:
18 tiny fragments of small porcelain bowl, Inv. Nos. Te.3.19, Te.3.20, Tg.3.4 (collective number).
42 tiny fragments of small bowls out of imitation porcelain, Inv. Nos. Te.3.4b, Te.3.6, Te.3.7, Te.3.8, Te.3.10 (collective number).

Lead

Te/g.3.26–Te/g.28

Musket balls, 26 and 27 with casting seam.

Caliber: 13.2–15.1 mm.
Weight: 11, 15, 17 g.
Finds Table 13.
Inv. Nos. Te.3.21, Tg.3.5j, Tg.3.5d.

Te/g.3.29–Te/g.3.32

Musket balls, 29 and 31 with casting seam.

Caliber: 18.2–19.5 mm.
Weight: 37, 39, 38, 39 g.
Finds Table 13.
Inv. Nos. Tg.3.5g, Tg.3.5b, Tf.3.1a, Tg.3.5h.

Te/g.3.33 –Te/g.3.34

Musket balls, 34 with casting seam.

Caliber: 20.0–21.0 mm.
Weight: 46, 46 g.
Finds Table 13
Inv. Nos. Tf.3.1b, Tg.3.5c.

Te/g.3.35–Te/g.3.36

Fragmented musket balls, deformed as a result of firing. 35 with casting seam.

Caliber of 34 was 20 mm, caliber of 35 no longer determinable.
Finds Table 13.
Inv. Nos. Tg.3.5e, Tg.3.5f.

4.3.6. Find Complex Ti.6

At the interface between the underlying burnt layer and the clay screed on the ground floor, very few.s appeared (see 3.3.2e). The scarcity of objects indicates that the interior of the Utse had been completely evacuated before the fire. The sedimentation of the layer probably occurred during the 17th and early 18th centuries.

Porcelain

Ti.6.1

Small rim fragment of a small bowl. On the interior, two narrow blue stripes. On the exterior, remnants of an extensive, no longer precisely discernable blue decor. High concentrations of iron, cadmium und manganese.

Not illustrated.

Inv. No. Ti.3.4.

Ti.6.2

Small wall fragment of a small bowl (?). On the exterior, fragmented blue stamp (seal script?).

Finds Table 11.

Inv. No. Ti.3.5.

Bone

Ti.6.3

Fragmented ring, crafted from a tubular bone. 11 mm in width. Sawed from a blank, polished surface. Blackish discoloration from fire.

Finds Table 13.

Inv. No. Ti.2.

4.3.7. Find Complex Ud.3

Find complex Ud.3 originated from a waste disposal site, which had been deposited outside of the main fortress in the angle between enclosure wall W09/49 and the corner tower East Ta Dzong (see 3.3.5c.). This settlement layer consisted of grayish-black, compacted clay, and besides animal bones, included tiny particles of charred wood and the artifacts presented below. The layer was nestled against the wall course mentioned above and spread out over an area of about 20 m². In the center it measured 0.5 m in thickness, tapering off towards the northwest and northeast. The deposit lay directly on the leveled, natural clay, respectively, on the building horizon of the adjacent walls and was covered with wall debris.

The sedimentation occurred during the entire occupation period of Drapham Dzong. Therefore, the finds originated from the 16th to the early 17th centuries.

Coarse Ceramics

Ud.3.1–Ud.3.8

Rim fragments of pots. Wheel-turned ware, mostly reduction-, partly oxidation- (Ud.3.3) fired. Coarse, mica-rich tempered. Curved, protruding, unthickened, rounded rim, short neck. Soot deposits on exterior.

Type Group A1. Finds Table 5.

Inv. Nos. Ud.3.3a, Ud.3.3b, Ud.3.3.16e, Ud.3.3.11a, Ud.3.5c, Ud.3.27a, Ud.3.30, Ud.3.16c.

Ud.3.9–Ud.3.10

Rim fragments of pots with handles. Wheel-turned ware, reduction-fired, coarse mica-rich tempered. Hand-shaped, rounded band handle, set flush with rim. Curved, protruding, unthickened, rounded rim, short neck. Soot deposits on exterior.

Type Group A1. Finds Table 5.

Inv. Nos. Ud.3.22, Ud.3.21.

Ud.3.11–Ud.3.18

Rim fragments of pots. Wheel-turned ware, mostly reduction–, occasionally oxidation- (Ud.3.18) fired. Coarse, mica-rich tempered. Curved, protruding, unthickened, rounded rim, short neck with edge on the interior. Soot deposits on exterior.

Type Group A2. Finds Table 6.

Inv. Nos. Ud.3.8a, Ud.3.4b, Ud.3.17c, Ud.3.17b, Ud.3.23a, Ud.3.6a, Ud.3.17a, Ud.3.6b.

Ud.3.19–Ud.3.27

Rim fragments of pots. Wheel-turned ware, mostly reduction–, occasionally oxidation- (Ud.3.26 and 27) fired. Coarse, mica-rich tempered. Curved, protruding, rounded rim with unevenly pronounced furrow at the interior. Short neck. Soot deposits on exterior.

Type Group A3. Finds Tables 6 and 7.

Inv. Nos. Ud.3.14a, Ud.3.14b, Ud.3.15a, Ud.3.14.c, Ud.3.4a, Ud.3.5a, Ud.3.5b, Ud.3.7b, Ud.3.2a.

Ud.3.28–Ud.3.29

Rim fragments of pots. Wheel-turned ware, reduction-fired. Coarse, mica-rich tempered. Protruding rim, horizontally beveled edge. Cylindrical neck. Heavy soot sedimentation on the exterior.

Type Group A4. Finds Table 7.

Inv. Nos. Ud.3.9a/b, Ud.3.9c.

Ud.3.30–Ud.3.35

Rim fragments of pots. Wheel-turned ware, mostly reduction–, occasionally oxidation-(Ud.3.33) fired. Coarse, mica-rich tempered. Mildly protruding, slightly thickened funnel rim, angular, obliquely beveled towards the exterior. Short neck, rising directly from shoulder. Heavy soot sedimentation on the exterior.

Type Group A5. Finds Table 7.

Inv. Nos. Ud.3.10a, Ud.3.10b, Ud.3.10c, Ud.3.19a/b, Ud.3.28a/b, Ud.3.17d.

Ud.3.36–Ud.3.39

Rim fragments of pots. Wheel-turned ware, mostly reduction-, occasionally oxidation-(Ud.3.37 and 38) fired. Coarse, mica-rich tempered. Short, horizontally flaring rim, rounded or beveled. Thickened neck with unevenly pronounced knick edges on the interior. Soot sedimentation on the exterior.

Type Group A6. Finds Table 8.

Inv. Nos. Ud.3.16f/g, Ud.3.16b, Ud.3.16h/i, Ud.3.16a.

Ud.3.40–42

Rim fragments of pots. Wheel-turned ware, reduction-fired. Abundant mica-rich, partly coarse tempered. Horizontal, angular rim beveled towards the exterior, short neck. Soot sedimentation on shoulder.

Type Group A7. Finds Tables 7 and 8.

Inv. Nos. Ud.3.16d, Ud.3.26a, Ud.3.25a.

Ud.3.43

Rim fragment of a pot, two join sherds. Wheel-turned ware, oxidation-fired. Rather fine, mica-rich tempered. Rounded, steep rim, bulging towards the exterior, interior furrowed. Rim sits without neck on shoulder.

Type Group D. Finds Table 8.

Inv. No. Ud.3.7a/b.

Ud.3.44–Ud.3.46

Rim fragments of pots. Wheel-turned ware, 44 and 45 reduction-fired, 47 oxidation-fired. Mica-rich tempered. Horizontally protruding rim, angularly beveled. Steep shoulder.

Type Group E. Finds Table 8.

Inv. Nos. Ud.3.18c, Ud.3.18b, Ud.3.18a.

Ud.3.47–Ud.3.49

Rim fragments of pots. Wheel-turned ware, reduction-fired. Mica-rich tempered. Horizontal protruding rim, rounded. Steep shoulder. Interior with traces of a matt, colorless glaze.

Type Group E. Finds Table 8.

Inv. Nos. Ud.3.24b, Ud.3.24a, Ud.3.24c.

Ud.3.50a/b

Two rim fragments of a pot (join sherds). Wheel-turned ware, reduction-fired, exterior with black coating. Mica-rich tempered. Wide, rounded, bulging rim, upper side with slight indentation. Rim sits directly on the flat shoulder, which exhibits a decor of horizontally arranged, slightly oblique notches.

Type Group F. Finds Table 8.

Inv. No. Ud.3.47a/b.

Ud.3.51–Ud.3.52

Wall fragments of pots. Broken rims ground to irregular oval. Apparently game tokens.

Finds Table 8.

Inv. No. Ud.3.48, Ud. 3.49.

Ud.3.53

Incense stick holder. Hand-formed cube, finely tempered. Bored holes on two sides.

Finds Table 8.

Inv. No. Ud.3.50.

Iron

Ud.3.54

Fragmented arrowhead, heavily rusted. Narrow socket. Flat blade with lancet-shaped contour.

Length: 81 mm.

Finds Table 13.

Inv. No. Ud.3.51.

Ud.3.55

Fragmented arrowhead, heavily rusted. Tang broken off. Narrow, elongated point with rhombic cross-section.

Length: 87 mm.

Finds Table 13.

Inv. No. Ud.3.52.

Ud.3.56

Fragmented arrowhead. Socket missing, still discernible in the neck. Broadhead point with rhombic cross-section, compressed in front.

Finds Table 13.

Inv. No. Ud.3.53.

Ud.3.57

Attachment plate with round clamp. Rhombus-shaped contour, visible surface with parallel ornamental notches. Clamp ends missing. Probably from furniture piece.

Finds Table 13.

Inv. No. Ud.4.1.

Bone

Ud.3.58

Sawn-off tip of a horn core. Functional purpose unknown.

Finds Table 13.

Inv. No. Ud.3.58.

4.3.8. Find Complex Na/b.3

In excavation sector Na/b, outside of enclosure wall W8/2, a settlement layer rich in finds up to 40 cm in thickness appeared (see 3.3.4a.). It consisted of blackish-gray, humous clay and lay partly on the sloped slab paving bordering the weakened walls W10/64a and W10/64b; partly on wall plinth W9/59 built in front of the enclosure wall; and, partly on the natural substrate of yellow clay. Downhill, the layer tapered off. The variety of finds, chiefly animal bones and coarse ceramic fragments, indicates that this deposit is a waste disposal site. Apparently, at this site all kinds of waste were disposed of from the western wing over the enclosure wall onto the slope. The disposal site could have been in use during the entire period of occupation. Thus, the finds derive from the 16th until the early 17th centuries.

Coarse Ceramics

Na/b.3.1–Na/b.3.3

Rim fragments of pots. Wheel-turned ware, partly reduction-, partly oxidation-fired. Mica-rich, rather fine tempered. Curved, protruding rim, unthickened, rounded, short neck. Exterior partially encrusted with soot.

Type Group A1. Finds Table 9.

Inv. Nos. Na.3.2c, Na.3.2d, Na.3.2e.

Na/b.3.4–Na/b.3.5

Rim fragments of pots. Wheel-turned ware, reduction-fired. Mica-rich tempered. Curved, protruding rim, interior furrowed. Mouth beveled. Short, slightly thickened rim. Exterior partially encrusted with soot.

Type Group A3. Finds Table 9.

Inv. Nos. Na.3.2a, Na.3.2b.

Na/b.3.6

Rim fragment of a pot. Wheel-turned ware, reduction-fired. Mica-rich tempered. Curved, protruding, slightly thickened rim. Mouth obliquely beveled toward exterior. Exterior encrusted with soot.

Type Group A4. Finds Table 9.

Inv. No. Na/3.2.

Na/b.3.7

Rim fragment of a pot (two join sherds). Wheel-turned ware, reduction-fired. Mica-rich tempered. Horizontally, outside-turned rim, obliquely beveled. Short neck. Exterior with soot crust.

Type Group A7. Finds Table 9.

Inv. No. Nb.3.5a–b.

Na/b.3.8

Rim fragment of a pot. Wheel-turned ware, reduction-fired. Mica-rich, rather fine tempered. Rim inwardly turned, obliquely beveled, without neck merging directly into shoulder. Mouth section glazed.

Type Group C. Finds Table 9.

Inv. No. Na.3.3.

Na/b.3.9

Rim fragment of a pot. Wheel-turned ware, reduction-fired. Mica-rich tempered. Rim rounded, thickened, horizontally, outward-turned, without neck sitting directly on shoulder. Traces of a glaze.

Type Group F. Finds Table 9.

Inv. No. Nb.3.27.

Na/b.3.10

Rim fragment of a pot. Wheel-turned ware, reduction-fired. Mica-rich, rather fine tempered. Flat, outwardly turned, rounded rim. Short neck, cylindrical, slightly bulging wall. Exterior with soot crust.

Type Group G. Finds Table 9.

Inv. No. Nb.3.3.

Na/b.3.11–Na/b.3.12

Foot fragments of pots. Wheel-turned ware, reduction-fired. Bulging bottom, merging, rounded, in belly. Exterior with soot crust.

Matches all profile groups. Finds Table 9.

Inv. Nos. Nb.3.20, Nb.3.15.

Na/b.3.13

Fragment of a handle of a pot. Hand-formed, oxidation-fired. Saddle-shaped band handle, two vertical decorative grooves.

Matches all profile groups. Finds Table 9.

Inv. No. Nb.3.13.

Na/b.3.14

Spout of a vessel of unidentifiable form. Hand-formed, reduction-fired. Rebate aligned with rim, beak-shaped spout, conically tapered, obliquely sunk towards the exterior. Exterior with soot remnants.

Finds Table 9.

Inv. No. Nb.3.9.

Na/b.3.15

Wall fragment of a pot (?). Wheel-turned ware, reduction-fired. Mica-rich tempered. Exterior with two decorative grooves.

Finds Table 9.

Inv. No. Nb.3.16.

Na/b.3.16–Na/b.3.17

Wall fragments of pots. Wheel-turned ware, reduction-fired. Exterior with crisscross, comb-like decor.

Finds Table 9.

Inv. Nos. Nb.3.14, Nb.3.17.

Na/b.3.18

Wall fragment of a pot. Wheel-turned ware, reduction-fired. Exterior with oblique, continuous comb-like decor.

Finds Table 9.

Inv. No. Na.3.5.

Fine Ceramics

Na/b.3.19

Rim fragment of a small bowl. Wheel-turned ware, oxidation-fired. Fine, mica-rich tempered. Rounded, steep rim, bulging wall.

Finds Table 11.

Inv. No. Nb.3.10.

Na/b.3.20a–c

Three rim fragments of a small bowl. Wheel-turned ware, oxidation-fired. Fine, mica-rich tempered. Rounded, steep rim, exterior with horizontal decorative groove. Bulging wall.

Finds Table 11.

Inv. Nos. Na.3.2, Na.3.3a–b.

Not included in the catalog:

3 tiny fragments of fine ceramics (wall pieces), Inv. Nos. Na.3.4.

Porcelain

Na/b.3. 21

Rim fragment of a small bowl. Genuine porcelain, rounded, slightly protruding rim. White glaze, interior and exterior each with two blue horizontal stripes.

Finds Table 12.

Inv. No. Nb.3.21.

Na/b.3.22

Rim fragment of a small bowl. Genuine porcelain, rounded, slightly protruding rim. White glaze, interior and exterior each with one blue horizontal stripe. Exterior wall with extensive blue decor, probably stylized flower pattern.

Finds Table 12.

Inv. No. Nb.3.22.

Na/b.3.23

Rim fragment of a small bowl. Genuine porcelain, rounded, slightly protruding rim. White glaze, inside as decor in blue horizontal stripes and plant pattern.

Finds Table 12.

Inv. No.Nb.3.23.

Na/b.3.24

Wall fragment of a small bowl. Genuine porcelain. White glaze, inside lavish, non-identifiable decor in blue.

Finds Table 12.

Inv. No. Nb.3.24.

Iron

Na/b.3.25

Heavily fragmented arrowhead. Narrow socket, form of the point no longer identifiable.

Finds Table 13.

Inv. No. Nb.3.25.

4.3.9. Find Complex Go.4

In the interior of the gateway, which occupied excavation sector Go, under a clay infill of up to 1.8 m in thickness, there was an only weakly defined settlement layer, 1 to 4 cm in thickness, made up of blackish-gray—and, in parts, reddish—clay (see 3.2.11d. and 3.2.11c.). The layer covered most of the floor surface of the interior space of the gate and also extended further in the narrow gate passageway Gp. Find complex Go.4 from this layer yielded only a few inclusions, which nonetheless deserve attention on account of their composition. Since room Go together with the gate passageway Gp was filled in during the late period of the complex, the sedimentation of the settlement layer containing find complex Go.4 must have been deposited before the late phase of the timespan of the use of the complex. Thus, the few finds belong to the 16th or early 17th century.

Coarse Ceramics

Go.4.1

Rim fragment of a pot. Wheel-turned ware, oxidation-fired. Coarse, mica-rich tempered. Exterior with soot crust.

Type Group A6.
Finds Table 10.
Inv. No. Go.4.1.

Go.4.2 (Collective Number)

Sixty-one mostly small wall fragments of pots, partly oxidation-, partly reduction-fired, strongly tempered, broken rims clearly rounded. (Evidence of reworking or sherding.)

Not illustrated.
Inv. No. Go.4.3.

Porcelain

Go.4.3–Go.4.4

Two small wall fragments of small bowls. Genuine porcelain. White glaze, Go.4.3 on the exterior, Go.4.4 on the interior blue decor with plant and diamond pattern.

Finds Table 12.
Inv. Nos. Go.4.5–6.

Stone

Go.4.5

Pebble in form of an ellipsoid. Origin/source unknown. Length: 19.5 cm, greatest diameter: 10.1 cm. Surface artificially polished. Sacred function probable.

Find Location: Infill over underlying settlement horizon.
Dating: 16th/17th century.
Finds Table 10.
Inv. No. Go.4.2.

4.3.10. Find Complex Sf.3

Outside of the southeastern enclosure wall W9/37, which originated from Phase 2, a thin settlement deposit appeared. Measuring a maximum of 5–20 cm in thickness, it rested directly on the step-like, downward-sloping boulder as well as on the crown of bulwark W9/54. Towards the northeast it ended at the large, towering boulder, over which wall W9/37 extended. The settlement deposit consisted of gray-brown clay and contained only a few artifacts. In contrast to the other find complexes, these mainly included iron objects, which justifies their being summarized in a separate find complex. The fact that the settlement layer was nestled against wall W9/37 means that the finds must be dated to Phase 2, i.e., to the late 17th or early 18th century.

Porcelain

Sf.3.1

Small wall fragment of a small bowl. Genuine porcelain. White glaze, blue, extensive decor, not further determinable.

Not illustrated.

Inv. No. Sf.3.3.

Iron

Sf.3.2–Sf.3.3

2 fragments of arrowheads, heavily rusted. Socket missing, still recognizable in the trace of the rebate. Point with lancet-shaped contour and rhombic cross-section.

Finds Table 13.

Inv. Nos. Sf.2.1–Sf.2.4.

Sf.3.4–Sf.3.5

2 fragments of arrowheads, heavily rusted. Sockets preserved in the rebate. Point broken off, rhombic cross-section and probably lancet-shaped contour.

Finds Table 13 (Sf.3.5 not illustrated).

Inv. Nos. Sf.2.2, Sf.2.3.

Sf.3.6

Fragmented arrowhead, heavily rusted. Socket broken off. Point with rhombic cross-section and lancet-shaped contour.

Finds Table 13.

Inv. No. Se.7.2.

Sf.3.7

Small iron ring, 11 mm in diameter, round cross-section, 1.5 mm in diameter. Circle discontinuous. Function uncertain, being part of a chain mail not ruled out.

Finds Table 13.

Inv. No.Sf.2.6.

Not included in the catalog:

Amorphous tiny fragment of rusted iron, Inv. No. Sf.2.5.

4.3.11. Individual Finds

In some excavation sectors, isolated individual finds appeared, partly in the primary debris or in slipped off, secondary mixed deposits, and partly in the faintly distinct settlement layers. The pieces were distributed over the entire compound, and due to the haphazardness of their find locations, cannot be combined into a find complex. Most of the pieces do not require more precise presentation in the catalog. There are, however, some objects, which deserve attention in terms of the typological or functional framework of the find inventory as a whole. Therefore, they will be listed below individually under respective details of the find location according to the catalog. The assigned dating depending on the find location.

Tc.2.1

Crafted stone slabs shaped to a crude parallelogram.

Side length: approx. 20 cm.

Squared-off sides coarsely hewn. On the surface, two artificially applied, conical holes of 4.3 and 4.6 cm in diameter and approx. 2.5–3 cm in depth.

Use/interpretation unclear. Both cavities could have served as receptacles for lamp butter.

Find Location: Secondary debris in excavation sector Tc. Probably built into the masonry as plundered spoils.

Dating: probably $16^{th}/17^{th}$ century.

Finds Table 14.

Inv. No. Tc.2.2.

Gl.2.1

Small fragment of clay plaster. Traces of painting with reddish-ochre colored ground and black stripes.

Find Location: Secondary debris in area Gl.

Dating: probably 17th century.

Not illustrated.

Inv. No. Gl.2.1.

Nc/d.3.1–Nc/d.3.6

Six broken pieces of at least two crucibles. Thick-walled, brick-red fired clay, coarse tempered. Hand-formed ware. Wall at least 25 mm in thickness. Only exterior side preserved, interior side darkly discolored by heat and crumbled away. Nc/d.3.1 Foot fragment with bulge.

Find Location: Thin settlement deposit in area Nc.

Dating: 17th century.

Finds Table 10 (only nos. Nc/d.1–2 illustrated).

Inv. Nos. Nc/d.3.4–9.

Nc/d.3.7

Rim fragment of a pot. Wheel turned, coarsely tempered ware, reduction-fired. Bulging rim turned outward, sits directly on shoulder.

Type Group F. Finds Table 10.

Inv. No. Na.3.3.

Ea.2.1
Broken piece of a millstone.

Length: 32.5 cm.

Grinding surface with conical depression (diameter: 3.7 cm, depth: 3.2 cm).

Roughly hewn grooves, arranged criss-cross, each 1.2 cm in width and 0.5 cm in depth. The coarse surface is due to the variable hardness of the sedimentary rock.

Total diameter not determinable.

Find Location: Secondary debris in excavation sector Ea. The piece could well have been built into the masonry as plundered spoils.

Dating: 16th/17th century.

Finds Table 15.

Inv. No. Ea.2.1.

Fh.2.1–Fh.2.4
Four slick stones. Stream gravel from the bed of the Chamkhar River. Ground flat on one or two sides. Found in completely intermixed and relocated wall debris.

Dating: 16th century to early 18th century possible.

Finds Table 10.

Inv. Nos. Fh. 1–4.

Fh.2.5
Whetstone, rectangular-shaped, ground gravel from the bed of the Chamkhar River. Found in intermixed and relocated wall debris.

Dating: from 16th up to early 18th centuries possible.

Finds Table 10.

Inv. No. Fh.1.5.

La.2.1
Deformed arm bangle in brass (for alloying, see Appendix 2). Made out of two strands, each 3 mm in diameter, twisted midsection. Outer parts attached. Long-wrought, trapezoidal-shaped contours. Axially symmetric decor, tooled and engraved. Reconstructed inner dimensions: approx. 4 × 5 cm, which indicates a woman's arm bangle.

Find Location: Slipped-off, intermixed debris in area La.2.

Dating: probably 17th century.

Finds Table 13.

Inv. No. La.2.2.

Lb.3.1
Rim fragment of a coarse ceramic pot. Wheel-turned ware. Dark gray fired. Coarse, mica-rich tempered. Rim rounded, protruding.

Profile Group A3.

Find Location: Thin settlement layer in area Lb.

Dating: late 17th or early 18th century.

Finds Table 10.

Inv. No. Lb.3.1.

Lb.3.2
Fragmented arrowhead. Heavy humps of rust corrosion. Point missing, long wrought, narrow socket.

Finds Table 13.

Inv. No. Lb.3.7.

Lc.2.1

Wall fragment of a small bowl. Genuine porcelain. White glaze, on the exterior side extensive, dark blue decor, probably flower or plant pattern.

Find Location: Secondary debris in area Lc.

Dating: 17th or early 18th century.

Finds Table 12.

Inv. No. Lc.2.2.

Fi.2.1

Fragmented brick-red and weakly fired chunks of clay. Broken rims, very rounded. One area with six parallel, extended finger furrows. Colored with ochre. Function unknown.

Find Location: Secondary debris in area Fi.

Dating: probably 17th century.

Not illustrated.

Inv. No. Fi.2.2.

Ua.2.4

Broken piece of a millstone.

Length: 29.5 cm.

Grinding surface with conically rounded out cavity and roughly hewn grooves of approx. 1–1.5 cm in width and 0.5–0.8 cm in depth. Total diameter not ascertainable.

Find Location: Secondary debris in excavation sector Ua. The piece could have been built into the masonry as plundered spoils.

Dating: 16th/17th century.

Finds Table 15.

Inv. No. Ua.2.1.

Ua.3.1

Spherical gravel, surface colored with ochre.

Find Location: The piece originated from the large gravel depository at the foot of the Utse wall W9/41b (areas Ua and Ue).

Intended use not clearly determinable. Projectile or rather sacred function conceivable.

Dating: 17th century.

Not illustrated.

Inv. No. Ua.3.6.

Ub.2.1

Foot fragment of a small bowl. Genuine porcelain. Bellied wall, rudiments of a standing ring still preserved. Ground color white with light bluish tint. Exterior side with brown coating, inside on the bottom blue decor, with irregular areas, of two concentric circular lines.

Find Location: Relocated, slipped down debris over wall W9/45.

Dating: probably 17th century.

Finds Table 12.

Inv. No. Ub.2.1.

Ub.2.2

Roundish stone slab, fragmented.

Diameter: 19–22 cm.

One side of the slab, with a maximum thickness of 4 cm, indicates five roughly crafted cavities of 2.5–3 cm in diameter. A sixth one at the edges remains uncertain.

Edge and surface of the slab apparently not overly crafted. Explanation of the piece is uncertain. Holes are too small for absorbing lamp butter. One interpretation as base of a game has not been ruled out. However, the found ceramic game tokens appear too large for the holes.

Find Location: Secondary debris in area Ub.2. Presumably built into the masonry as plundered spoils.

Dating: probably 16th or 17th century.

Finds Table 14.

Inv. No. Ub.2.2.

Ud.4.1

Small plate fitting with right-angled clamp, heavily rusted and fragmented. Contour not determinable.

Find Location: Secondary infill in putlog hole of a door lintel of W9/40.

Dating: 16th or 17th century possible.

Finds Table 13.

Inv. No. Ud.4.5.

Ue.3.1

Rim fragment of a pot, coarse ceramic. Wheel-turned ware, oxidation-fired. Mica-rich tempered. Horizontally protruding, rounded rim, steep wall without neck. Interior with matt, colorless glaze, exterior with soot remnants.

Type Group A6.3

Find Location: weakly pronounced settlement layer in area Ue.

Dating: 16th or 17th century possible.

Finds Table 1.

Inv. No. Ue.3.1.

Ue.3.2

Padlock, rusted to amorphous clump. X-ray shows a rectangular casing and parts of the mechanism, namely, a V-shaped lock spring.

Find Location: same as Ue.3.1.

Dimensions: 70 × 40 × 31 mm.

Finds Table 13.

Inv. No. Ue.3.2.

Za.2.1

Lead musket ball. Caliber: 12 mm.

Weight: 10 g.

Find Location: Secondary debris at the foot of the small tower, directly over rock level (settlement layer missing).

Dating: probably about 1700.

Finds Table 13.

Inv. No. Za.2.2.

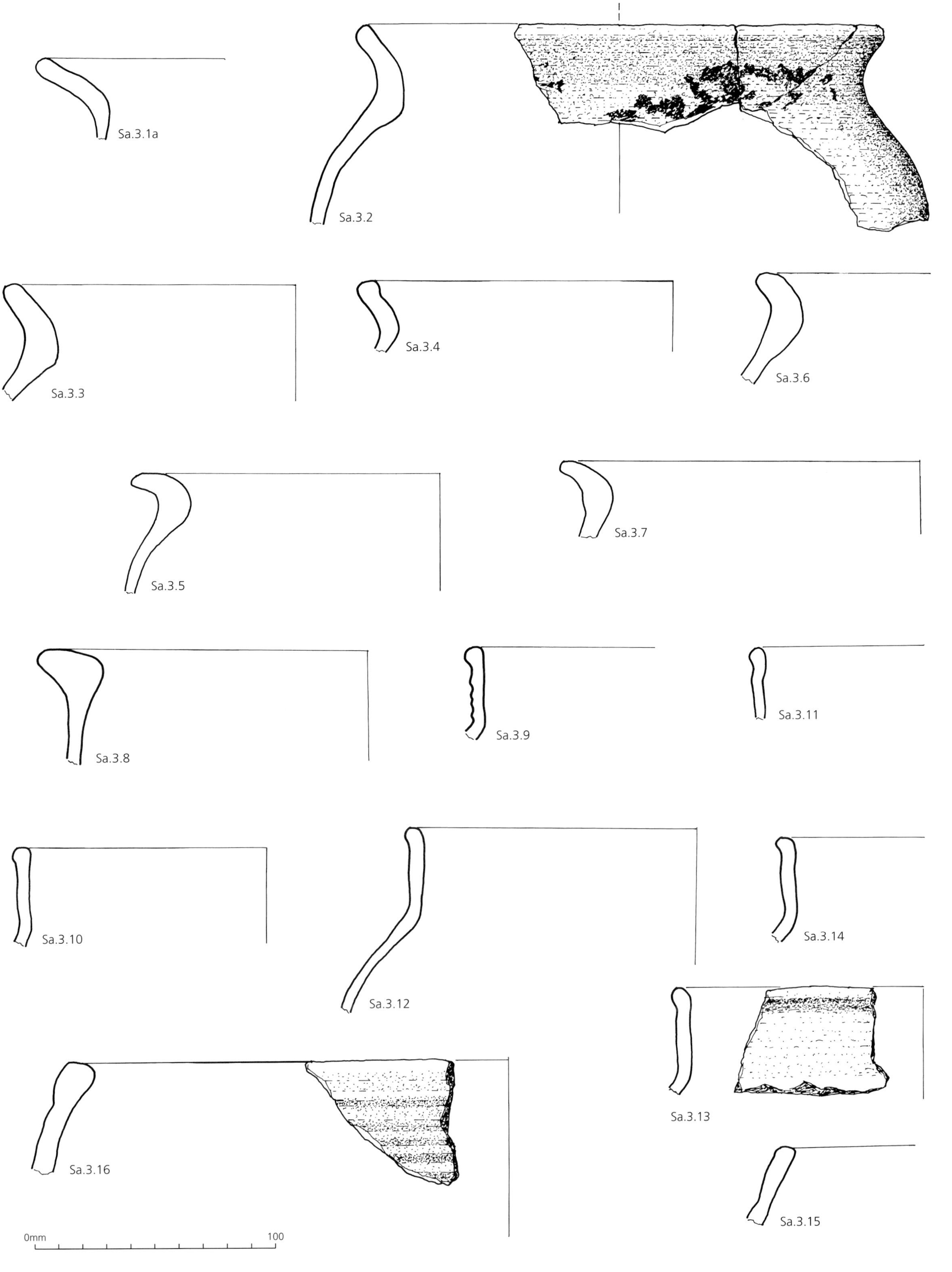
Sa.3.1a
Sa.3.2
Sa.3.3
Sa.3.4
Sa.3.6
Sa.3.5
Sa.3.7
Sa.3.8
Sa.3.9
Sa.3.11
Sa.3.10
Sa.3.12
Sa.3.14
Sa.3.13
Sa.3.16
Sa.3.15
0mm
100

1

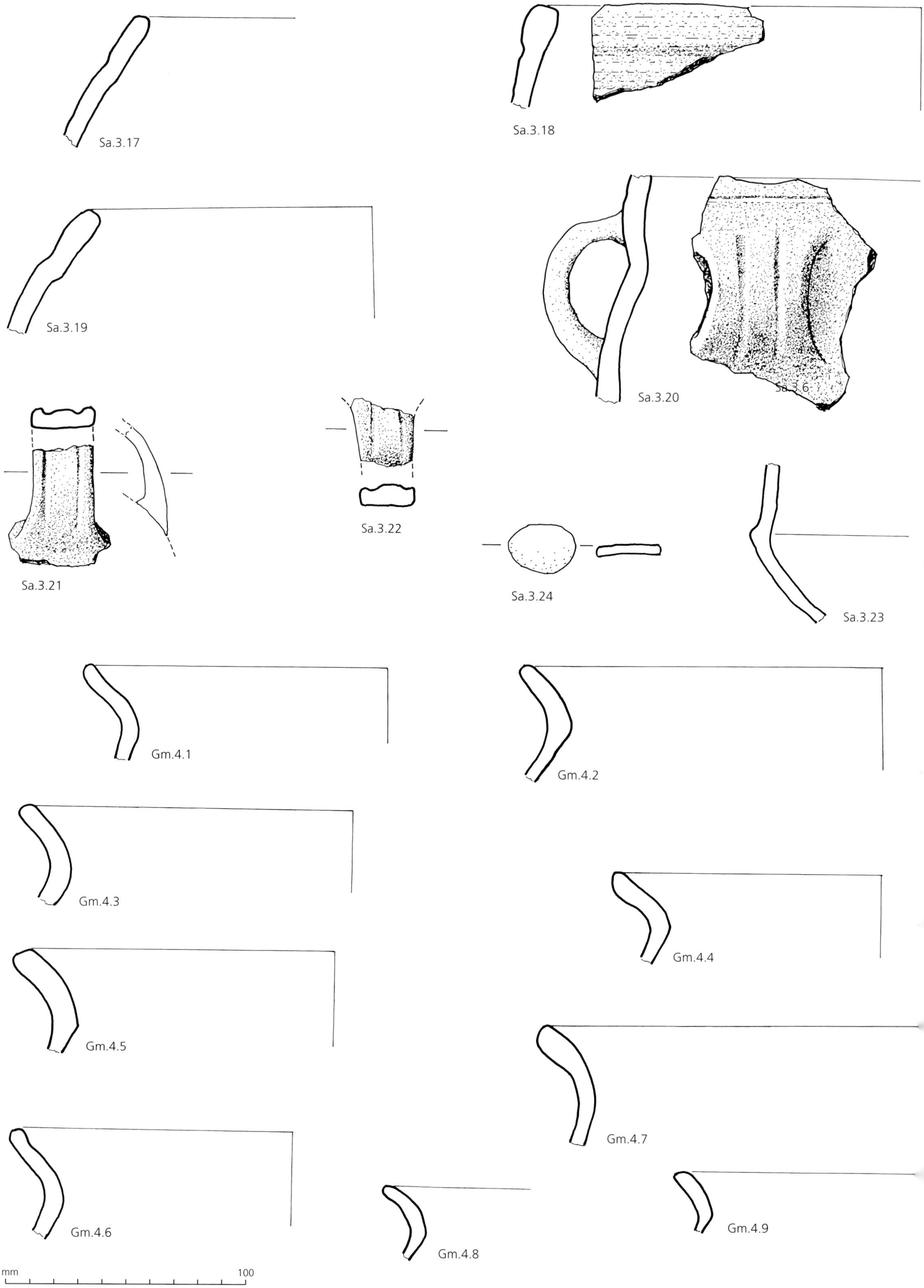
Sa.3.17
Sa.3.18
Sa.3.19
Sa.3.20
Sa.3.6
Sa.3.21
Sa.3.22
Sa.3.24
Sa.3.23
Gm.4.1
Gm.4.2
Gm.4.3
Gm.4.4
Gm.4.5
Gm.4.7
Gm.4.6
Gm.4.8
Gm.4.9
0 mm
100

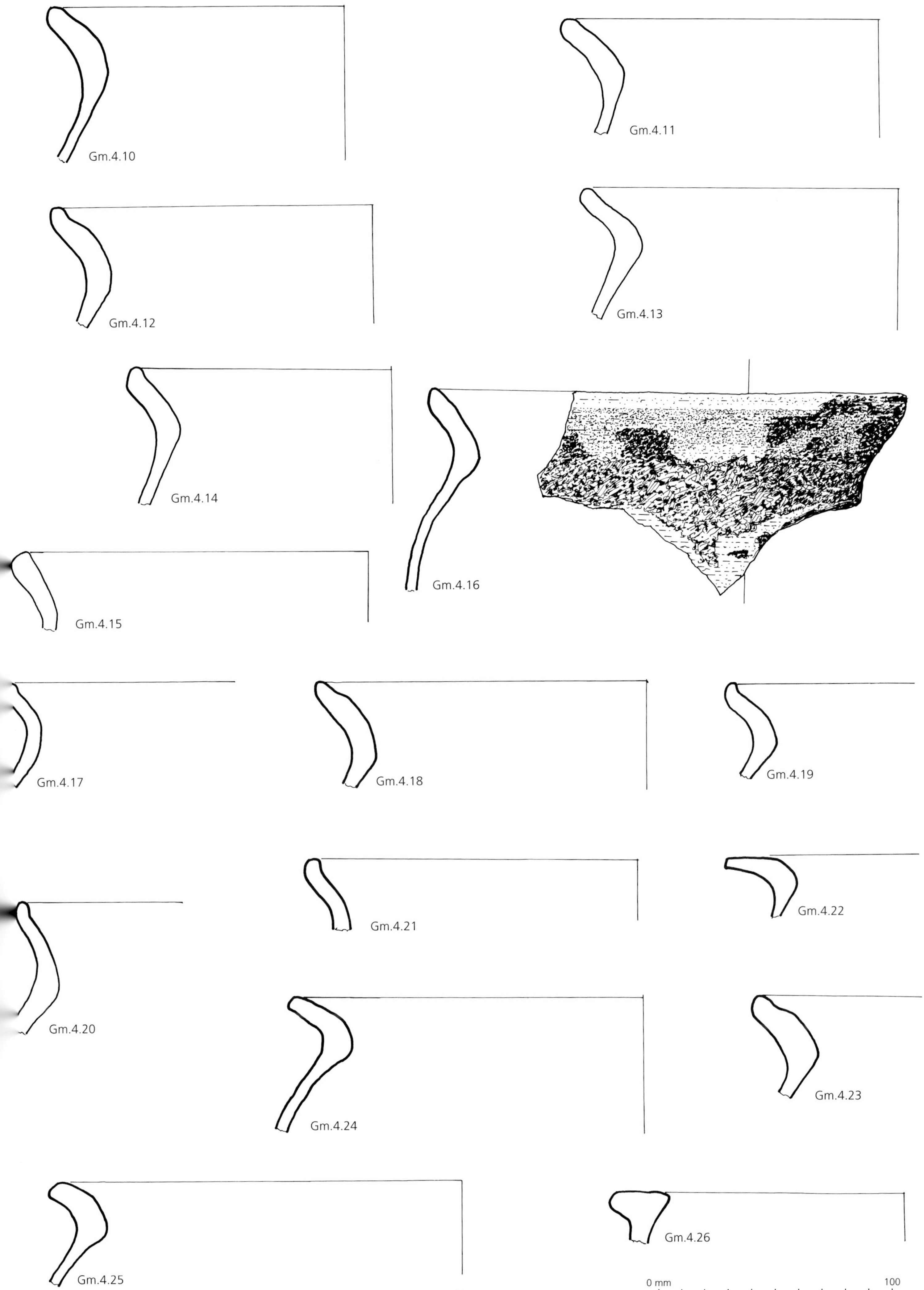
Gm.4.10
Gm.4.11
Gm.4.12
Gm.4.13
Gm.4.14
Gm.4.16
Gm.4.15
Gm.4.17
Gm.4.18
Gm.4.19
Gm.4.21
Gm.4.22
Gm.4.20
Gm.4.24
Gm.4.23
Gm.4.25
Gm.4.26
0 mm
100

3

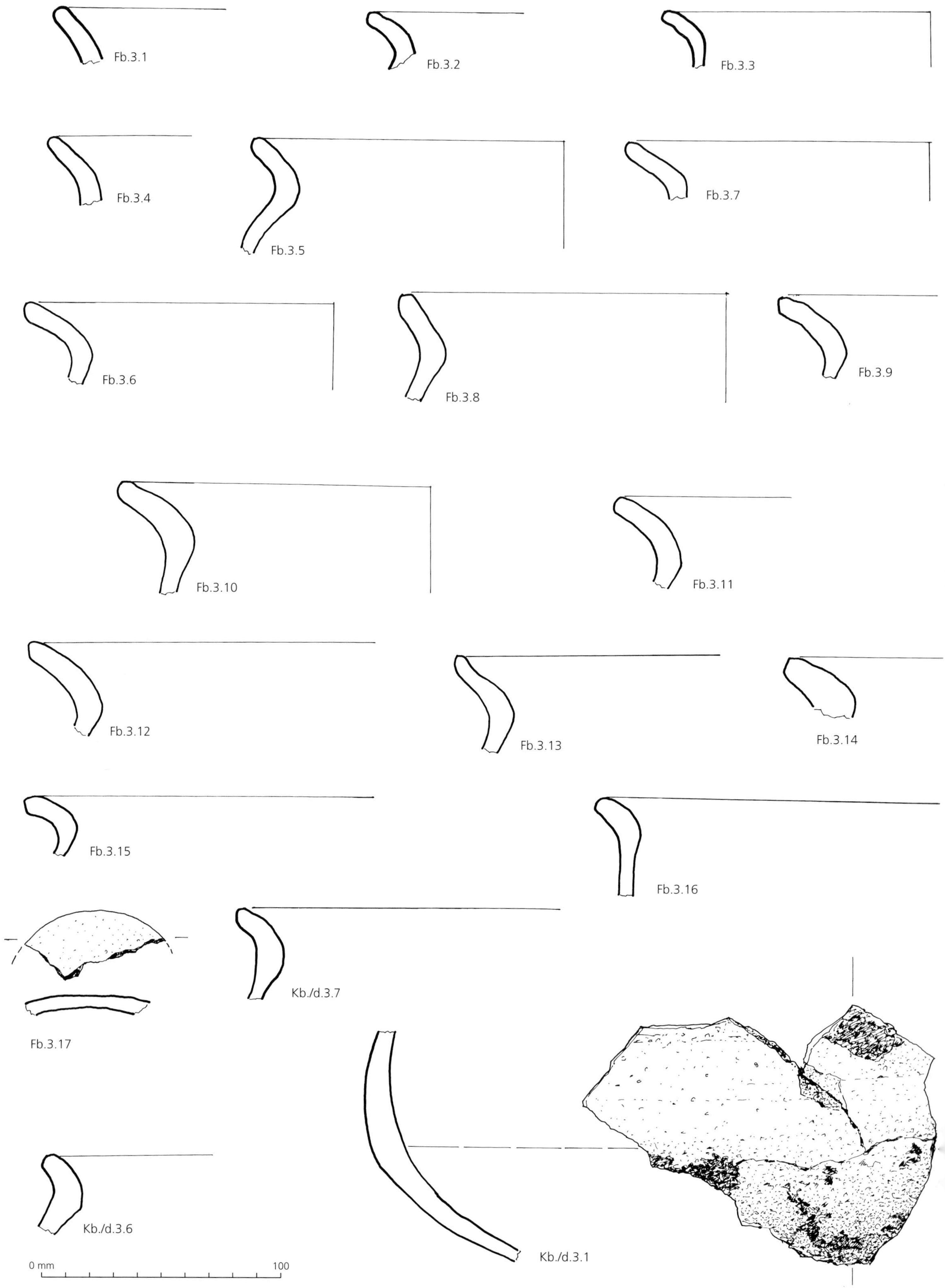
Fb.3.1
Fb.3.2
Fb.3.3
Fb.3.4
Fb.3.5
Fb.3.7
Fb.3.6
Fb.3.8
Fb.3.9
Fb.3.10
Fb.3.11
Fb.3.12
Fb.3.13
Fb.3.14
Fb.3.15
Fb.3.16
Fb.3.17
Kb./d.3.7
Kb./d.3.6
Kb./d.3.1
0 mm
100

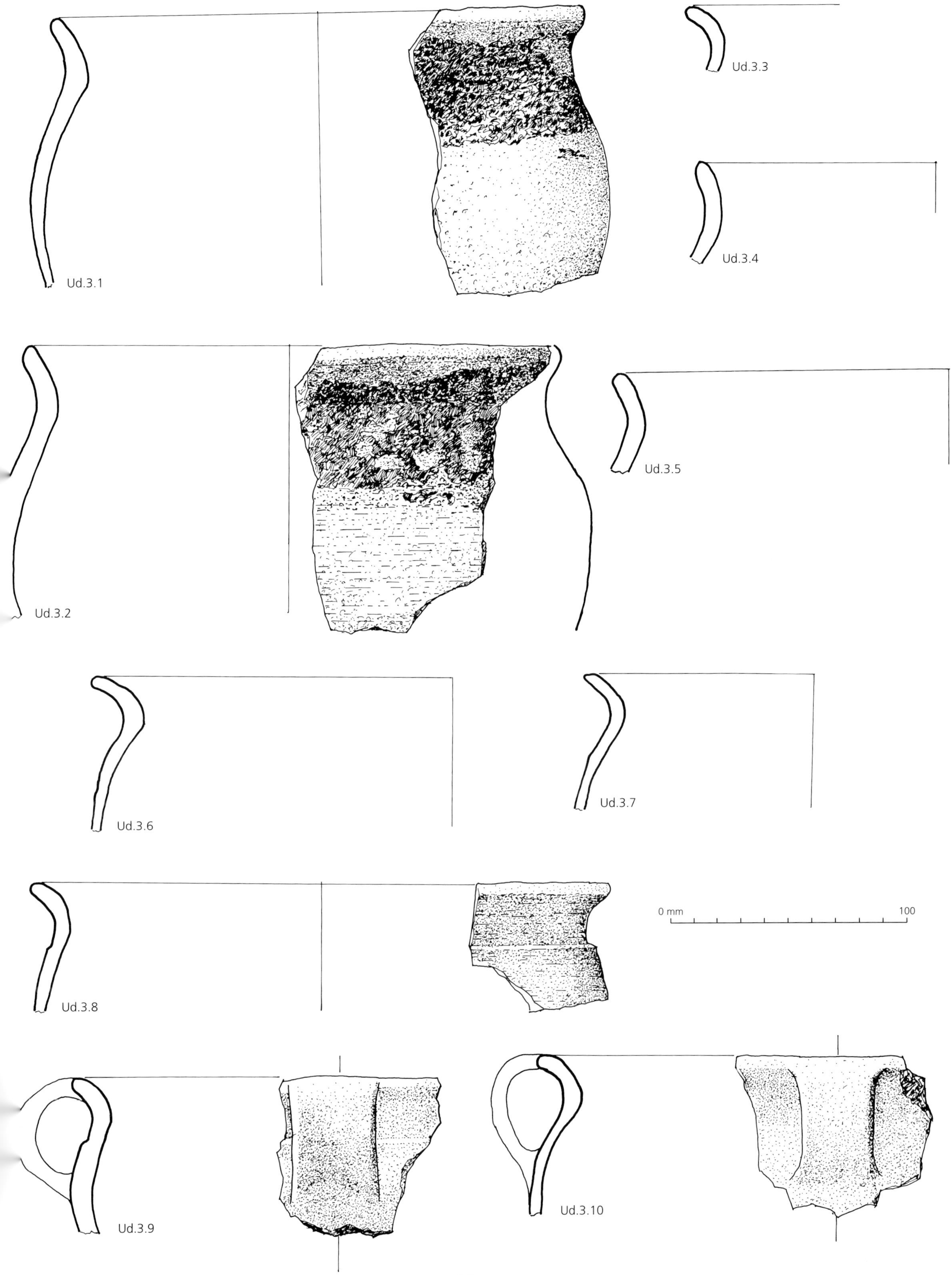
Ud.3.1
Ud.3.3
Ud.3.4
Ud.3.2
Ud.3.5
Ud.3.6
Ud.3.7
Ud.3.8
0 mm
100
Ud.3.9
Ud.3.10

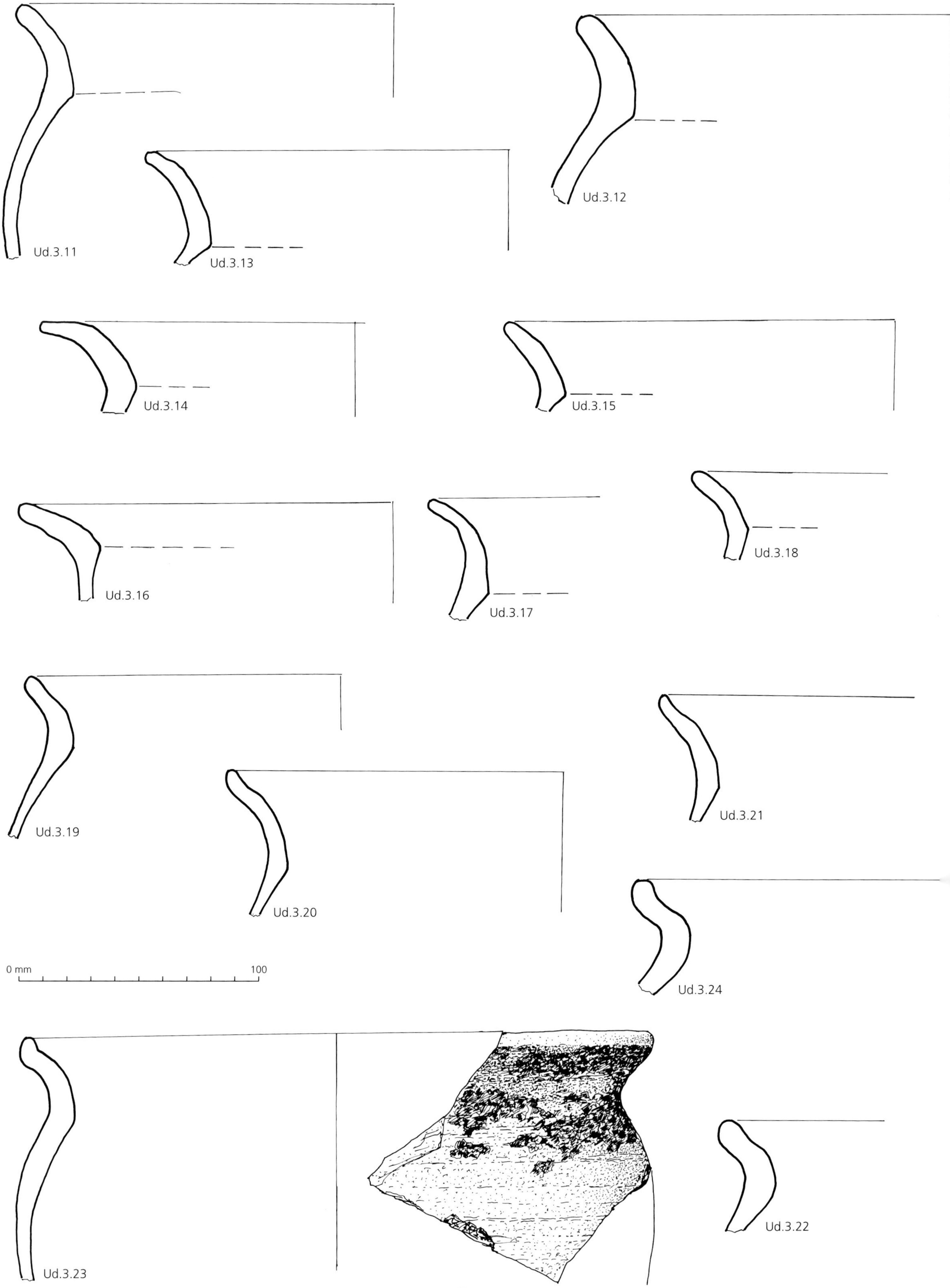
Ud.3.11
Ud.3.12
Ud.3.13
Ud.3.14
Ud.3.15
Ud.3.16
Ud.3.17
Ud.3.18
Ud.3.19
Ud.3.20
Ud.3.21
0 mm
100
Ud.3.24
Ud.3.23
Ud.3.22

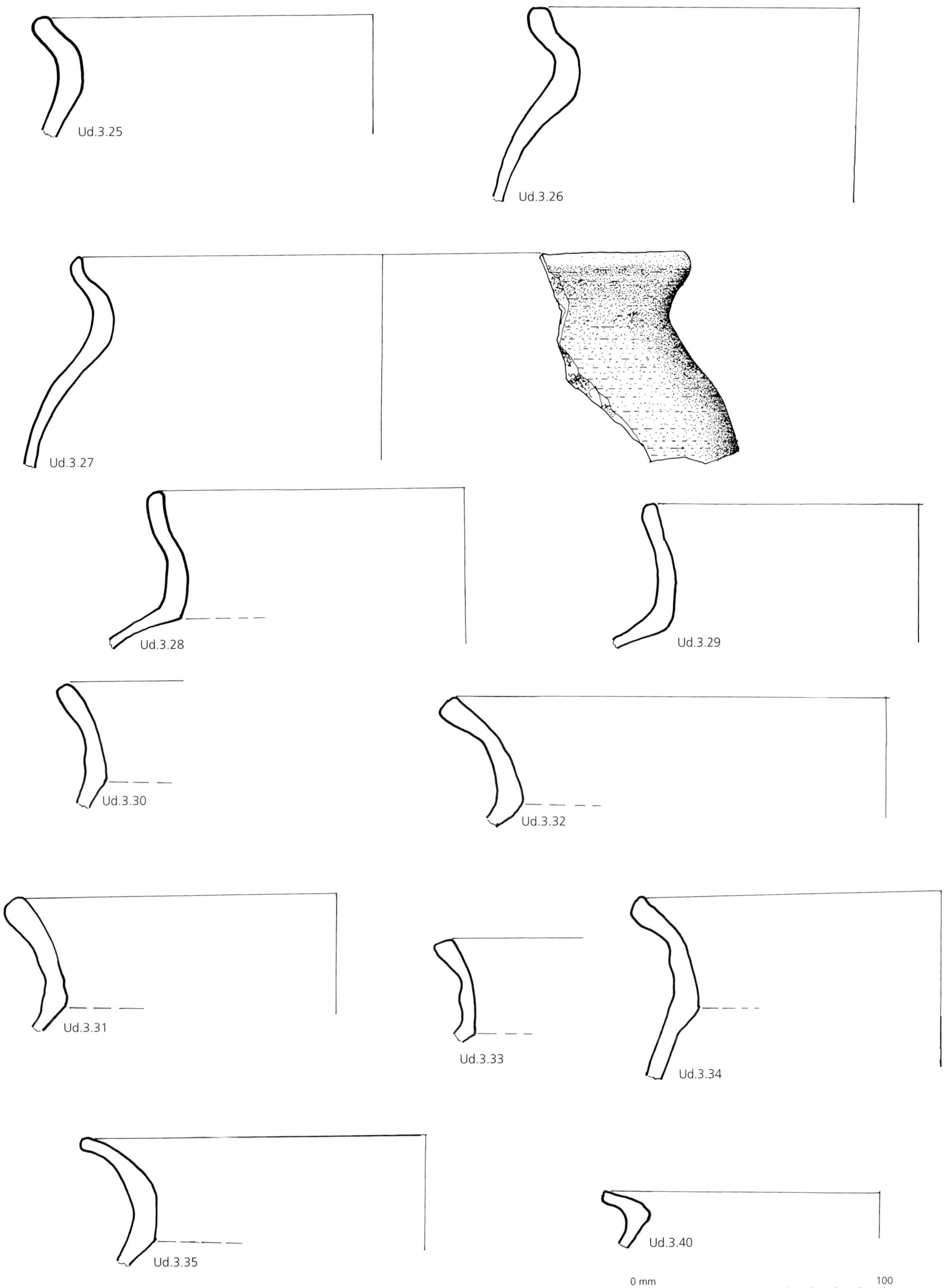
Ud.3.25
Ud.3.26
Ud.3.27
Ud.3.28
Ud.3.29
Ud.3.30
Ud.3.32
Ud.3.31
Ud.3.33
Ud.3.34
Ud.3.35
Ud.3.40
0 mm
100

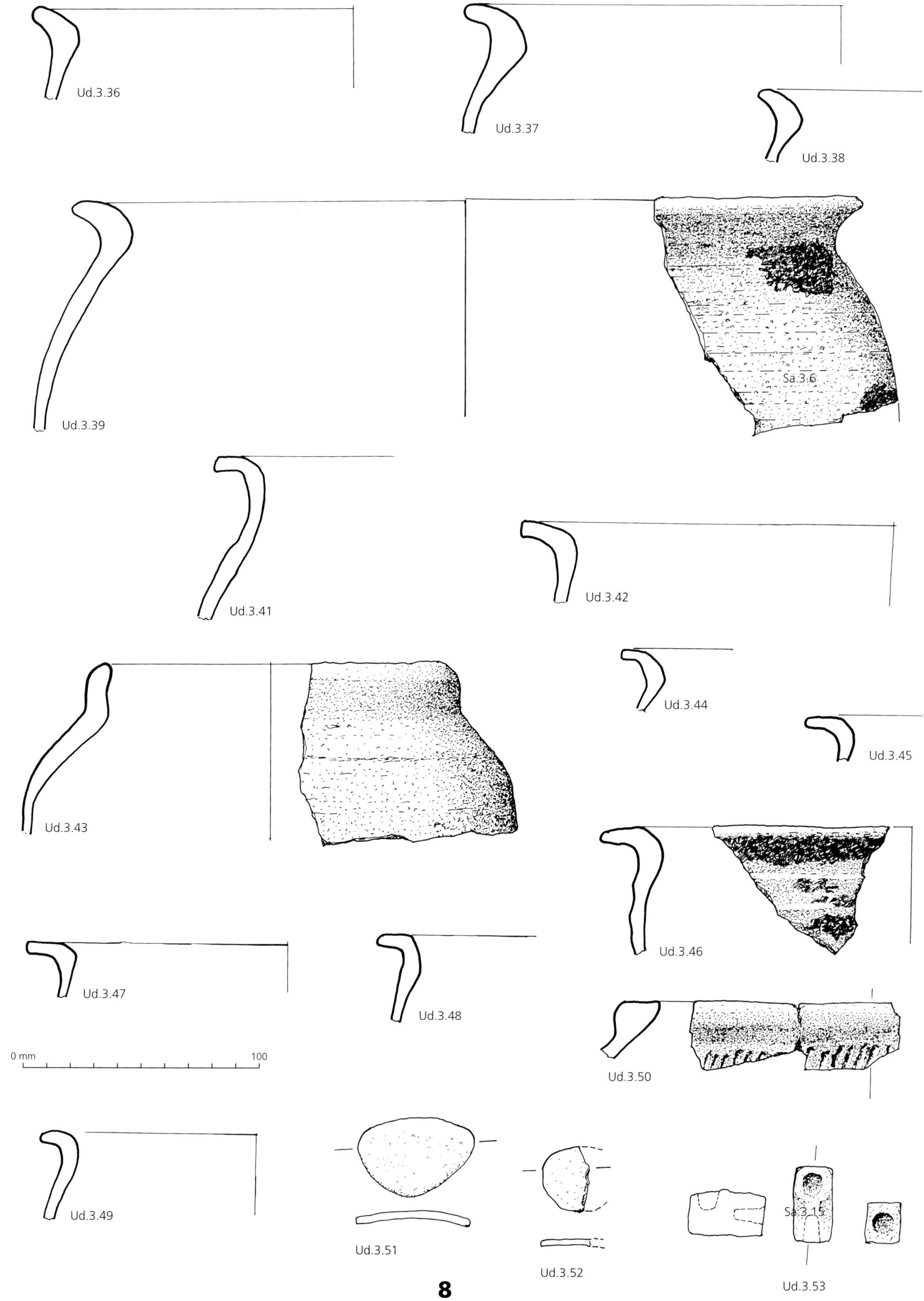
Ud.3.36
Ud.3.37
Ud.3.38
Ud.3.39
Sa.3.6
Ud.3.41
Ud.3.42
Ud.3.43
Ud.3.44
Ud.3.45
Ud.3.46
Ud.3.47
Ud.3.48
Ud.3.50
0 mm
100
Ud.3.49
Ud.3.51
Ud.3.52
Sa.3.15
Ud.3.53

8

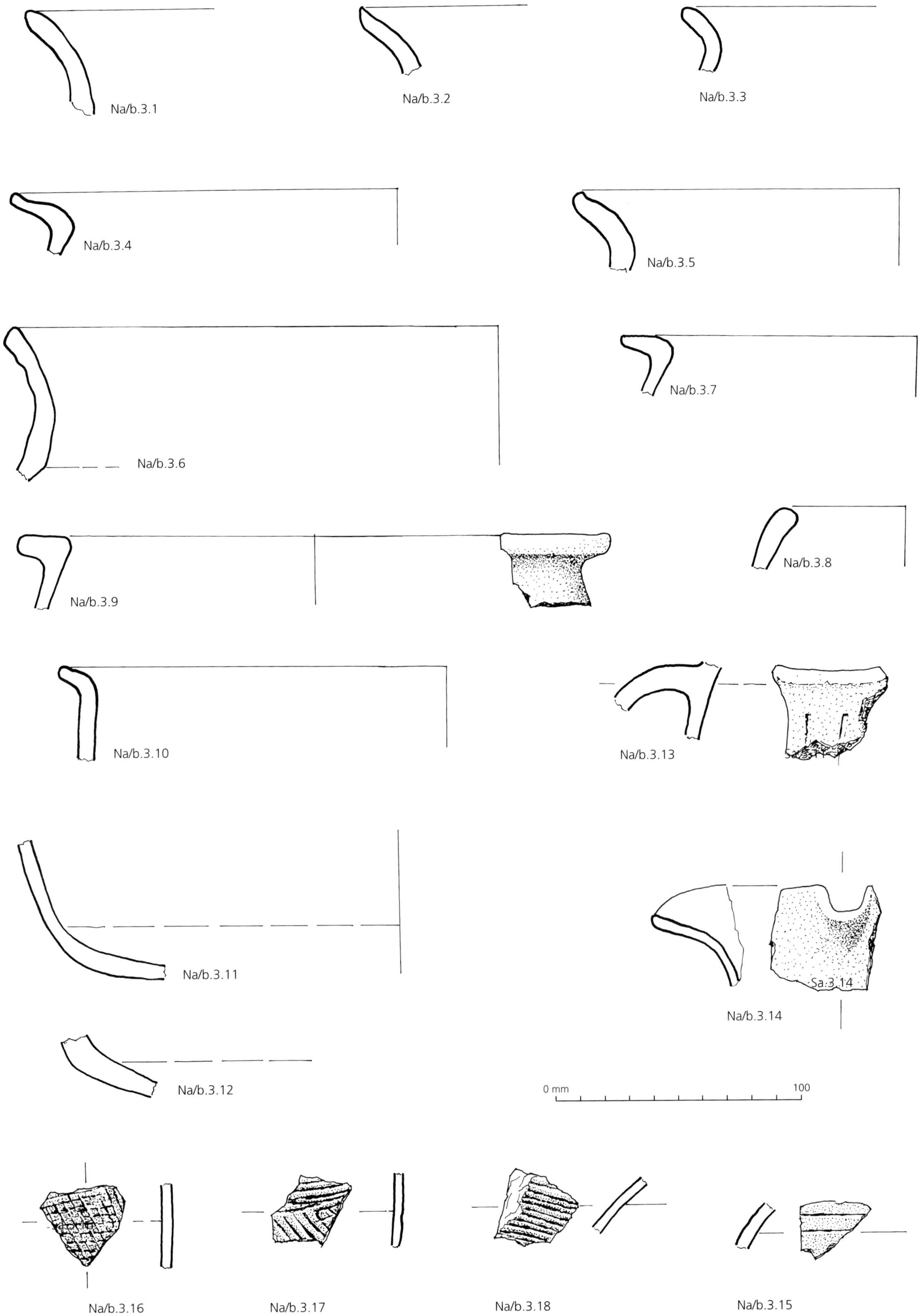

Na/b.3.1
Na/b.3.2
Na/b.3.3
Na/b.3.4
Na/b.3.5
Na/b.3.6
Na/b.3.7
Na/b.3.8
Na/b.3.9
Na/b.3.10
Na/b.3.13
Na/b.3.11
Na/b.3.12
Sa.3.14
Na/b.3.14
0 mm
100
Na/b.3.16
Na/b.3.17
Na/b.3.18
Na/b.3.15

Go.4.1

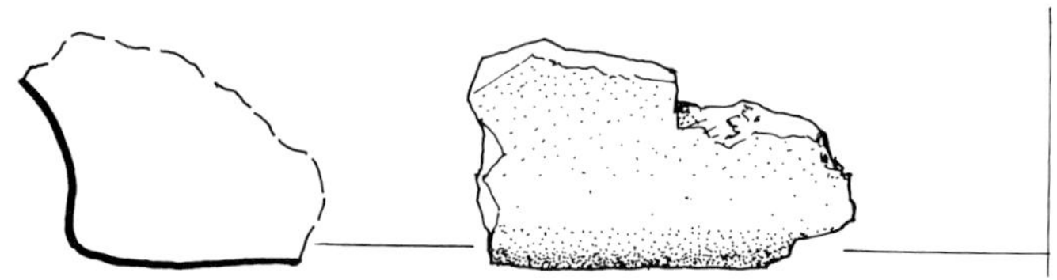

Nc/b.3.1

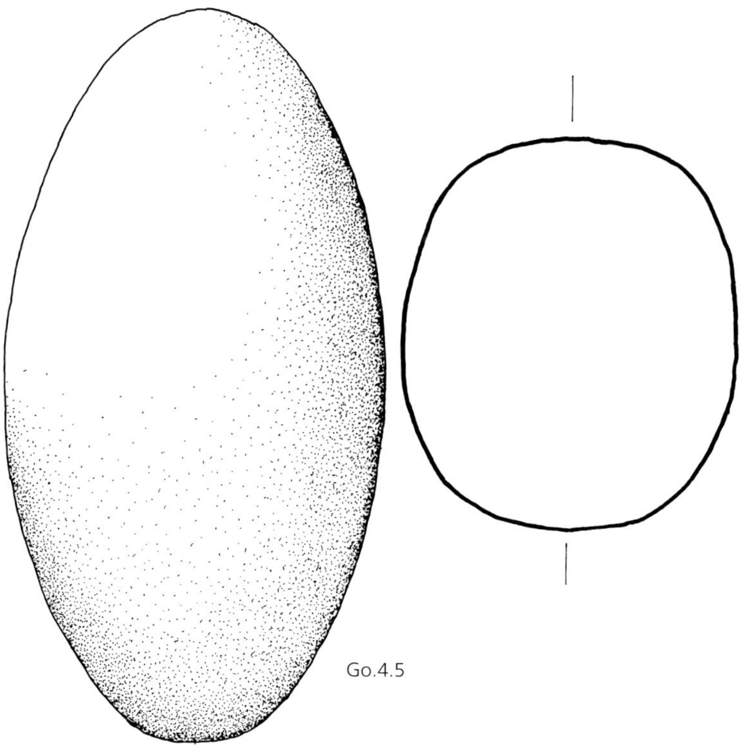

Go.4.5

Nc/b.3.2

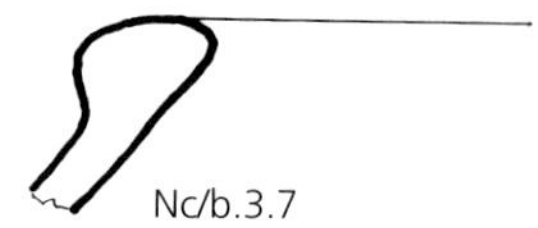

Nc/b.3.7

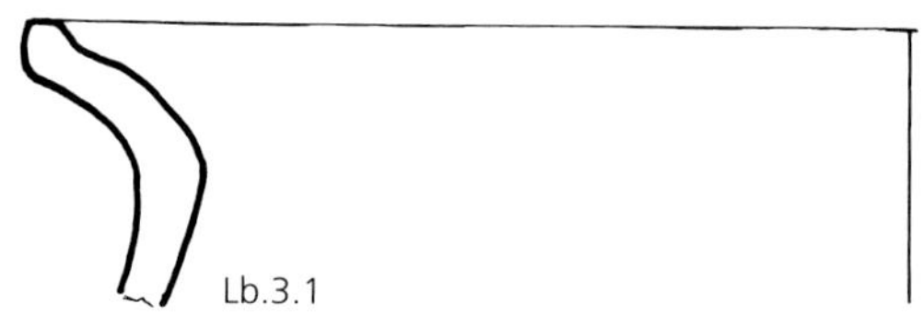

Lb.3.1

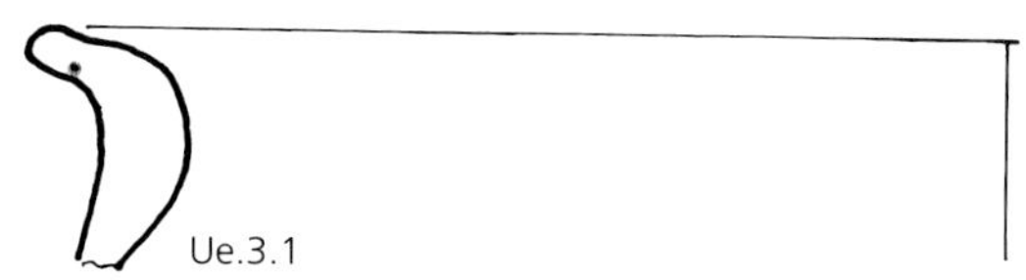

Ue.3.1

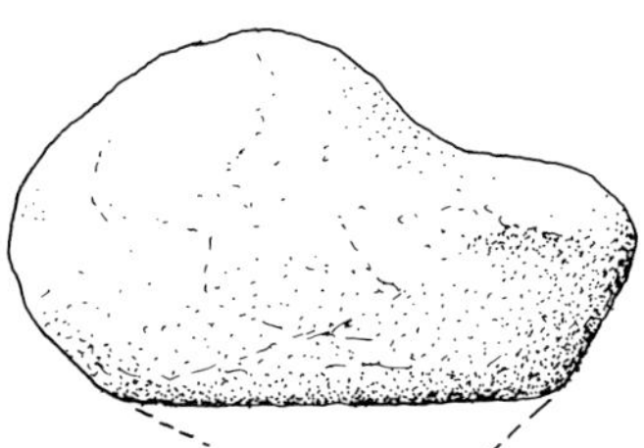

Fb.3.18

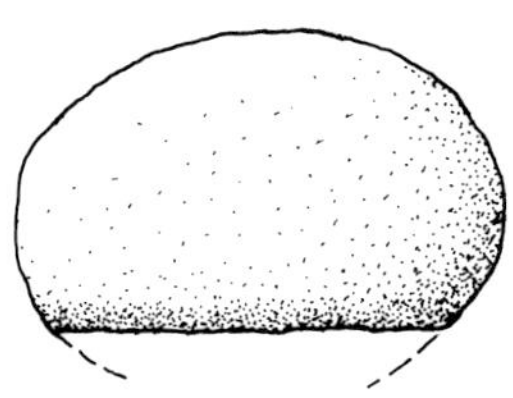

Fb.3.19

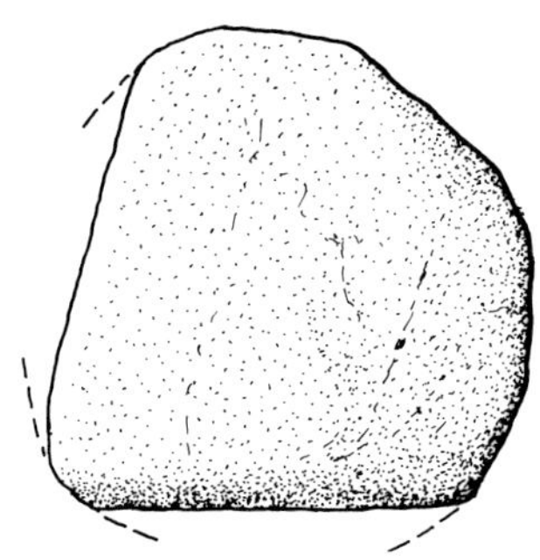

Fh.2.1

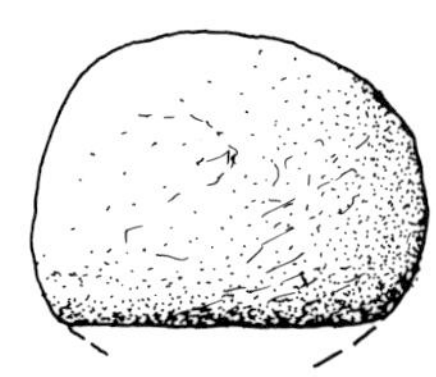

Fh.2.3

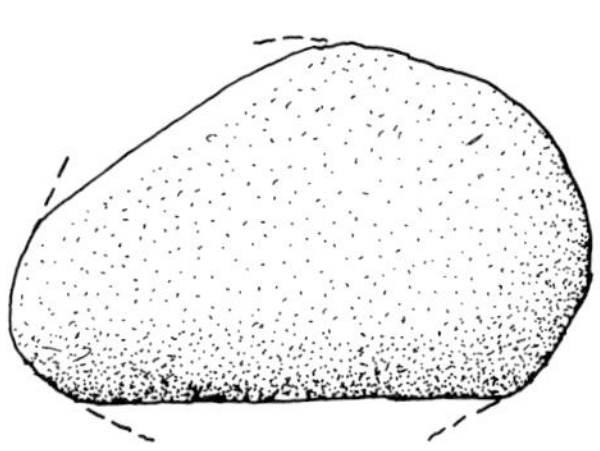

Fb.3.20

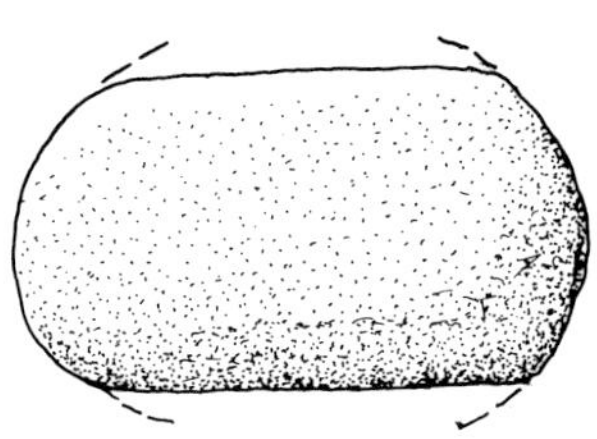

Fb.3.21

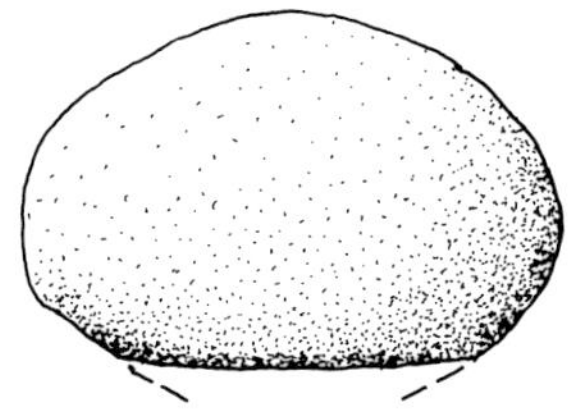

Fh.2.2

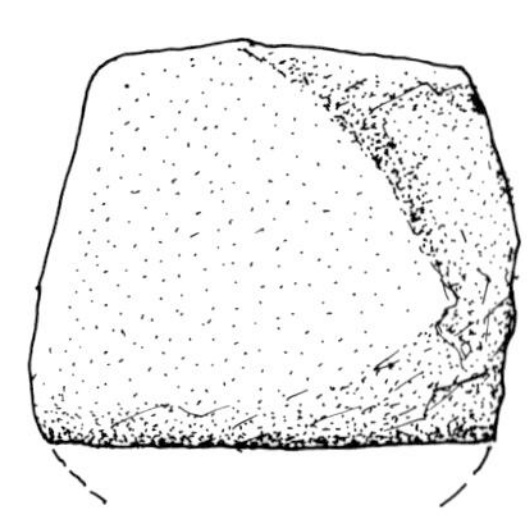

Fh.2.4

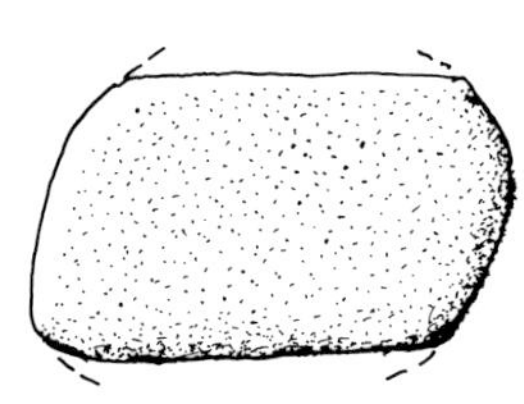

Fh.2.5

0 mm 100

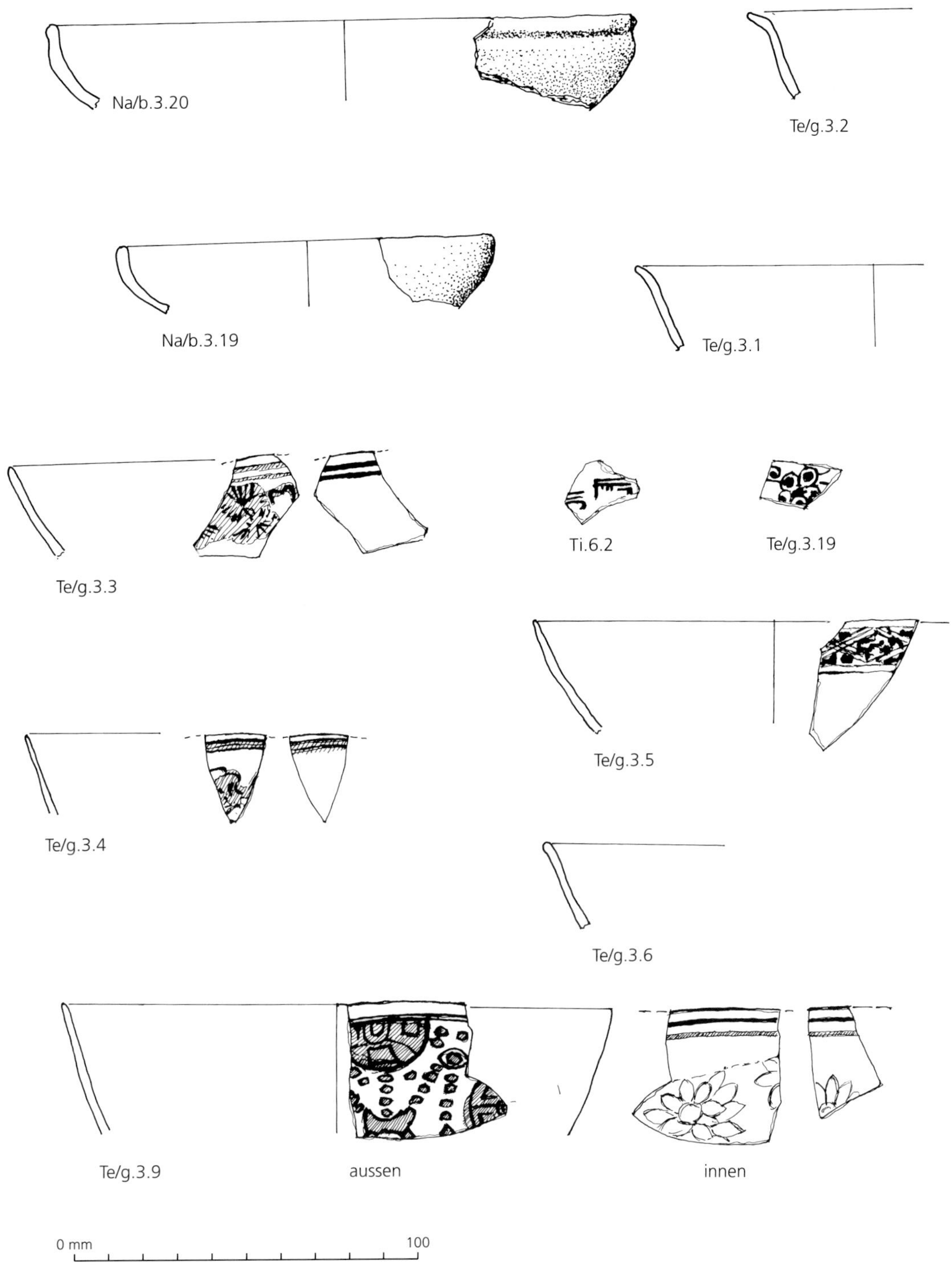
Na/b.3.20
Te/g.3.2
Na/b.3.19
Te/g.3.1
Te/g.3.3
Ti.6.2
Te/g.3.19
Te/g.3.5
Te/g.3.4
Te/g.3.6
Te/g.3.9
aussen
innen
0 mm
100

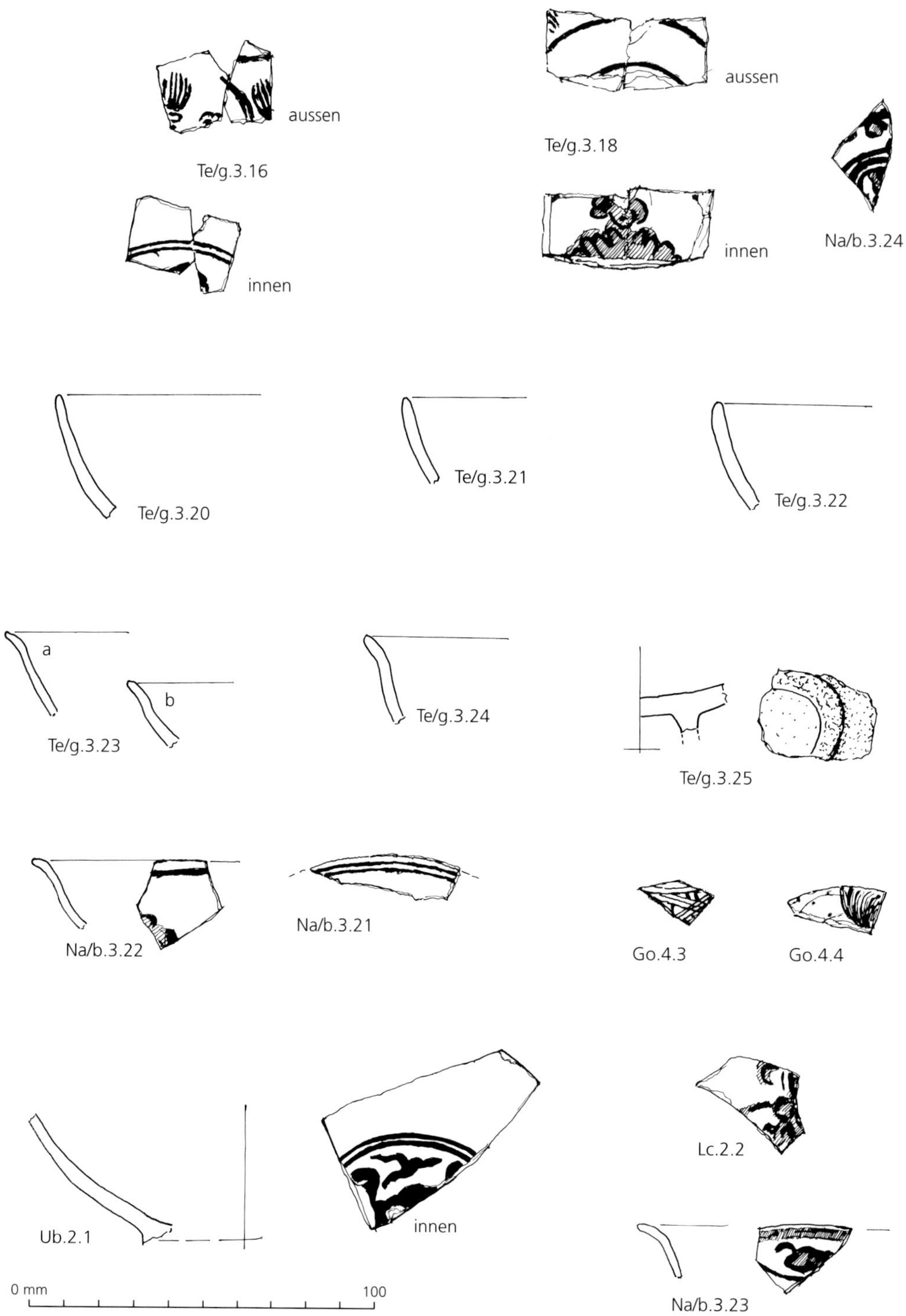
Te/g.3.16
aussen
innen
Te/g.3.18
aussen
innen
Na/b.3.24
Te/g.3.20
Te/g.3.21
Te/g.3.22
Te/g.3.23
a
b
Te/g.3.24
Te/g.3.25
Na/b.3.22
Na/b.3.21
Go.4.3
Go.4.4
Ub.2.1
innen
Lc.2.2
Na/b.3.23
0 mm
100

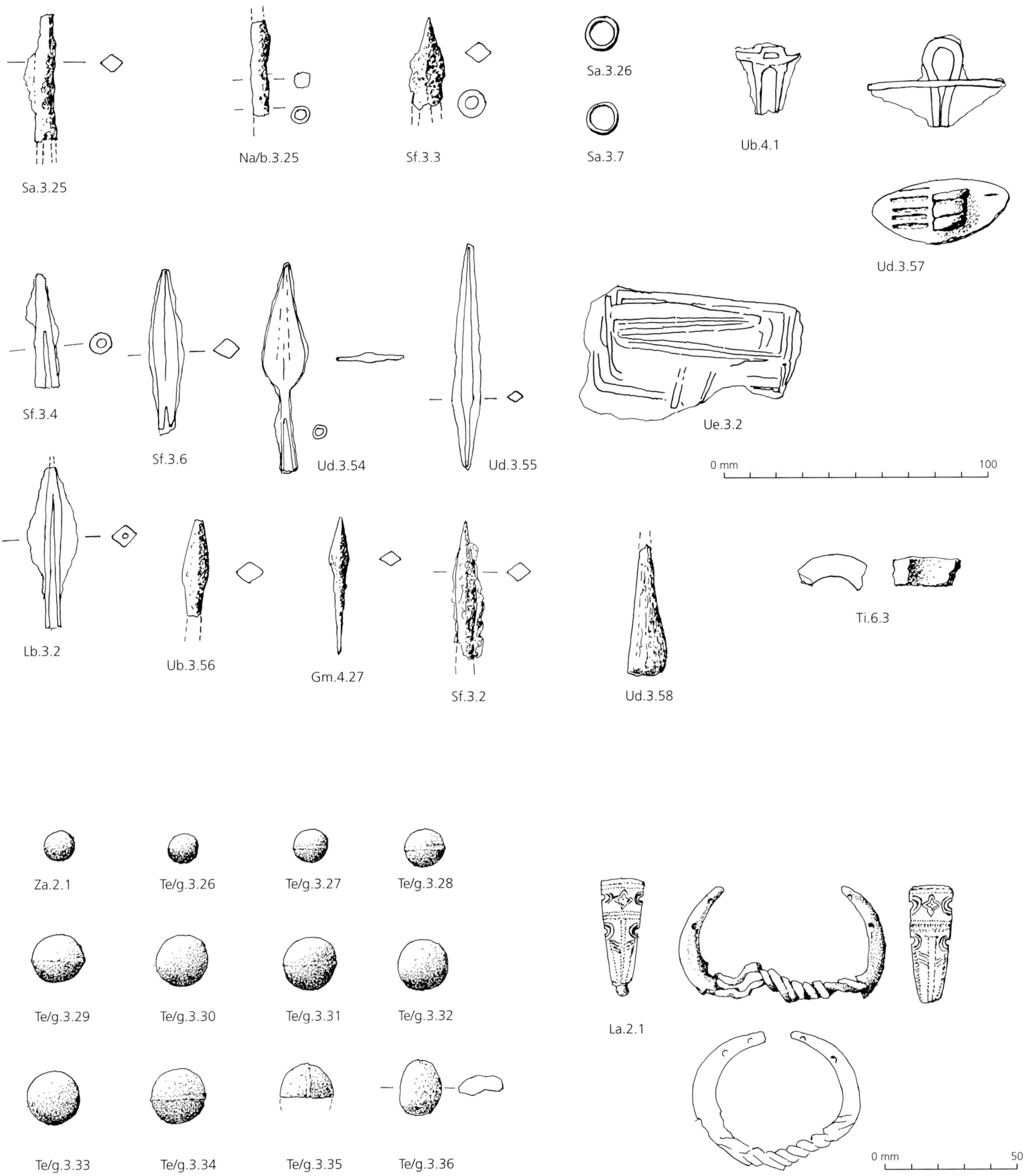
Sa.3.25
Na/b.3.25
Sf.3.3
Sa.3.26
Sa.3.7
Ub.4.1
Ud.3.57
Sf.3.4
Sf.3.6
Ud.3.54
Ud.3.55
Ue.3.2
0 mm
100
Lb.3.2
Ub.3.56
Gm.4.27
Sf.3.2
Ud.3.58
Ti.6.3
Za.2.1
Te/g.3.26
Te/g.3.27
Te/g.3.28
Te/g.3.29
Te/g.3.30
Te/g.3.31
Te/g.3.32
Te/g.3.33
Te/g.3.34
Te/g.3.35
Te/g.3.36
La.2.1
0 mm
50

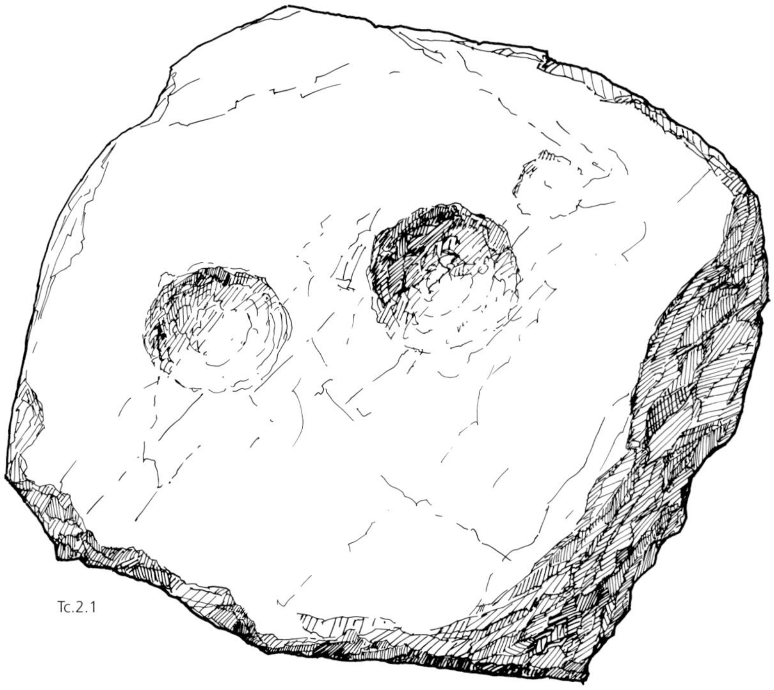

Tc.2.1

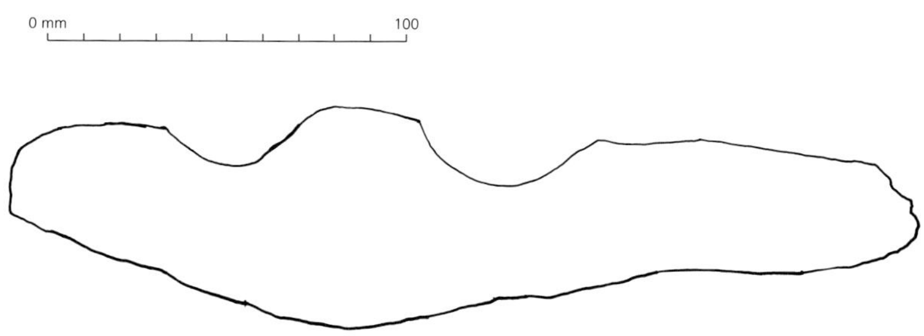

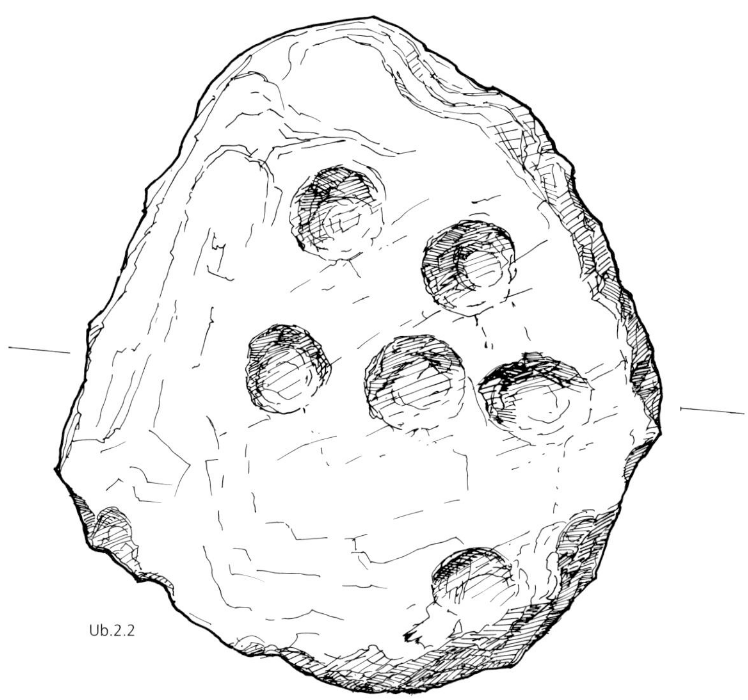

Ub.2.2

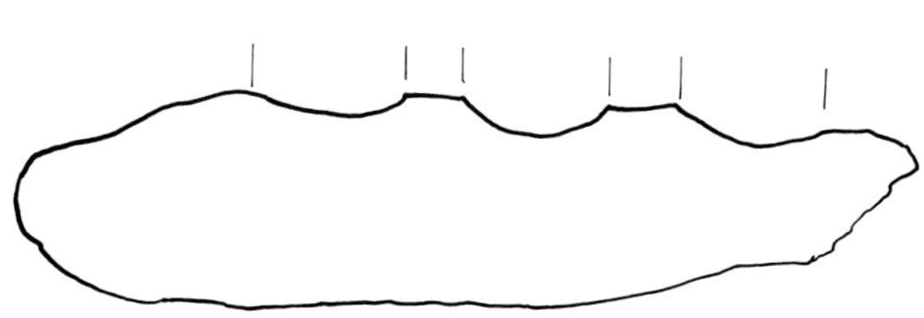

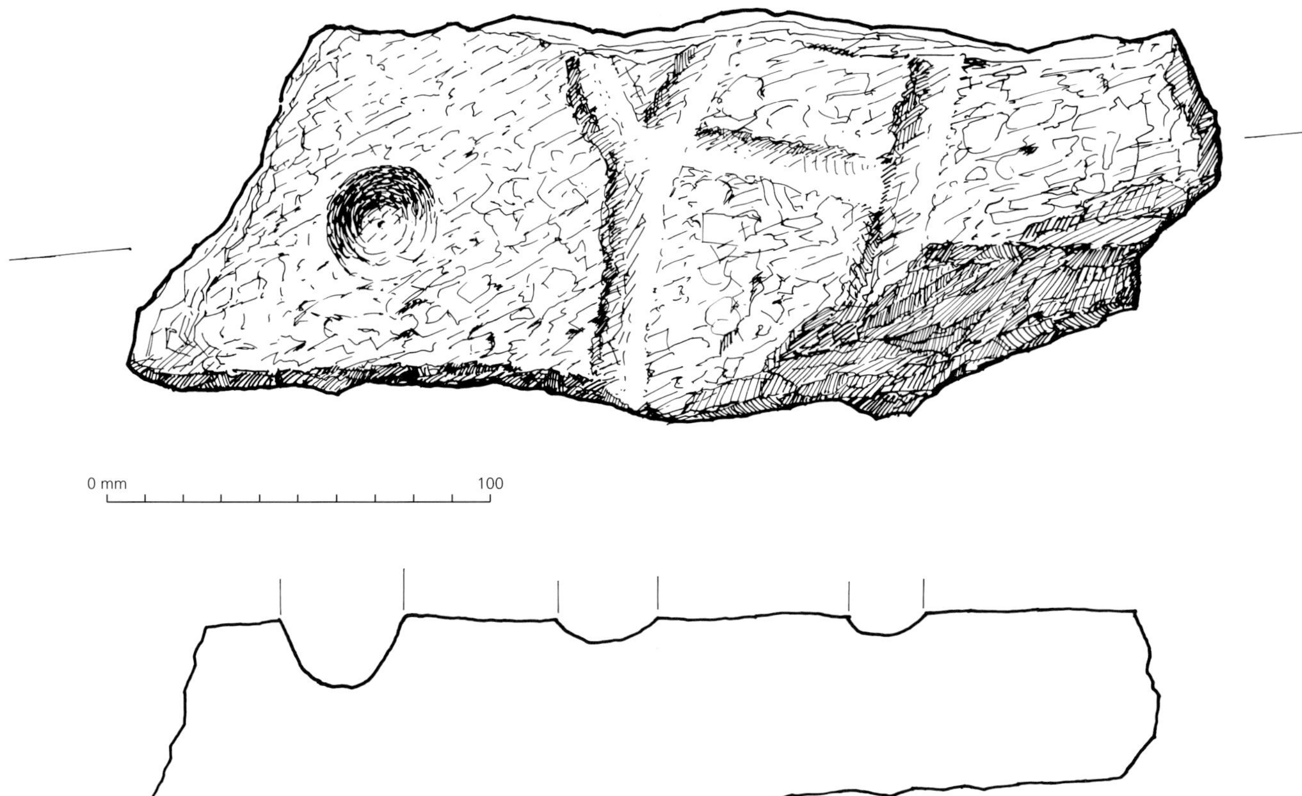

Ua.2.4

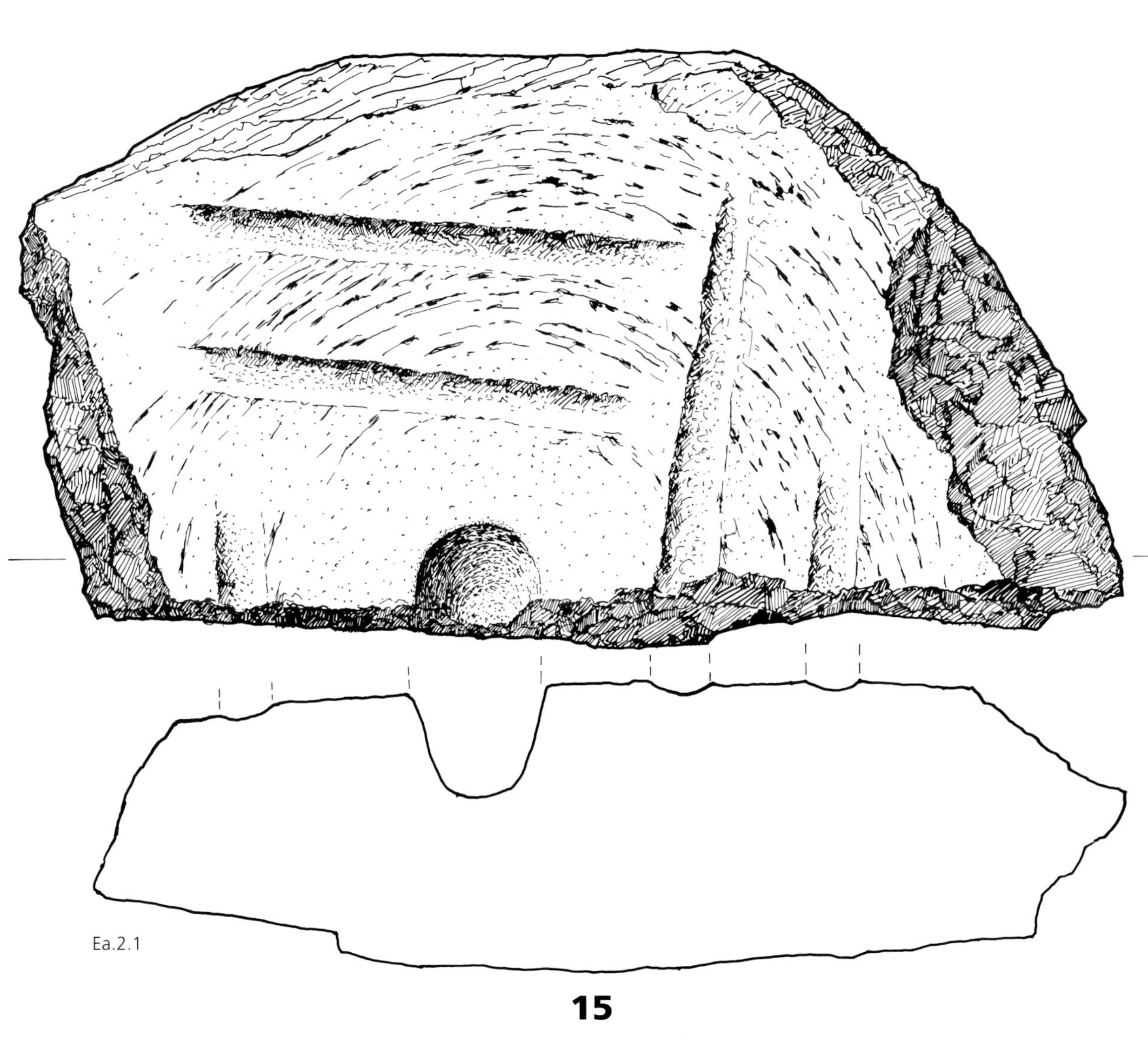

Ea.2.1

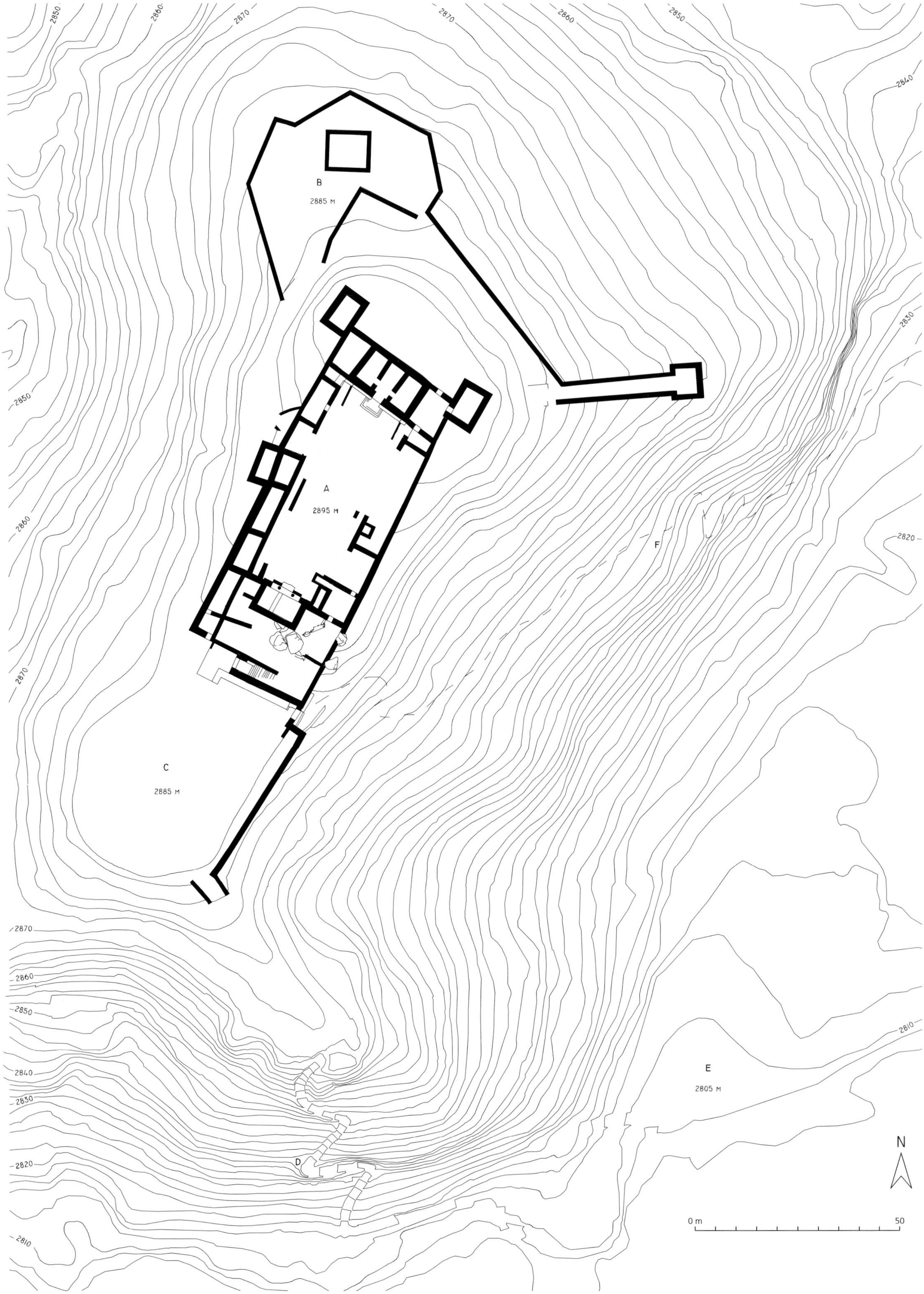

Fig. 126

5. Interpretation and Dating

5.1. Ground Plan Disposition

5.1.1. Entire Compound

The longest axis of the entire compound of Drapham Dzong extends from northwest to southeast over a length of approx. 500 m. The transverse northwest-southeast axis measures approx. 200 m. The visible and only partially excavated remains of human labor—walls, buildings, terraces, ditches—evidence the development of the area of a site of varying density, whereby to be noted, is that the outer parts, i.e., the northern and southern baileys and valley settlement, have not been archaeologically recorded, and still remain underground with an unknown number and extent of buildings ruins that might be uncovered.

Within the entire compound, the main fortress on the highest knoll of the fortress hill forms a compact block arranged as a rectangle with a densely clustered fabric of development grouped around an inner courtyard (see. 5.1.2.). Within the entire compound, the defensive-representative, trapezoidal walled-in structure seems isolated and withdrawn; with the exception of the outer gate at the eastern front (sector Sd), no architectonic connections can be observed between the main fortress and the site area of the two baileys. The possibility that the enclosure walls of the two baileys, however, were hung together on the western flank of the mountain, is not to be excluded, which thereby would have formed a ring wall outside of and in front of the main fortress. Since the slope is covered by massive wall and slope debris, very elaborate surface excavations would be necessary for clarification. A constructional correlation between the southern bailey and valley settlement can be clearly demonstrated in the Gestalt of a turreted stairway, even though its lowermost segment lies hidden at the junction in the valley settlement under wall und slope debris.

In contrast to the ground plan of the main fortress, which seems to be strictly laid out symmetrically and according to right angles, the enclosure walls of the baileys and the valley settlement adapt to the given conditions of the natural, unevenly flowing topography. This is especially apparent at the northern bailey, where the ring wall assumes a mostly obtuse-angled, broken course. The attempt to articulate the wall in primarily long, straights segments is, however, unmistakable.

Also, the connecting passages, which extend out radially from the peripheries of the two baileys, stretch to the protruding defensive towers—as far as recognizable—in extended alignment. Only the lower segment of the stairway that leads down to the valley settlement is laid out as a zigzag to accommodate the steeply sloping terrain of the site. The presence of two access ways seems rather unexpected: next to the stairway that rises up from the valley settlement, there is even a second ascent, which leads from the saddle at the eastern foot of the fortress rock directly to the southeastern corner of the main fortress.

Fig. 126 Topographic plan. J.O.

Fig. 127 Upper section of non-excavated connecting corridor between southern bailey and valley settlement. View from the main fortress towards southeast. W.M.

Fig. 128 Overall view of valley settlement. View from main fortress towards southeast. W.M.

127

128

129

Fig. 129 Overview of excavation site. Left, sector Ba at southern corner of southern bailey. Right (in background), main fortress. View towards northwest. W.M.

Fig. 130 Main fortress. Construction phases. J.O.

On the two baileys there are few wall traces indicating a building development compound. The preserved, clearly identifiable remains reveal the ground plan of elongated rectangular buildings—inwardly pushed against the ring walls—, which, however, occupy only a small part of the total area of the site. Most of the defensive towers at the periphery of both baileys also possess a rectangular footprint. An exception is a tower at the northern bailey, which has a trapezoidal ground plan.

Without archaeological clarification, the question of whether the irregularly shaped depressions in the southwestern area of the southern bailey are to be interpreted as traces of buildings, must remain unanswered. In any case, all in all, there is no indication on the 3,200 m^2 total surface area of the two baileys of a large building development compound, which ultimately provides hardly any grounds in answering the question of the purpose of the vast area of the site. A manmade walkway level, e.g., in the form of paving, has not been observed on the exposed surfaces of the southern bailey. (This contradicts claims by older locals, who remember slab paving at the southern bailey.)

The situation is different in the valley settlement at the southeastern foot of the fortress hill. Following the edge of the natural terrain, the enclosure wall, reinforced with a tower, is only to be perceived as a wall of rubble. The exact alignment could not be determined until after exposure, it seems, however, that individual segments—in contrast to the enclosure walls of the main fortress and the baileys—had been curved to conform to the topography. On the other hand, the remains of the buildings that were still visible seem to be laid out at right angles, namely, suggesting the ground plan of a centrally located, large rectangular building, singly and transversely subdivided, plus an adjacent, trapezoidal, walled-in structure of unknown function to the west. As well, lying to the southeast outside of the enclosure wall on a lower tier of the terrain, there is a ruin of a building with a rectangular footprint, which locals refer to as a mill.

It would be possible to undertake an extensive ground plan analysis only after comprehensive excavations at the valley settlement and two baileys.

5.1.2. Main Fortress

As noted elsewhere (5.2.2.), the main fortress of Drapham Dzong was built in the process of two clearly separate construction phases that were conducted at different times. Whether the expansion of the compound in Phase 2 had already been envisioned at the time of the completion of Phase 1, has to be considered as unlikely. As the constructional changes undertaken in Phase 2 entailed such extreme interventions in the southern segment of the main fortress (zones L, G, and Z), it's difficult to imagine that

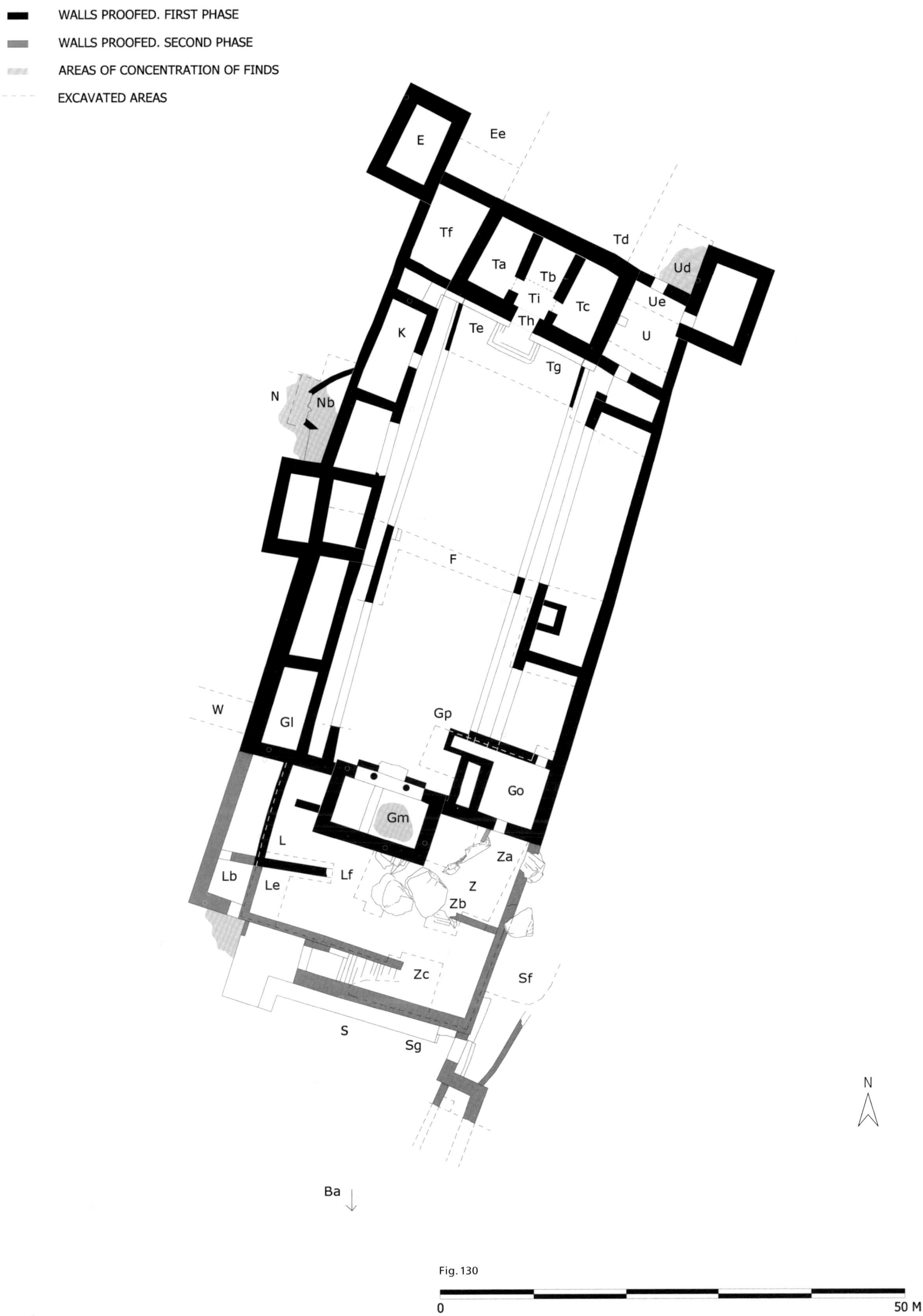
WALLS PROOFED. FIRST PHASE
WALLS PROOFED. SECOND PHASE
AREAS OF CONCENTRATION OF FINDS
EXCAVATED AREAS
E
Ee
Tf
Td
Ta
Tb
Ud
Ti
Tc
Ue
Te
Th
U
K
Tg
N
Nb
F
W
Gl
Gp
Go
Gm
L
Za
Lb
Le
Lf
Z
Zb
Zc
Sf
S
Sg
N
Ba
0
50 M

Fig. 130

the building stock constructed in Phase 1 was conceived as temporary, i.e., most likely, its redesign was already planned from the start. The interpretation of the ground plan disposition—assumptions about the design of the upper floors remain speculative—has accordingly to begin with a consideration of the building remains of Phase 1.

Even if an exact, properly dimensioned, and truly right-angle plan might not have existed for the footprint at the beginning of construction, nonetheless, it is likely that a clear concept—be it as a sketch or an idea in the minds of those in charge of the building project—had prevailed concerning the arrangement of the compound and its parts. This can be surmised, e.g., from a drainage channel, which was intended to divert rainwater from the inner courtyard (Doche) to the south: This channel ran directly on top of the natural rock stratum or, respectively, the clay horizon and must have been laid out before the walkway level of the courtyard was filled in and the walls of the small tower (South Ta Dzong) were built. This means that a central inner courtyard was planned from the start, even if the surrounding buildings—except for the Utse at the northern narrow side—were only built in Stages 2 and 3 of Phase 1.

Within the limits of the possible and purposeful, the rough architectonic forms adhered to an axial symmetry based on right angles. This proceeded from a longitudinal axis that linked the Utse and the small tower with one another. (Concerning the deviation in Stage 1 of the Utse from the right-angle axial system of the rest of the compound, see 5.2.2.) The integration of the small tower into adjacent wall courses, respectively building parts, demonstrates that the planning of subsequent buildings was already undertaken at earlier stages. Built during Stage 2, the small tower initially existed as an isolated volume, whose transverse axis was aligned exactly on the center of the entrance to the Utse. The narrow sides of the small tower were laid out in such a way that the same amount of space was left for the adjoining buildings of the western and eastern wings erected in Stage 4. Accordingly, proceeding on both sides of the small tower, the end wall of the trapezoidal, walled-in fortification could be executed with nearly the same length. This was made possible in that in Stage 3, the correction of the alignment of the western enclosure wall was already envisioned when the ground plan of South Ta Dzong was being staked out. The aim to build as much as possible at right angles resulted in tolerating an unusual constructional consequence, which positioned the southeastern corner of the small tower tightly beside the peak of the abutting massive erratic to the south. (In the building of fortresses in Europe, such crags, regardless of the striving for right angles, would have been integrated into the foundations of the tower.)

Comparing their ground plans, the fact that the Utse and South Ta Dzong do not share the same dimensions, but demonstrate practically the same proportions (1:1.6), can hardly be a coincidence. An attempt to explain this correlation, however, would result in pure speculations, especially as the other towers of the main fortress exhibit significantly different proportions.

The intended axial symmetry, which was oriented according to a line running from northeast to southwest, was only roughly maintained. Several deviations occurred in construction Stages 3 and 4, and not only in architectonic details that would hardly have been noticeable, e.g., outside of the corner towers at the northeastern front, which are aligned on both sides, a projecting flanking tower is located only along the western longitudinal front, while for unknown reasons, no such corresponding tower is to be found on the opposite side to the southeast. The transversal subdivisions of the two longitudinal wings were also conceived to be unsymmetrical. Their internal partition walls divided the wings into rectangular rooms of unequal length. These were accessible at ground level from the courtyard-side of the projecting loggias, also partially connected directly with each other by doors in the transversal walls. The ceilings of larger spaces were supported by girders and wooden columns, whose stony base slabs—partly *in situ* and partly scattered or dumped in the debris—have been preserved.

131

Fig. 131 Zone G. Southern corner of interior courtyard. Left, entry into gateway (sector Gp). Right, to the rear, wall W8/10a of small tower. In the middle (at the edge of the destroyed slab paving), wall W9/34 of loggia. View towards southeast. W.M.

Another aberration from axial symmetry resulted inevitably through the positioning of the gate tract in the southeastern corner of the trapezoidal, walled-in fortification. Positioned at the outskirts in front of the southern bailey, what the ascent to this gatehouse had looked like in Phase 1, can no longer be determined on account of the structural modifications executed in Phase 2 (see 5.2.2.). The first gate that was verified was inserted into wall W9/38. Passing through its portal, an approximately square room (sector Go) was reached. From here, a door at ground level led through wall W10/69 directly into the adjacent eastern wing, while to the left, there was a passage (sector Gp), 5 m in length, accessible through wall W9/32. With a door at the entrance, this passage continued under the loggia and ended on a steep, wooden staircase, 1.2 m in width, by which the inner courtyard was accessed.

Due to the narrowness of the passages, steepness of the stairs, and bending angulation of the access, this gate complex was easy to defend, but possessed hardly any representative character, since from outside it barely appeared as a building volume. Standing out all the more then from this uninviting entrance are the gate portals of both towers, which are oriented opposite the Doche, i.e., the Utse gateway, with an open or outside staircase and the massive portal of South Ta Dzong with its imposing wooden columns.

The meager representative impact of the entrance built in Phase 1 might have been the incentive to re-design the entire southern front in Phase 2. During these construction measures, which were divided into two stages and accompanied by extensive infill and leveling work, the massive erratic south of the small tower had to be taken into consideration. At the same time, there was apparently an effort to maintain the overall impression of a compact, rectangular, walled-in compound. Between the western segment of the new enclosure wall (W9/35b) and the eastern segment of the ring wall (W9/37b) that proceeded further south, a gap approx. 2.5 m in width opened up, and, in the course of a second stage of construction, into which a door complex with projecting stair ramp (W9/36) was inserted. A protruding gate that was built into the enclosure wall of the southern bailey, where it abutted against the southern corner of the main fortress (sector Sd), underscored the defensive-representative nature of the new access.

Architectural development of the interior of the extended area of the site appears to have only been carried out in the western part (zone L). In its western corner, a possibly tower-like building (Lb) with a square footprint was erected. A ground-level door connected this structure with an adjacent, elongated tract to the northeast. The entire building compound correlated with one wall course, which rambled at right angles around the small tower and still originated from Phase 1. The buildings in zone L were given their own access. This led from the middle platform of the ramp of steps across a wooden balcony to a separate entrance at the southern front of building Lb.

In Phase 2, through lateral fill (0.3–1.5 m in thickness) introduced throughout the newly walled-in sector, the walkway level was increased in height. Exposed sectors received a stone slab floor (see 5.2.2.). All in all, the ground plan—realized in two phases through several stages—tended towards a more generous use of area, enhanced defensive-representative exterior, and more rigorous, regular-symmetrical articulation of the building volume. The compound reveals stately and residential tendencies, which go far beyond the requirements of a purely functional military building.

5.2. History of Construction

5.2.1. Construction Technology and Process

Although only a few traces of the construction technology procedures had been preserved in the excavation feature, the masonry and stratigraphy provided a whole series of clues, from which the construction process can be roughly deduced. In contrast, evidence of manual construction techniques could scarcely be observed, even though the preserved walls and layers of destruction and lateral fill allow many conclusions to be made about construction procedures.

Unfortunately, the feature yielded only vague information about manual construction techniques. Apart from a few slick stones, which had served in spreading clay plaster, no other tools have emerged. Even when assuming that the work was undertaken with very simple equipment, hoes, hammers, trowels, axes, carrying devices, and other utensils must have existed to serve in performing the various procedures. Since traditional ways of building using long-established equipment are still employed today in Bhutan, especially in rural areas, the various ways of working by which Drapham Dzong was most likely constructed, can be inferred from conventional artisan methods still being practiced today.

Direct traces, however, as already indicated above, are rather rare and cannot always be interpreted conclusively. In this sense, perhaps two stratigraphically registered piles of fine gray and red sand, each with approx. 5 m^3, located at the southeastern foot of the Utse (Ub/Tg) might be read as the remnants of a deposit of building material. But all in all, no or at most only occasional traces have survived of the manifold work procedures that certainly must have taken place. There were no indications of specific places, where wood was chopped or hewn into shape, stones were worked on, or clay was mixed. In addition to the devices already mentioned above, in the corpus of the finds, except for a few specimens, there were hardly any iron nails, which led to the conclusion that iron nails were used neither for the scaffolding nor for the wooden interior finishings. (To be noted, is that the bamboo poles and hardwoods probably used for construction would have been difficult to nail.)

Careful evaluation of the documented excavation features, nevertheless, provided some evidence of individual work procedures. A few positions of posts for the scaffolding could be observed in the ground (see 3.3.5c.), and, on the masonry rising above the foundation, there were horizontal holes with a diameter of 10 cm and extending 0.6–1.0 m in depth, occurring in an irregular arrangement, which may have served to hold the scaffolding lever. Where impressions of the scaffolding wood in the interior of the holes in the clay had been preserved, this showed an angular profile and, in part, also the negative of the wood grain. This means, that for the scaffolding, not only were bamboo poles—imported from the south and approx. 10 cm in diameter—used, as is generally common today in Bhutan, but also roughly split or chiseled hard- or softwood. (Unfortunately, there was no wood substance found in any of the scaffolding lever holes that could be identified botanically.)

A horizontal ledge, 10 cm in width and 0.8 m in length, carved in the boulder in front of the southeastern corner of the small tower (South Ta Dzong), might have served as the underlay for a scaffolding platform. The aforementioned lack of iron nails in the find material revealed that the individual elements of the construction scaffolding were not nailed, but tied together with cords made of plant fibers (bamboo?). Hoists, even simply via rollers, were probably unknown. Loads on the scaffolding were presumably transported higher via stairs or steeply ascending ramps assembled out of planks. Optional equipment for carrying might have included the common four-sided piece of cloth on the user's back, still used today, and pole stretchers requiring two persons. While the use of pack animals is feasible, nothing about an actual application is known.

Apart from masonry in general, foundation trenches—described elsewhere—can be considered as further evidence of manual construction work. The trenches were dug

Fig. 132 Sector Sf. Foundation area of enclosure wall W9/37a. Constructed wall element skillfully adapted to natural rock formation. View towards northwest. W.M.

Fig. 133 Sector Za. Southern corner of small tower. Corner bond touches massive erratic block and underpins it in foundation area. View towards southwest. W.M.

132

133

Fig. 134 Detail of the door construction in wall W9/38 (sector Za): thin stone platelets as base for support beams embedded in the reveal/sconcheon. W.M.

134

step-by-step in the soft soil of the construction site. At those places where the soil seemed particularly unstable, the wall course was preceded by a bulwark measuring 1–2 m in width in order to prevent slippage, possibly also in order to impede undermining of the foundations in case of siege.

Since most of the timberwork is burnt or rotted—moreover, perhaps usable parts were carried off in the process of abandoning the fortress—, there are only a few parts that permit observations concerning woodworking, e.g., the door lintel in Gp or the embrasure or (arrow) slit in Tc. They revealed that the beams were not sawn, but rather chiseled or chopped, probably with an adze or with a machete (kichu). Wood elements such as ceiling joists or door and window frames were installed in stone walls during the building process. Putlog holes inserted afterwards are nowhere to be found. In the western wing (sector Fd), where enclosure wall W9/57a was built before the wing building was definitely planned and construction started, a bulwark or additional wall in front had to be constructed in order to support the ceiling joists. Studies of the remains of the wood species used in the construction confirmed fir (*Abies*) and cypress (*Cupressus cashmeriana*).[22]

As already mentioned, the outer shells of the higher walls had been built at an inclination of approx. 6°, which is typical in the cultural region of the Himalayas. This would have been construed as follows: First, the corner edges were spanned to the intended inclination with string. Then two to three layers of the edge or corner bond (or joint) were constructed with especially carefully hewn or selected stones, whereby the edge followed the line of the string. Proceeding from this corner edge, the wall shell could be built up at the intended inclination according to a horizontally stretched alignment string, which had to be re-spanned every two or three layers. Although this method did not leave any clear traces behind, it corresponds to the usual procedures still used today in restoration.

Completion of the work on the finished shell entailed, first of all, applying clay plaster, namely, surface treatment with slick stones. Indeed, these tools emerged scattered irregularly across the site (see 4.2.5.), and plaster remains have been preserved on various interior and exterior walls demonstrating that large wall surfaces were colored red, black, and white.

Considerable quantities of material were moved for construction purposes. However, quarries or clay pits, which would have been exploited for the production of building materials for Drapham Dzong could not be detected. Because of the hardship of transporting materials on the backs of men or four-legged creatures, i.e., in carrying cloths and wicker baskets that were hauled by one or two men, it is therefore to be assumed that, wherever possible, building materials were sought in close proximity to the construction site. Whether useful building materials were gained from the former substrate in the deep trench dug to protect the valley settlement, remains an open question.

With the gradual increase of the wall courses in height and length, supplying building materials—stones, clay, wood, and fill material—to the upper fortress site area became increasingly more difficult and cumbersome. The fact that ground-level gaps were left open in the wall courses that had been started until all of the material had been brought to its destination, is a tribute to a well-organized construction site. Only after all deliveries had been completed were the gaps closed, a procedure that is evidenced by the butt joints, which remained visible. As well, the reason for constructing the walls at the northeastern front (W9/60 and W9/49) between the three towers only at a later building stage is probably also traceable back to the need to keep transport routes open.

Overall, amazing masses of construction and fill material were handled and processed. Alone for the buildings of the upper fortress, approx. 10,000 m^3 of stone and clay—in an approx. proportion of 3 : 1—were required in Phase 1. In addition, there were

22 Processing of the wood remnants by A. Schlumbaum, IPNA, and Isabel Figueial-Rowe, Centre de Bio-Archéologie et d' Ecologie, Montpellier.

also large, indeterminate amounts of lumber, besides stone slabs for about 1,250 m^2 of courtyard paving (Phases 1 and 2), as well as incalculable cubic volumes of clay with pebbles for the floors of multistoried, roofed buildings. Not to be forgotten is the water that was indispensable for various parts of the work, which—whenever the supply collected and stored in containers during the rainy season wasn't enough—had to be fetched from the stream in the ravine at the southeastern foot of the fortress hill. Compared to these massive amounts of diverse materials, the quantity of paint and the like needed for finishing the completed structure appears quite meager. The limestone required for the whitewash was probably gained from erratics in the immediate vicinity of the construction site. The bulk material consisting of moraine clay for various infill work completed in Phases 1 and 2 may have originated from nearby. The terraces visible on the mountain flanks might possibly have been created in the process of extracting bulk material.

On account of the many variables and unknown factors, it is hardly possible to conclusively calculate—or even attempt to roughly estimate—how many workers were required for extraction, delivery, and handling of the building materials. What can be claimed with some certainly is that men and women were equally involved in the work, even though exceptional specialists were more likely to have been men. In terms of the logistics, however, there are many uncertainties. It's possible to estimate, e.g., that a trained mason could accomplish 1 m^3 of masonry per day—provided that the provision of materials functioned well. But there is no way of knowing where the construction workers came from—were they locals or immigrants?—and how were their basic needs met. How many weeks per year—considering the months of the monsoon rains and the probable necessity that local people had to work in the fields to raise and harvest food—could building activities even take place? How many people could be employed simultaneously without getting in each other's way or overtasking the capacity to supply materials? It can be estimated that for every mason, who was engaged in building up a wall on the scaffolding, approx. ten persons were necessary for acquiring material, as well as for pre-treatment, and then making it available for installation. According to the butt joints, it's possible to determine which buildings and walls were worked on simultaneously, i.e., were built within one and the same stage. Based on these various factors, it can be estimated—although, roughly—that per stage, 15–20 walls could be built, meaning that a total of 150–200 persons had to be working simultaneously on the construction project. Excluded from this admittedly very uncertain extrapolation, are auxiliary laborers responsible for providing for the construction workers' basic needs (food, shelter, etc.), and those who had to extract and deliver building materials over long distances, such as from the bed of the Chamkhar River.

These somewhat speculative estimates lead to the even more difficult conjecture as to the duration of the Drapham Dzong construction period. Assuming, under the conditions described above, that a mason could manage to build 1 m^3 of masonry per day, and that, on account of seasonal weather conditions and field work, full employment in construction is likely to have been about six months per year, a construction period of four to five years can be conjectured for the completion of the shell of the main fortress in Phase 1, including lateral filling/embankments and wood construction. Construction activities at the two baileys and in the valley settlement remain outside the scope of this calculation. Although it can be assumed that these outlying fortification compounds were already being worked on while the main fortress was still under construction, at this time more certain statements cannot be made, as there are no available archaeological features to serve as a basis of such interpretations.

Fig. 135 Sector Za. Clearly distinguishable butt joints between wall W9/43 (Phase 1, right) and wall W9/37a (Phase 2). W.M.

Fig. 136 Sector Go. Interior of gate building. Doorway in wall W9/38 after removal of walling-up construction. Threshold built in Phase 1 lies approx. 30 cm lower than slab paving, abutting from outside, in sector Za builit in Phase 2. View towards southwest. W.M.

5.2.2. Construction Phases, Stages, and Segments

As repeatedly mentioned, the nearly 8,000 m^2 enclosed compound of the main fortress has been developed in the process of several phases and stages. From the stratigraphy, it is clear that the settlement period, which occurred in the 16th and 17th centuries and ended in the early 18th century, could have encompassed only one period. Construction activities, however, can be clearly divided into two phases. Their subdivision into several stages can especially be extrapolated from the butt joints. However, caution is advised with their interpretation, because the investigation of the masonry structure in the foundation area has shown that with individual building volumes, e.g., the Utse, the foundations were joined at the same time, while above the foundations, the construction period of the walls was staggered. Therefore, different construction stages must be divided into several construction segments, which are also separated from one another by butt joints. This assessment also applies to the gaps left open in the walls, which facilitated transport of the material during construction.

The continuity of the settlement is certain, as there is no evidence of any break between the two phases of construction or between individual stages of construction.

The only absolute means available of dating the beginning of the settlement at the site area of the upper fortress—and, along with it, that of the two baileys—are radiocarbon dates. These stem from charred building timber, which explains the time span of the oldest samples. According to the probes, the average value—with possible deviations of 25–30 years earlier and later—varies between 1475–1590 AD. This means, that the beginning of construction (Phase 1/1) could be estimated in the period around 1550. Since excavation in all zones was carried out down to the natural, glacial moraine substrate without uncovering any traces of settlements from earlier epochs, Drapham Dzong must have been founded around the middle of the 16th century on new territory. All speculations about Drapham Dzong having been founded earlier are thereby untenable.[23]

135

136

Admittedly, several open questions interface with this scientifically validated claim, how, e.g., according to the dating of the stone cist grave at Kuenchosum/Bumthang (approx. 100 A.D.),[24] the Chamkhar Valley was already inhabited much earlier, which suggests that the pass route leading through the valley towards Tibet had already been in use in protohistoric times. In addition, the radiocarbon dates of the slag slope north of Drapham Dzong go back as early as the 12th/13th centuries. Iron extraction in the valley is therefore much older than the fortification compound, yet it is safe to assume that the builder of Drapham Dzong had had his hands so-to-say in the mining business.

These features and considerations made it seem conceivable that the valley settlement at the southeastern foot of the fortress hill had existed as a stopover point and

23 All radiocarbon probes were analyzed by J. van der Plicht, Faculty of Mathematics and Natural Sciences, Isotope Research—Energy and Sustainability Research Institute Groningen, University of Groningen.

24 Documentation in 2009 by A. Springer and G. Weber, according to the excavation materials of Drapham Dzong 2009.

site of mining and related trades even before the erection of the fortress. Conclusive answers could only be found through archaeological clarification. In any case, it is clear that around the middle of the 16th century, Drapham Dzong is set up within an already longstanding settlement and economic region.

In broad terms, the development of the building process in Phase 1 from the northeast to the southwest and from the exterior to the interior can be established. At the beginning of the construction, i.e., in Stage 1, the goal was to erect the Utse at what would later become the northeastern periphery of the main fortress. First, the foundation was laid for its complete ground plan, then the main walls were built, and finally—with butt joints—both interior partition walls were executed, which divided the interior of the Utse into three parts.

In Stage 2 the small tower (South Ta Dzong) was created opposite the Utse at the other end of the courtyard. Its erection was also carried out in several segments of construction. First, the sewage channel was laid out, which cut diagonally through the ground plan. Then, the stony shell of the gatehouse with its representative, courtyard-side entrance was erected, after which the frame of joists was added at ground level over the—partly artificial, partly natural—cellar room that had been excavated in the western portion. Finally, the interior partition wall was built, and the eastern part filled with soil.

It appears that surveying of the area was not carried out. In Stage 2, when execution of the small tower was tackled, and as the longitudinal axis of the main fortress following the natural topography was defined, it became apparent that the Utse was incorrectly oriented, i.e., its footprint deviated 10° from the alignment with the longitudinal axis. In order to be able to maintain the ground plan concept, which was based on right angles and axial symmetry, corrections of alignment had to be carried out in subsequent stages of construction. Of the corner towers laid out in Stage 3, the eastern one (East Ta Dzong) was rotated 6° from the Utse axis. At first, it stood as an isolated building volume. The northern corner tower (North Ta Dzong) was also angled 6° opposite the Utse, and its enclosure wall W8/2, which extended out from its southern corner up to the flanking tower (West Ta Dzong), was also given a course rotated an additional approx. 5°. West Ta Dzong, however, defined an actual kink, whose exterior course deviated a full 18° from the transverse axis of the Utse. Erected during a later construction segment of Stage 3, the northern part of the western wing (West Shab Khor) adopted the orientation of the ring wall. In this way the pre-conditions were created, which enabled the final development of the upper fortress in Stage 4 defining a rectangle oriented along the longitudinal axis. Thereby, it was only this Stage 4 that transformed the sprawling construction site into a closed fortification compound.

During Stage 4, which was sub-divided into several segments of construction, quite a few details still had to be improvised and dimensions corrected, e.g., the width of the interior courtyard was expanded from north to south by approx. 0.5 m. Its level increased from the south to the north by approx. 0.6 m, and the lengths of the two enclosure walls extending from South Ta Dzong differ by approx. 1 m.

Why the northeastern front between the Utse and the two corner towers was only closed in Stage 4 cannot be answered with certainty. The most likely grounds are constructional—material transports departing from the northern bailey. Such a motive was probably also the reason why the southern front with the gatehouse was not completed until the fourth and final stage of Phase 1.

What should not be overlooked, is that in reconstructing this sequence of construction, which is subdivided into stages and segments, the entire Phase 1—excluding major disruptions, for which there is no archaeological evidence—could be completed over a period of no more than four to five years for the shell. The question, as to when parts of the main fortress, e.g., the Utse, were in a useable state, is difficult to answer considering the uncertainties about the construction process of the upper stories. There is no archeological information available concerning the—presumably representatively regarded—finishings of the new access to the interior courtyard that was completed in Phase 2.

The launching of this Phase 2, which completely re-designed the southern front oriented towards the southern bailey, probably occurred after a longer interim. Above all, the aim was to create a defensive-representative impression at the access, respectively the gate compound. Two construction stages can be distinguished. The first—based on the southern front of Phase 1—defined the expanded ground plan through the erection of the enclosure wall and its backfill at a higher level; the second consisted of the design of the gate compound and the ascent from the southern bailey into the interior courtyard. Because the original gateway in wall W9/38—built in Phase 1—had become completely nonfunctional, it was walled shut. The small walled-in rectangular structure Fi in the eastern wing was probably also built in Phase 2, because, along with its fixtures, the entire interior of the wing with the beamed ceiling had to be changed. Such constructive measures are likely to have been only launched some time after the completion of the eastern wing in Stage 4 of Phase 1. According to radiocarbon dates, the construction activities of Phase 2 can be dated to mid-17th century. Other small wall courses, which are butt-jointed with larger structures, cannot be attributed to any particular stage. However, they hardly change the overall impression of the steadily progressing building process.

Still to be kept in mind is the fact that in both construction phases during each stage, not only were wall courses erected, but also extensive lateral fills and leveling were undertaken.

Indeed, it seems that the client, or respectively the construction manager had developed a rough idea at the beginning of the work about the future appearance of the main fortress, and, along with it, also of the ground plan. However, there was apparently no precise overall plan available. A *Gesamtwerk*, as described in the individual stages, was completed step-by-step, whereby from the beginning, a fixed, yet flexible basic concept was implemented through improvisation to accommodate the challenges of architectonic reality.

5.2.3. End of Drapham Dzong

The written and oral narratives about the downfall of Drapham Dzong are strongly penetrated by legendary and topical elements, and therefore remain historically of questionable value. Indeed, the excavations have delivered meaningful features, but leave a wide scope open to interpretation and raise a whole series of questions, when all the references to the destruction, respectively the abandonment of the compound are juxtaposed.

Without a doubt archaeologically, the downfall of Drapham Dzong was definitely accompanied by a catastrophic fire. However, traces of a blaze are quite differently pronounced in the individual building tracts. The most clear and impressive burnt remnants are located inside of the three-part Utse. The massive burnt layer with charred beams, tempered, discolored-red inner shells of the masonry, and fragments of the clay plaster that were cracked by the heat clearly tell their own story. The complete lack of small finds in the burnt layers could indicate plundering of the interior of the tower before it was set on fire, and, thereby suggest a combat-related torching of the Utse. What has to be taken into consideration, however, is that the walkway level and lowest layers have only been exposed on a small sector in the middle room (Ti), which is why surprising finds not yet exposed in the rest of the interior of the tower are still conceivable.

Curiously, in terms of their explicitness and magnitude, traces of a catastrophic fire are mainly attributable only to the Utse. Restricted to a few square meters, the burnt layer in the interior of the small tower (South Ta Dzong) stemmed from a collapsed cooking hearth. Charred fragments of beams without a pronounced burnt layer were to be found in the primary debris of the northern corner tower Ea (North Ta Dzong). As well, in the other excavation sectors that have been exposed down to the walkway level, only meager amounts of burned substance have occurred. In the interior courtyard (Doche) and in the outskirts of the gate (zones S and Z), blaze traces are completely absent. Accordingly, it might then hardly seem strange, that, except for in the interior of the Utse, masonry, which has been discolored red and damaged by heat, could not be observed on any building remains at the main fortress.

Even so, besides fire traces, there were still other signs of violent interventions, e.g., at the Utse and other wall courses, the good cornerstones were torn out just above the ground. Likewise, some of the floor slabs in the interior courtyard (Doche) seem to have been carried away. Incidentally, to be noted is that in many parts of the main fortress, especially in the southern parts of the eastern and western tracts as well as in zone L, the walls are worn down to below the most recent settlement horizons, which led to the erosion of the deeper-lying infill layer. Therefore, possible burnt traces on the masonry or most recent walkway level would therefore no longer be preserved.

Direct signs of combat actions could only be observed as an exception. They were limited to a dozen musket balls, some of which had been deformed by the impact against a wall. The few arrowheads stemming from waste layers cannot be interpreted as evidence of a battle. At most, the specimens could have been fired from the foot of the southeastern ring wall (sector Sf) with the intention to do harm. However, if there had been a massive assault with bow and arrow, substantially more iron arrowheads would have had to be found.

Overall, there is no indication of a long, systematic siege. No projectiles were fired from catapults or heavy artillery. Also, no traces of attempts to undermine the foundations are evident at the enclosure walls and flanking towers. However, it is important to remember that battles for fixed locations, which—as is generally well known—can take place in very different forms, do not necessarily leave archaeologically identifiable traces. As has already been noted, the features from Drapham Dzong leave a broad scope open to interpretation. In any case, conclusive assessment is only possible when the two baileys and the site area of the fortified valley settlement have been explored archaeologically.

The possibility that the downfall of Drapham Dzong occurred without any enemy action cannot be ruled out entirely on the basis of the excavation results. The lack of small finds in the interior of the Utse could also be explained by the fact that at the outbreak of the fire—triggered, e.g., by lightning—the inhabitants had managed to escape in time to the open with the chattels when the fire broke out, although some of the porcelain would have been broken in the process. Because of their small numbers, the musket balls that had been fired are not proof of a major attack with subsequent destruction. They could also stem from another occurrence having nothing to do with the downfall of the fortress. It could also be argued—perhaps somewhat pedantically—that shooting practice was occasionally held in the interior courtyard of the upper fortress. Allowing the imagination to continue fantasizing, in the period following the burning of the Utse, the rest of the fortress compound could have been abandoned and its useful building components could have been robbed.

However, this interpretative version is anything but compelling. It does not answer, e.g., the obvious question as to why the Utse was not rebuilt after it had burned, but rather the entire compound was abandoned. Generally, the fate of fortification compounds after destruction is still poorly researched. This is especially true concerning reasons that prevented rebuilding. Destruction in itself, even when it is carried out thoroughly, still offers no explanation for the definitive abandonment of a place. For such an occasion, different causes are possible, which, however, can hardly be determined on the basis of archaeological observations. Basically, military, political, stately, societal,

Fig. 137 Sector Ti. Interior doors of the Utse in wall W9/40. Charred remains of wood lintel *in situ*. W.M.

Fig. 138 Sector Ti. Burnt layer in interior of the Utse. End piece of charred beam. W.M.

Fig. 139 Sector Ti. Traces of fire on interior wall W9/39 in interior of the Utse. Completely annealed clay plaster, detached from the wall surface. W.M.

137

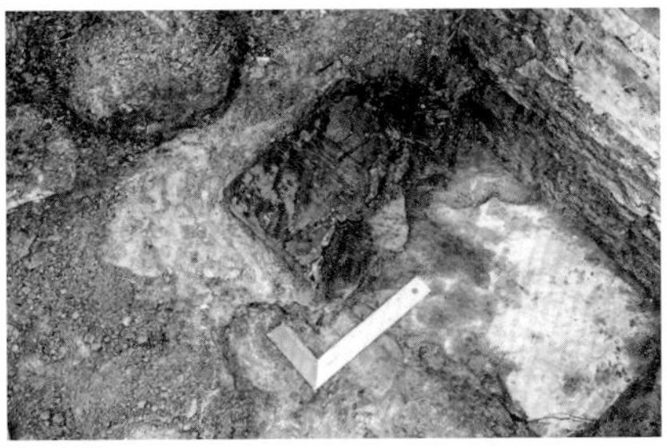
Fig. 138

Fig. 139

and economic situations have to be considered, which could have hindered reconstruction. Due to the lack of written sources, only conjectures can be proposed for the causes of the definitive abandonment of Drapham Dzong in the early 18th century.[25] What can be inferred from the excavation features is that Drapham Dzong formed the center of a stately-administrative, economic, and military commodities/goods and legislative complex. Only its dissolution or restructuring, e.g., by shifting the center, introduced the precondition for closing down the fortification compound. Until archaeological evidence provides evidence to the contrary, it is still conceivable that the location of Drapham Dzong would have become untenable by the diminishing of the iron ore deposit, and that the stately center was relocated to a more favorable place further down in the valley.

Accordingly, there are other interior and exterior reasons to be considered that might have caused a violent change or even destruction of the political, respectively stately-administrative structures, which then prevented reconstruction of the destroyed fortress. This question cannot be answered using archaeological measures. If the abandonment is to be considered as a result of warfare destruction—which is plausible, but is not supported by all the arguments—, the following events, which are based on the excavation features, could be viewed as relevant:

Troops, partly equipped with muskets, fight their way through the gate compound into the inner courtyard and storm the Utse. (The strength of the resistance remains unclear.) In the outer entrance area, an exchange of shots involving muskets and bows and arrows takes place. After seizure, the Utse is plundered and torched. In so far as the defenders manage to escape, they are captured or killed (whereby, to be noted is the fact that no remnants of human skeletons have been found). In the following period, the demolished, remaining building complexes are robbed, torn town in places, whereby individual fires break out. Subsequently, the ruin serves as a quarry, especially for the extraction of floor slabs, stair steps, and cornerstones.

Overall, the archaeological features, supported by legendary lore, speak rather in favor of a violent end of Drapham Dzong. However, its seizure must not be imagined as a major military event—in the sense of a protracted siege. It was probably rather an event in which troops on both sides were involved as company forces. Much larger formations would have left more traces in the ground and on the masonry.

Determining the chronology of the demise is of central importance for positioning Drapham Dzong in the history of the country. According to written and oral lore, this took place in 1676, the year of the great Tibetan invasion, which was accompanied by terrible devastation.[26] As a result, the temptation to attribute the violent end of Drapham Dzong to this catastrophic event is great. However, the archaeological observations clearly contradict this dating, which in itself is not implausible.

The most recent radiocarbon dates—they stem from waste deposits and cooking hearths—belong to the early 18th century, around approx. 1720–1730.[27] Accordingly, the fortress must have been inhabited up to this period. Historical processes that could be related to the demise of Drapham Dzong should be sought within this period. Combative events occurring in the early 18th century have actually been attested to.[28]

As has already been mentioned, all archaeological features, which could have stemmed from combative actions, or respectively warlike destruction belong to the end phase of the settlement period. There were no traces of restoration work, which would have been undertaken after interim devastation. There was no archaeological evidence left at Drapham Dzong by the catastrophic year of 1676. This does not exclude a former seizure of the fortification by the Tibetans, yet such a conquest would remain without archaeological traces. Nevertheless, what can be contemplated is that the constructive measures in Phase 2 might have been undertaken in response to the looming danger of the Tibetans, which, however, would lead to an atmosphere of ambiguous speculations because of the vague dating.

25 See footnote 27 below.

26 Yonten Dargye, *Fortress of the Defeated Enemy*. Kuensel, March 29 and 30, 2013; Ugyen Norbu, *Oral History of Drapham Dzong*, Coekbhor gewog, Bumthang Dzongkhag, Bhutan, n.d.

27 Radiocarbon Probes Nos. 9/3 (approx. 1730), 9/4 (approx. 1730), 10/5 (approx. 1700).

28 John A. Ardussi, «Introduction,» in Michael Aris, *Sources for the History of Bhutan*. Delhi 2009. p. XIV.

5.2.4. Reconstruction Attempt

The attempt to reconstruct Drapham Dzong using drawing has to be limited to depicting the rough constructive forms of the main fortress. Due to the lack of archaeological excavations, the appearance of the fortified valley settlement and the two baileys must remain open to speculation. This also applies—with the exception of the outer gate in sector Sf—to architectonic connections between the bailey areas of the site and the main fortress. Therefore, the latter appears in the reconstruction drawing as an isolated building complex. Yet this is to be imagined as a core zone of a vast stronghold structure, equipped with fortified walls and towers, which from a distance, especially from the base of the Chamkhar Valley, must have offered an incomparably imposing spectacle.

Considering the question of the possible appearance of the missing upper stories, roofs, and crowns of the enclosure walls, excavation results provide few useful answers. The cubature of the wall debris conveys approximate indications of the height of the individual buildings and wall courses. From the composition of the destruction rubble, it can be concluded—hardly a surprise—that roofs had been covered with wooden shingles Deeply extending wall breaches, as they especially can be observed at the Utse, are probably due to wooden structures that were spanned between the stony wall parts. Or, they came about through the collapse of the masonry, which was statically weakened by large window openings arranged one above the other.

Considering the general state in Bhutan of the transmission of history and lore, it hardly seems strange that there are no available descriptions or images depicting Drapham Dzong stemming from the 17th or 18th centuries. Important references about the former appearance are generated through comparisons with the architecture of preserved Dzong compounds, e.g., those at Jakar, Tongsa, or in the Paro Valley.[29] In view of the strong traditionalism in the field of Bhutanese architecture, engineering, and construction, morphological similarities play a subordinate role in relation to questions of dating. However, to be considered is the fact that various solutions have been found for recurring construction problems. This applies, e.g., to the connection between masonry and roof beams, which can sit directly on top of the wall crown or on a top of a wood construction up to 1.5 m in height that has been set on the wall crown. Which solution was applied at Drapham Dzong cannot be concluded.

The main fortress of Drapham Dzong is depicted in an isometric view as a bird's eye view towards the northeast. The drawing reflects the presumed state in Phase 2 (after approx. 1650). As to the appearance of the southeastern front access in Phase 1—as already stated—, there is no information available. The portrayed height of the buildings and freestanding walls has been construed by feature, function, and analogy, but this figure is taken from the lower spectrum of the probable range. The possibility that individual buildings, e.g., the Utse or small tower might have loomed even higher, is not to be excluded. The monumentality characterizing the entire building complex was enhanced by the fact that all of the exterior walls had been built into the slope, whereby the footing of the wall came to lie 3–6 m lower than that of the level of the interior courtyard.

The 6° inclination of the roof lies within the scope of the generally applied range. The forms of the roofs in the drawing are borrowed from examples of preserved Dzongs, but ultimately remain hypothetical. For the smaller towers, the simple solution of the tent roof has been proposed. For the Utse, a double-tiered hip roof can be taken into consideration. In the reconstruction drawing, the two longitudinal wings have been given a vast hipped roof, which, of course, is not imperative. A saddleback roof would also be conceivable, but the question remains as to whether the roofs would have been articulated by different building heights of the two wings. In addition, it is unclear whether upper stories had still been placed on top of the two courtyard-side loggias (gallery corridors), which would have reached up to the line of the eaves of the roof.

[29] Re Dzong architecture, see: *An Introduction to Traditional Architecture of Bhutan*. Department of Works, Housing, and Roads. Royal Government of Bhutan, 1993, pp. 52–94.

Fig. 140 Drapham Dzong, Main fortress, proposed reconstruction. Isometric view from west. J.O.

Preserved Dzongs offer different solutions, which would have equally been options for Drapham Dzong. Here, the strongly cantilevered roof edges can be considered as relatively certain. In the case of the preserved compounds, an outward projection of the line of the eaves by approx. 1.5–2 m is the general rule.

In the reconstruction drawing, reproducing hypothetically reconstructed details has been mostly avoided. Only those doorways have been noted, which were proven archaeologically. The façade, however, is to be conceived with copious woodwork and numerous window openings of different sizes. What is not representable is the colorfulness of the façades. As proven by archaeological traces, the stone masonry was extensively tinted in white, black, and red ocher, and the wooden parts were certainly painted polychromatically. How the upper end of freestanding walls was designed remains unclear. Covered wall walks and wood oriels or bays can be presumed by analogy, e.g., as exist at the preserved Dzong at Jakar. However, to depict such constructions in a drawing would result in something purely speculative. Even prayer wheels, which were probably placed in rows on the plinth walls in front of the Utse and in the entrance parts, have been omitted.

For these reasons, the reconstruction might strike the viewer as somewhat abstract and inanimate. However, in broad terms, it possibly corresponds to the constructional reality of the period after approx. 1650.

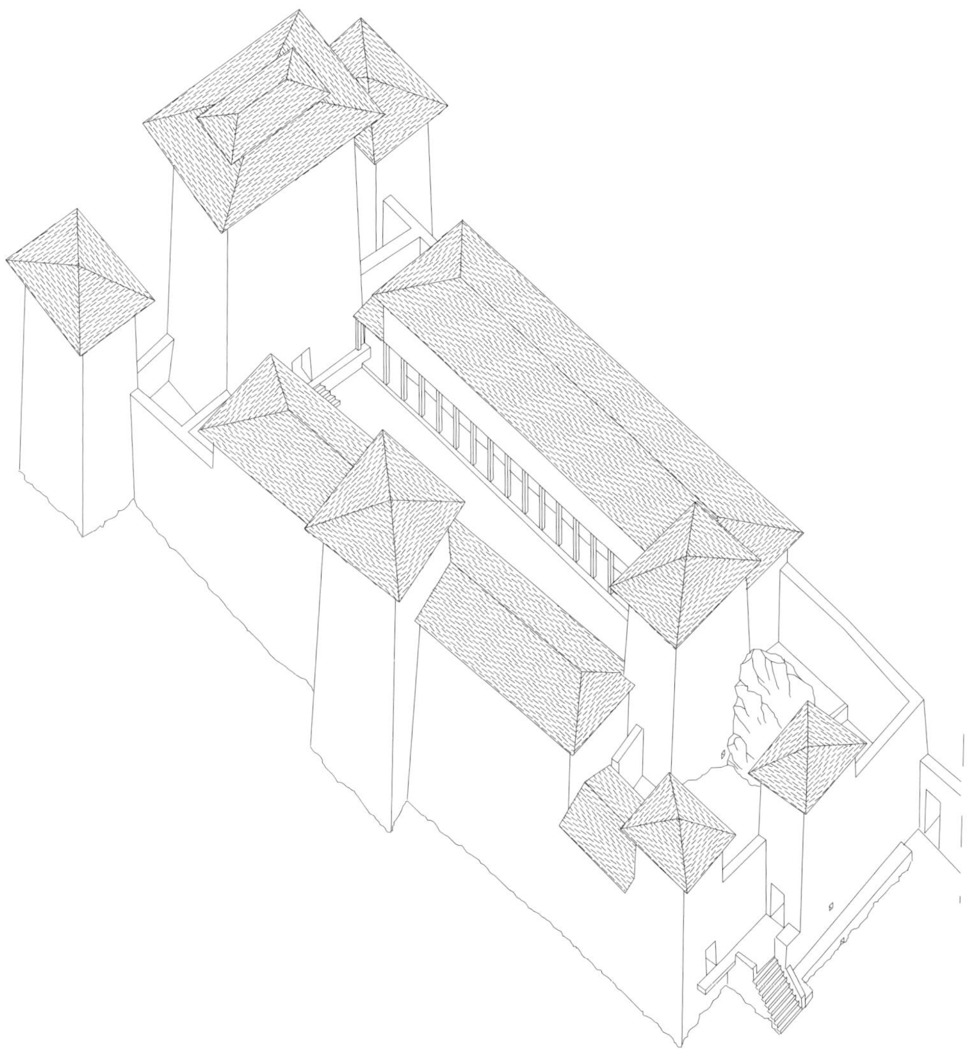

Fig. 140

5.3. Lifestyle

5.3.1. Traces of Everyday Life

The incompleteness and one-sidedness of the finds and features excavated during 2008–2010 permit only fragmentary, disjointed glimpses of everyday life at Drapham Dzong.

Difficulties already begin with trying to more accurately determine the number of residents and their social structure. However, the remains and dimensions of the fortification compounds (including the outer structures) allow conclusions to be made as to how many men fit for military service would have been required to defend the entire stronghold against a larger besieging army—i.e., approx. 1,000 men (see 5.3.4.). What remains still open is if ever such a large garrison was stationed at the fortress, and, if so, then for how long. However, besides soldiers, at Drapham Dzong there must have also been handworkers, namely construction workers, as well as dignitaries and servants responsible for maintaining the royal household of the ruler and his family, which resided in the Utse, and furthermore, administrative officials of different ranks, e.g., for the collection of taxes and customs duties, and presumably also priests and monks.

Entirely unknown is the number of women living at Drapham Dzong. Likewise, archaeological features do not allow any conclusions to be made about the distribution of the inhabitants in families and, along with this information, the presence of children. Find objects, which could conclusively prove the presence of women, did not emerge, what, however, does not speak categorically against their presence. Tending hearths, associated with the procurement of firewood and cooking (see below), could well—though by no means exclusively—have been part of the range of duties of women.

Considering all of the archaeological traces and the deducible presumptions they allow, provides a rough and uncertain estimate ranging from approx. 100—120 persons, who might have lived at Drapham Dzong. Not included in this estimate is the military garrison, which in normal times could as well have amounted to 100 men (see 5.3.4.). When gauging the presumed number of residents—including women and children—the bareness of the high mountain valley should be considered. Its agricultural yields are likely to have hardly provided enough to feed a larger garrison for longer periods. Massive military units would have been dependent on food supplied from more distant parts of the country.

The constructional remains show—to the extent they have been exposed—only a few traces of everyday life. Although how a niche measuring 1.9 meters in length and 0.45 m in depth (the height is unknown), which was found in the northern end wall of the eastern wing, is to be interpreted, remains open (see 3.3.8a.), a reading as a quasi «built-in» container intended for storage is conceivable. The drainage canal, which begins in the inner courtyard and empties in the southern bailey (see 3.3.1b., 3.3.3.) provides insights. It contained hardly any disposable objects and had not carried anything of the kind to be left at its outlet. Accordingly, the canal did not serve as a means of waste removal, but rather only for rainwater drainage. This addresses a general aspect of everyday life, namely the problem of maintaining a supply of water, especially for drinking. Apparently, rainwater was not collected in cisterns—e.g., in contrast to hilltop fortresses of Europe and in the Near East—, but rather the need for clean water was met in another way (see 5.2.1.).

Hearths provide limited insight into everyday life. The one that was detected *in situ* in sector Le, was apparently only in use temporarily (see 3.3.6.). A small hearth in the eastern corner of room Lb may have served to heat the ground floor. The third was located in the interior of the small tower (South Ta Dzong) and had crashed down from an upper story onto the level of the ground floor (see. 3.3.3.). As indicated by the collapsed remains, the hearth surface consisted of floor-level laid stone slabs.

Evidence of a cooking and heating hearth on an upper floor of the small tower supports the conjecture that in other buildings, namely in the eastern and western wings as well as in the Utse, there must have been additional hearths on the upper, no longer existent stories. That would mean that the actual living quarters were not on the ground floor, but rather were located on the upper floors.

Aside from coarse ceramics, which are to be assigned to the kitchen area (see 5.3.2.), and porcelain fragments, which convey a refined lifestyle that was cultivated in the Utse, hardly any remains of moveable household goods have appeared at Drapham Dzong. The majority of the objects needed for everyday life were made of wood, bamboo (also used for wickerwork), hides, and textiles from plant or wool fibers. Museum collections give an idea of the diversity of such objects.[30] Of all these, none were found in the ground at Drapham Dzong. Valuable objects such as vessels and utensils made of metal or jade, which with a high probability had previously existed at Drapham Dzong, were presumably stolen or carted away. An isolated unique piece, a fitting plate with an iron clamp, cannot be interpreted further.

The question of possible means of artificial lighting is difficult to answer. It was certainly necessary for all kinds of tasks in view of the rapid setting of nightfall after sunset. Dim illumination of the living quarters was provided by the fires of the open hearths. Butter lamps, as far as they were not intended for worship, may also have cast some light. The possible use of moveable light sources made out of plant material—e.g., torches or pine chips—is archaeologically not feasible. Since also during the day the living quarters were dimly lit, because of the generally rather small windows, activities that required good illumination took place outdoors under the covered loggia corridors or inside the building near the windows.

Besides work, eating, and drinking, amusement was also part of everyday life (see 5.3.2.), of which a few archaeological finds testify. The arrowheads need not only to have been used for military activities. They could also be interpreted as evidence of the practice of archery, which is still extremely popular today. Particularly noteworthy are those round, polished fragments of coarse pottery, which, without hesitation, can be called game tokens. However, they give no information about the kind of board games that were played at Drapham Dzong. What remains unanswered is whether small, occasional gravel—it comes from the riverbed in the valley—also had served as game tokens or simply had originated from the clay-gravel floors from the interiors of roofed structures.

All in all, the claim can be made that the small finds represent only a small fraction of the diversity of everyday life at Drapham Dzong, whereby evidence of a peaceful existence significantly outweighs traces of a combative nature.

5.3.2. Diet and Waste Disposal

Concerning the array of questions about diet, the excavations have only supplied little, disjointed information. Ground-level hearths, which were used for cooking, have emerged at various points. Apparently, there was no central kitchen at Drapham Dzong. The inhabitants prepared their meals in groups. The only traces preserved, however, of the kitchen equipment and utensils are numerous fragments of ceramic cooking pots.

A particularly impressive hearth was detected in the small tower (South Ta Dzong). It was located on an upper floor and collapsed with the destruction of Drapham Dzong. Its wreckage, scattered stone slabs, lay approximately in the middle of the room, so that they could have been collected in a circle around the fire. Metal objects—e.g., fragments of copper kettles, etc.—, which could be conclusively attributed to the kitchen area, did not emerge. Likewise, vessels made of wood as well as containers out of wickerwork, were also missing in the collection of finds, which, with certainty, must have existed.[31]

30 Abundant material in: Kunzang Thinley, R. Dampnier: *The Folk Heritage Museum*, Thimpu 2006.

31 See Thinley (Ibid.), as well as: Blance Chr. Olschak and Augusto Gansser, *Bhutan. Land der verborgenen Schätze*. Bern, Stuttgart 1969.

Traditionally of great importance in the Himalayan region, plant-based foodstuffs are only vaguely detectible archaeologically. Slurry probes from settlement deposits have provided some remnants of cereal grains (presumably rice and buckwheat) from plant fibers. Also to be recalled in this context are the fragments of millstones.

On the other hand, the animals that were eaten left significantly more traces than the plant-based foodstuffs. In the settlement deposits numerous bones have appeared. These were not just from cooking remains and food leftovers, but also slaughter waste. Apparently, directly at the fortress, animals were slaughtered and cut up, and the pieces that were not intended for eating were disposed of on site. The greatest density of animal bones was located in actual waste deposits, while at other excavation sectors, only occasional skeletal remains were found. These could have been the remnants of waste that scavenging animals, especially dogs and ravens, had carried off.

A superficial examination of the bone material indicated that these were the remains of domestic animals, i.e., the bones of cattle, sheep, goats, pigs, and chickens. Remnants of wild animals were not represented—or only as an exception—in the collection of finds, which speaks against an art of hunting practiced by the inhabitants of Drapham Dzong. Remnants of fish are also lacking among the finds, whereby to be noted is that skeletal parts of fish are very poorly conserved in the ground. For the time being, there is no useful comparative material from other sites that could serve as the basis for a precise determination of the animal remains. The total amount of excavated animal bones indicates that meat played a fairly important role in the diet of the fortress inhabitants.

On most of the excavation sectors, only very weakly formed settlement layers with sparse waste remains were detected. Apparently, the inhabited rooms and the inner courtyard were kept clean, and the waste was deposited at designated places outside of the ring wall, at the footing of the northeastern tower (excavation sector Ud), in front of the western enclosure wall (excavation sector Wa), and, in Phase 2, near the open or exterior staircase to the inner gate (sector Sa). Sector Nb in the angle between the western tower and the ring wall proved to be especially informative. Here there was a triangular walled-in dumpsite, which presumably had also accommodated feces. Above this waste deposit in the ring wall, toilets were presumably installed, of which no traces have been found anywhere else on the fortress compound.

The location of the waste deposit next to the open or exterior staircase in the southern façade by the second gate (sector Sa) is puzzling. Since the access to the main fortress was seemingly designed in a representative fashion, the location of a stinking heap of garbage near the staircase is difficult to understand. All attempts to explain this situation lead into the vastness of vague speculation.

5.3.3. Working Environment/Handwork/Trading

Apart from references to the activities of construction handworkers (see 5.2.1.), excavations have only unearthed a few traces of small trade operations. Some iron slags evidence a connection with the extraction of iron, which was conducted northeast of the fortress hill, above the hamlet of Nag Lhakhang.[32] Fragments of smelting crucibles with traces of smelted iron masses complement the references to the metal trade. Where exactly and by whom this trade was practiced, remains unclear, especially since the blacksmith was socially marginalized. Not to be excluded is that traces of additional small trades could still be found in the two bailey compounds as well as in the valley settlement, where in 2008–2010 no archaeological excavations were conducted.

A building ruin in the valley settlement, situated outside of the fortification walls at the edge of a stream ravine, is referred to by locals as a former mill. A damaged millstone, which could be observed in the wall debris, appears to support this interpretation. This presumption, however, is still in need of proof on the basis of an archaeological investigation. The preserved wall remains in any case do not correspond to the

32 Dominique Oppler, Raphaëlle Soulignac, Vincent Serneels, *Entdeckung einer metallurgischen Industrie am Fusse des Hochhimalyas*. Hochwald 2013.

manner of construction of the old, partly still operating mills today in the section of the valley north of the fortress hill between Damsang and Nag Lakhang. Be that as it may, the final word as to whether and which small trades were conducted at Drapham Dzong, is still open.

A footpath leads over the saddle to the east below the fortress hill, as has already been mentioned, upon which the nomadic yak herders still drive their flocks, and which lately has begun to be used by trekking tourists. Apparently, it is a stretch of a pass route that connects the valley of Bumthang over the Himalayan ridge with Tibet. In earlier times, the path appears to have been used as a trade route for the exchange of goods between Bhutan, Tibet, and China. The fortified valley settlement at the foot of Dzong Drapham probably would have served as a place for resting and restocking provisions. The significance of the site was also enhanced by the fact that just to the south of the fortress hill at Sangling, a secondary route branched off into the Tang Valley.

The fragments of Chinese porcelain and also perhaps the brass arm bangle, which were uncovered during excavations, could be interpreted as archaeological evidence of the wide-spanning trade relations in which Drapham Dzong was engaged. Other goods, which might have been transported on the pass route, and, thereby, traveled past Drapham Dzong or were acquired by the fortress inhabitants, e.g., silk or salt, naturally would have left no archaeologically detectible traces in the soil. Conversely, it may be assumed that the iron extraction in the surroundings of Drapham Dzong was not only conducted to satisfy local consumption, but also served a clientele over—admittedly—unknown distances.

Considering the hardly not-insignificant value of Drapham Dzong as a whole for trading in the Himalayas, the complete absence of coins in the collection of finds is striking.

5.3.4. The Stronghold as Military Compound and Symbol of Ruling Authority

The realization that the combative potential of medieval fortresses in Europe not only accommodated the needs of practical defense, but also can be understood as a manifestation of the consciousness of power and ruling authority, also applies to fortification structures in non-European cultural areas, such as the fortresses in Japan and the Dzongs in Bhutan. Stronger than in European fortresses, religious functions are also to be considered in the fortification compounds in the Himalayas (see 5.3.5.).

There is no doubt that Drapham Dzong served as a fortification structure. The finds and features, however, which can be directly related to a combative context, did not turn out to be abundant. Hardly anything remains of the former weaponry. There are no polearms or grip/hilt weapons among the finds.[33] The few arrowheads of varying types, all of which showed up in the waste deposits, reveal nothing about the combative gear of Drapham Dzong. The lead musket balls, found in the courtyard in front of the Utse, could have been fired by attackers. As well, a couple of tiny iron rings, which may have originated from chain mail, are of little significance in and of themselves. The round gravel from excavation sectors Ua and Ue as well as Sb, which was left behind in depot-like mounds, cannot be identified functionally with certainty, even if the possibility that it could be either throwing or sling stone cannot be excluded. Be that as it may, these few finds are by far not sufficient to estimate the actual combative technological gear and equipment of Drapham Dzong. Between the scanty evidence of ranged and melee weapons and the vast, mighty fortification buildings, there is a mismatch that is difficult to explain. Nevertheless, it must be assumed that there must have been an extensive arsenal, namely, ammunition for ranged weapons of all kinds, stocked at Drapham Dzong.

The remains of the fortified compound—both, those that have been exposed at the main fortress and also those not yet investigated, but still visible at the baileys and

[33] Re weaponry in general, see: Donald J. LaRocca with essays by John Clarke, Amy Heller, Lozang Jamspol, *Warriors of the Himalayas: Rediscovering the Arms and Armor of Tibet*. New York/London 2006.

the fortified settlement at the eastern foot of the fortress hill—reveal a spacious, staggered concept of defense.

With the upper fortress more precisely connected with its southern bailey compound by a steep stairway—incidentally, however, apparently protected on the mountainside without a fortified wall—, the fortified settlement in the valley lowland formed an independent defense area. Tactically, this was not insignificant for the entire compound because of the talweg, which led through the walled compound, and therefore could be easily barricaded or blocked. The valley settlement was even more significant, however, on account of supplying the upper fortress with water, which had to be fetched from the mountain stream that flowed by to the east, and brought through the fortified settlement and over the stairway up into the main fortress.

The defensive settlement was fortified with an enclosure wall, which followed the irregular contour of the plateau edge, and at its eastern periphery a tower arose. At the northern side, where the natural terrain ascended, a deep, artificial trench had been dug in front of the enclosure wall. Without excavations, whether a gap at the northeastern side of the enclosure wall indicates the location of a gate or breach caused by the hand of the enemy, cannot be decided.

Another question to be raised is why the valley settlement was built on a terrace in the slope and not on the saddle further to the north, where the topography would have offered better possibilities for defense. Without archaeological clarification, which would also enable determining the function of the buildings in the compound of the valley settlement, the question cannot be answered. Considerations about supplying water provisions might have played a role.

In the tactical concept of the compound as a whole, the fortification set-up of the low-lying defensive settlement could be designated as outermost, most forward or projected line of defense. For the garrison, however, the enforcement or maintenance was a matter of survival, because, as mentioned earlier, the water supply depended on its possession. A second line of defense was formed by the enclosure walls of the two baileys. These also stretched along the edge of the plateau. They were not only protected by an angled projecting course and—on the northern side—a powerful square tower, but also by several, approx. 30–50 m in width protruding rectangular towers, which were each connected to the site area of the fortress through a radially outgoing wall walk. At its southwestern periphery, the southern bailey even possessed two consecutively staggered towers. The principle of widely protruding towers can also be found at other Dzong, such as Drukyel Dzong at the rear of Paro Valley. In terms of defensive techniques and technology, the task of these towers, together with the connecting corridors that were equipped with embrasures or openings for shooting, was to enable a flanking fire in good time at attacking troops. To fulfill this function, the garrison had to be sufficiently equipped with ammunition. A doorway in the southeastern connecting passage of the southern bailey (excavation zone B) could have served as postern for sorties against attackers in the eastern escarpment or steep slope.

What has remained unclear is how the enclosure walls of the baileys were connected with the closed, walled-in rectangular structure of the main fortress. The only place where an architectonic junction could be determined was at the southeastern corner, where an outer gate system was located (see 3.3.1a.). This gate was directly accessible via a zigzag path from the saddle at the eastern foot of the fortress hill, so that the upper fortress had two entrances, one via the direct way and the other via the stairway that led from the defensive settlement to the higher level.

The third and innermost line of defense consisted of the enclosure wall of the upper fortress, which was arranged as a rectangular, strengthened by protruding flanking and corner towers. Concrete defensive aims can be unmistakably recognized in the architectonic details, e.g., the angled gates prevented employment of a battering ram. Numerous embrasures or slit openings allowed for the use of bow and arrow (which has been proven experimentally), and cross-rectangular notch openings were probably intended for firing muskets or light guns.

As a whole, Drapham Dzong constituted an imposing, frightening fortification compound. In case of war, a garrison of at least 1,000 men would have been necessary to effectively occupy all three, i.e., one behind or next to each other, staggered lines of defense. An impressive number, which summons up an image of the military potential that stuck—or could have stuck—in Drapham Dzong.

In assessing the military value of a fortification compound, it is not enough to just analyze the architectonic elements of defense, i.e., the walls, towers, battlements, embrasures, or gate systems, as well as the moveable means of combat, in particular, the weapons. There are also factors that come into play, which can hardly be grasped in constructional-archeological features and only occasionally in written sources—if available. These include the sensitivities of the defenders, e.g., their numbers, their gear, and their supplies, as well as their dependability, their fighting morale, or their faith in their commander. In the end, such factors would depend on whether, with an attack, if there was any prospect of reinforcements, or what fate the defenders expected in case of conquest or surrender.

The actual strength of a stronghold must also be measured against the means, which a potential attacker has available. The number of troops, their gear and supplies or their besiegement equipment played an equally important role, as did the exact intentions of the commander. Attack or siege proceeded differently, when the opponent wanted to take possession of a fortress damaged as little as possible than when he intended to destroy it.

It is important to note, that an attack against a stronghold could be made in many different ways and with greatly variable resources. An extravagant way of systematic siege was not the only way. Also possible were *coup de main*, surprise assaults, or handovers without bloodshed arranged through threats or promises.

These scenarios demonstrate that the question of the military value of a defensive compound proves to be a very complex one, and, it is especially so for Drapham Dzong—which indeed was not just a military fortress—; so in employing the basis of the purely archaeological indications—verified written sources are not known to be available—the question of military value can only be answered very hypothetical.

The stronghold could be expected to be confronted with three major military tasks: halting, whereby the aim was to protect the fortified place itself from enemy access; barricading, which entailed, hindering an opponent from getting in through one or more passageway axes; and, finally, ruling or controlling, which manifested in the military control of space of varying dimensions. Thereby, it should be noted, that the distinction between purely military control and political-administrative rule was very fluid.

With its staggered, angled gate systems, guarded by well functioning sentries, the highly articulated compound would have been difficult to take by surprise. Under the pre-condition, that the entire fortified complex (i.e., the main fortress, as well as the armed valley settlement with walls and trenches) was outfitted with a sufficient, well-provided-for, and properly equipped squad—a minimum of 1,000 men would have been needed—, the stronghold could be maintained for some time, also against a strong besieging troop, whereby certain weak spots cannot be overlooked. Among these, e.g., was the problematic provision of drinking water. The masonry, nowhere more than 1.8 m in thickness and with many vulnerable parts made of wood, would not have been able to long withstand a massive bombardment with heavy powder weapons or guns. Without reinforcements, Drapham Dzong would have hardly been able to hold out longer than two to three weeks against a besieging troop proceeding systematically under a resolute commander.

The barricading effect towards the outside from Drapham Dzong is difficult to evaluate, as conditions of the passages at that time are unknown. Today's path, which

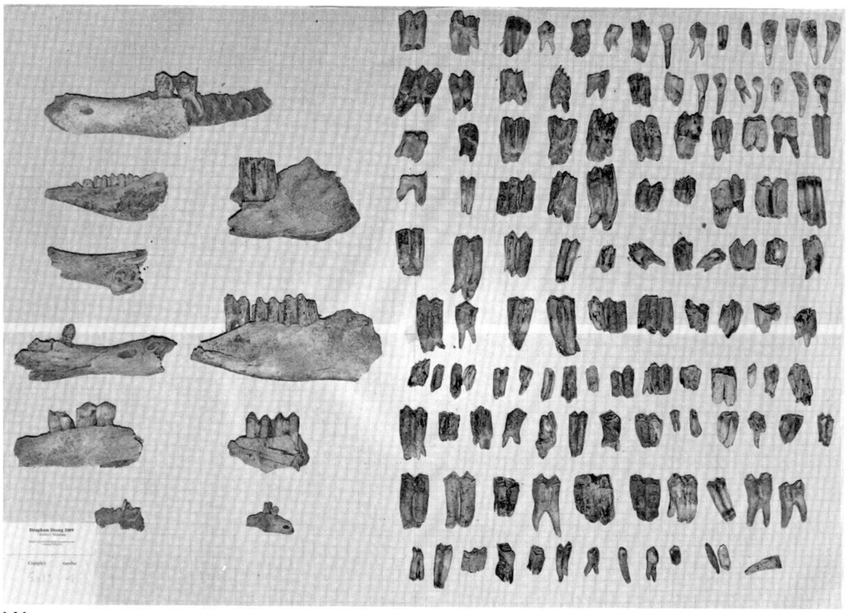

141

Fig. 141 Teeth and jaw fragments of slaughtered animal, found in the settlement deposit of sector Sa. S.S.

leads across the saddle to the east of the fortress hill, and probably represents the traditional valley or pass route based in the fortified valley settlement, could have been closed with little means. The valley settlement would have been quite suitable as a customs station, resting place, or market for provisions; but the fortification compound of the valley settlement would have been too weak to defend against an attempt by a strong troop to gain passage by force. In addition, it remains uncertain, whether Drapham Dzong could not have been simply avoided by armed forces at the base of the valley along the river or on the other side of the valley. A barricading effect in the military sense of the word is from the fortification structures of Drapham Dzong therefore only to be assumed to a certain extent, when the garrison would have been content to hide behind the fortress walls. In order to effectively barricade the valley, a mobile troop would have been required that would have also had to operate on the right side of the valley.

Concerning the military command of the valley dwellers, alone just for the area of the Chamkhar Bend, a larger, preferably mounted mobile force would have been necessary. In terms of a garrison square or plaza, the spacious bailey districts could have accommodated a military force of a few thousand men, but only for a short time. In the barren mountain valley, very soon there would have been a bottleneck in the provision of food supplies. With a small troop, e.g., of company strength, during normal, i.e., peaceful times, an armed maintenance of law and order including securing the pass route and protection of the iron mine, would have been definitely possible. The question remains open, as to how many men would have been required—as claimed by legendary, but little credible lore—to violently oppress and exploit the valley inhabitants over a longer period.

Stately, armed authority that emanates from a ruler, no matter what rank or title, always strives after visible symbols of power. The architecture of Drapham Dzong not only served practical defense and the concentration of military means, but also the demonstration of wealth and rule. Accordingly, in its architecture, different elements can be found that are not only based on the necessities of defense techniques and technology, but also on the need for the representation of rank, power, and sovereignty. Their traces are certainly not so clearly preserved as references to the former strength of defense. This representational character can be sensed, e.g., in the exterior stairways, the entrance framed by wooden columns in South Ta Dzong, and in the multicolored painting of the walls that is only detectible via fragmentary remnants. In terms of its external appearance—insofar as it can be reconstructed—, Drapham Dzong seems threatening, withdrawn, unapproachable, and protective, all at the same time.

To what extent the movable equipment and utensils of Drapham Dzong corresponded to the standards of the persons of upper rank, is difficult to assess due to the finds and features, especially since hardly any information is available about these claims. Besides the scanty remains of polychrome murals found at best in the courtyard in front of the Utse, fragments of Chinese porcelain dishes of the finest quality suggest that, at least in the main tower, a lavish lifestyle was cultivated. Drapham Dzong was certainly not only a military fortress, but also a royal residence with services provided by handworkers or even production facilities.

Reflected in the defensive character and in the representative elements of Drapham Dzong is the claim of the lord of the fortress for the exercise of legitimate power and reign.

5.3.5. Traces of Religious Life

As a rule, expressions of religious life leave few material traces, which can be conclusively interpreted—without reliance upon written sources, pictorial evidence, or living customs—in relation to their contextual and functional meaning. Therefore, it is not surprising that the finds and features from Drapham Dzong are able to convey only sparse and uncertain references to religious life.

With certainty it can be assumed that the inhabitants of Drapham Dzong from the 16th until the early 18th centuries had lived according to the teachings of Tantric Buddhism, in which many elements of an older, shamanic belief in gods and spirits was integrated.[34] Stemming from this foundation, the practiced religion was based on a wide range of instruments, which were employed in the numerous ceremonies and rituals of everyday life as well as at festivals. Many cult objects were made of perishable materials such as wood or fabric, and have decayed in the ground. Even more are likely to have been lost through being transported away or stolen. Whether the non-excavated burnt debris in the interior of the Utse contains valuable sacred objects—e.g., statues or ceremonial equipment—, remains vague speculation. The extremely sparse remnants of polychrome mural suggest, nonetheless, that different rooms were painted. About the motives and their possible religious significance, it is not possible to even make any conjectures.

Basically, the Dzongs of Bhutan incorporated, on the one hand, rooms for living quarters, working, and representative spaces for secular authorities, and, on the other hand, accommodations and cult rooms for monastic communities of monks. Unfortunately, the excavation features in Drapham Dzong provide no unambiguous determination of the function of the individual buildings and rooms, excluding the defensive towers and the periphery. The oversized entrance to the small tower (South Ta Dzong) could perhaps allow a sacred space on the ground floor of this building to be inferred. Concrete indications of the permanent presence of monks are lacking. Whether a monastic community had lived in Drapham Dzong must therefore remain open, even when it must be conceded, that in the elongated tracts on the western and eastern sides of the main fortress, plenty of space for a group of monks would have been available.

Constructional traces of religious life can be seen in the various stone plinths, which are positioned at several points in front of the outer walls of prominent buildings. They are to be found in front of the Utse (W10/65a and 65b, W9/48), before the outer gate (W9/54), in front of the enclosure wall in zone S between the outer and the middle gates (W9/42), the passageway of the middle gate (W9/56), and on both side of the entrance to the small tower (W8/17a and 17b). Completely useless structurally, most plausibly they can be interpreted as pedestals for sacral objects, namely, for serially arranged prayer wheels that would have been set in motion by passersby. Remaining uncertain is the interpretation of the two gravel deposits at the south-

34 Françoise Pommaret, *Bhutan*, Bremen 2006; B. Chr. Olschak, U. and A. Gansser, *Bhutan, Land der verborgenen Schätze*. Bern/Stuttgart 1969; Chr. Schickelgruber, F. Pommaret, *Festung der Götter*. Wien 1997/Basel 1998.

142

143

eastern foot of the Utse (sectors Ua and Ue) and in the angle between the enclosure wall (W9/37) and the outside or open staircase (W9/36) in zone 2. In the Himalayas, depositing stones is still practiced today as a common religious ritual. The interpretation of the two gravel deposits as the result of cultic customs is supported by the observation that individual gravel stones have been tinted with ocher.

A single gravel stone, polished to a regular ellipsoid (Finds Catalog. Nr. Go.4.5.) is likely to have also served sacred purposes. Otherwise, the find material contains only a few pieces that can be associated with religious conventions. A stone slab with two manmade indentations might have been part of the fittings of an alter, perhaps the traditional version of a small double butter lamp. Finally, a holder for incense sticks executed in ceramic was found, which was used for the everyday religious practice of burning incense.

All in all, the finds and features evidence the penetration of everyday life with religious mores. The fragmentary indications, however, do not provide a clear image. The notion, that on holidays religious dances were conducted on the inner courtyard of Drapham Dzong, remains left to speculative phantasy.

Fig. 142 In the shooting opening of wall W9/49 (sector Ue), the functional capability is tested using a bamboo bow. W.M.

Fig. 143 Sector Ua. Deposit of gravel at the foot of the Utse. W.M.

6. Results and Assessment

The excavation at Drapham Dzong has opened an archaeological window in the wall blocking our view into Bhutan's past, although not all of the questions existing at the beginning of the project have been answered, and at the end of the excavation, i.e., after the assessment, new questions emerged whose answers lie in the future.

The main conclusions include verification of the dating. Constructed in the mid-16th century and violently destroyed in the 18th century, Drapham Dzong can now be positioned in the chronology of Bhutan's history of events to the extent this can be deciphered from the written sources. Also, now the interpretation of legends needs to be re-examined. The historical development of the building construction of the upper fortress has been clearly established. A further goal achieved through the excavation is the proof of a single settlement period, which can be divided into two construction phases completed in several stages.

The attempted functional analyses of the individual buildings and rooms were not completely satisfying. Considering the lack of significant building components and small finds, in many cases the question as to what purpose one or another space served, had to remain unanswered. Obviously, buildings and wall courses equipped with embrasures or arrow slits were part of the upper fortress' defense system. However, also to be considered is the fact that the defensive facilities—comparable with aristocratic fortresses in the West—were not only intended to serve in warding off attacks, but also to represent stately dominion. Hearths—preserved *in situ* at the ground level or collapsed from upper stories—suggest dwelling spaces. More uncertainty exists as to which residues can be attributed to religious life. No evidence of a settlement of monks or a sacred use of specific rooms exists, which, however, does not support any compelling argument against their presence.

In addition, there are still some uncertainties regarding access to the upper fortress. The exterior parts of the access in Phase 1 were either removed or buried by the renovations in Phase 2, whereas conversely, the newly designed, inner gateway built in Phase 2 fell prey to warfare destruction and gradual erosion. What only is certain is that the outer gate with its open staircase received a representational character in Phase 2. The fact that only a small area within the Utse could be excavated down to the settlement horizon due to safety concerns meant a painful deficit of information. Nonetheless, lying under the masses of debris the burnt and settlement layers remain preserved intact, and in the future, when sufficient means are available to ensure for safety, could be studied in their original condition.

Important observations about the building technology and architectonic design could be made. In particular, evidence that the natural topography had been changed more drastically by massive lateral fill or embanking and infilling with clay than by the construction of walls, buildings, and towers, can be regarded as a discovery, which is to be paid special attention to in future excavations at analogous sites. The features provide only fragmentary insight into the use of wood in construction. The established presence of putlog holes and other notches in the masonry as well as the burnt remains imply an abundant use of timber for parts of the outer walls, intermediary floors, window cladding, and roof construction. Since stone arches and stone vaults apparently were unknown and sufficiently large stone slabs were not available, window and door lintels had to be executed using wooden planks. After their decomposition by fire or rotting, their supporting property then failed, which led to characteristic, breach-like breaks in the wall alignment. Thereby, a state of deterioration ensued, which particularly in the area of window openings entailed dramatic risks of collapse. These absolutely have to be considered in the planning of future excavations.

The analyses of the masonry and also the layers of destruction, i.e., burnt layers, yielded significant insights with regard to the defence value and violent downfall of the fortification compound, whereby the unexcavated but documented (albeit in summary form) fortress buildings of the two baileys and the valley settlement were able to round out the overall picture.

Revelations stemming from small finds fell short of expectations, especially because of their one-sided components being largely limited to animal bones and ceramics. Nonetheless, the analyses of the bones and information from the silt probes conveyed an approximate notion of the diet [of the fortress inhabitants]. Instructive results were provided by the assessment of the ceramics. The fact that the majority of its components were fragments of cooking pots, which were most likely produced locally, suggests that most everyday tableware—assuming it was not put on the fire—was made of wood, none of which has survived, for obvious reasons. The diversity of ceramic cooking pot forms enables the creation of a provisional typological ordering primarily based on the vessel rim shapes. The temporal and spatial validity of this ordering must be left to future research, whereby the question of regional distribution of individual types warrants particular attention.

The appearance of Chinese porcelain in the form of fragments of cup-like, apparently handle-less, small bowls was a surprise. These finds not only imply long-distance trade relations, but also a high standard of living, which reinforces the presumed notion of the compound being a noble residence.

The amount of metal finds turned out to be disappointing. At least it was possible to categorize the few gathered arrowheads according to various types and the lead musket balls prove the use of handguns at the beginning of the 18th century. The brass arm bangle represents an isolated single piece. Nonetheless, in correlation with its size, it can be interpreted as suggesting the presence of women.

Surprisingly, there was evidence of a connection between Drapham Dzong and a neighboring iron smelting works. Even though the latter has only until now been verified by prospecting-like means, it is clear there are striking analogies to medieval fortress building in the West, where in the meantime the link between fortress-based ruling aristocracy and iron mining has been observed archaeologically across a large area. Aside from these remains of extracting iron and hints concerning the craft of building, hardly any traces of applied arts and crafts appeared. Fragments of smelting crucibles point to metalworking, however, of an unknown scale. Whether or not a building ruin in the vicinity of the valley settlement actually was once a mill, as local lore claims, still remains to be verified archaeologically. In any case, it may be assumed that applied arts and crafts took place rather in the valley settlement or in the baileys than in the upper fortress.

By and large, the archaeological goals can be regarded as having been achieved. However, the results raise new questions, and have respectively allowed questions, which had already been raised at the beginning, to emerge into sharper focus. This pertains particularly to the historical context. Who built and inhabited Drapham Dzong, who destroyed it and what are the reasons why it was never rebuilt, are questions that the means of archaeology cannot answer. Here historians are called upon to integrate the archaeologically-secured data into the historical context of written sources and oral tradition.

Given the current state of research, the assessment of the find material can only deliver provisional and partial results. Not until comparative material from other, future excavation sites becomes available, can the wealth of information hidden in the ceramic fragments, skeletal remains, and other objects be accessed completely. For this reason, it is advisable to put further excavations at Drapham Dzong on hold, and for the time being, shift archaeology research to other sites in Bhutan, so that the broadest possible spectrum of comparative data can be compiled.

The completion of the first excavation at Drapham Dzong does not mean the end of archaeology in Bhutan, nor even the beginning of the end, but hopefully the end of the beginning.

7. Abstract

The excavations at Drapham Dzong in the Choekhor Valley (Bumthang) of Bhutan were conducted during the autumn months of 2008 through 2010. Initiated by the Swiss-Liechtenstein Foundation for Archaeological Research Abroad (SLSA) at the request of the Royal Government of Bhutan, they were conducted in collaboration with Helvetas Swiss Intercooperation and implemented by the Division for Conservation of Heritage Sites under the Department of Culture of Bhutan. Professor Werner Meyer of the Department of History, University of Basel, Switzerland, was selected to head the project, whose purpose was twofold: to conduct archaeological research on a ruin site in Bhutan, and to introduce a team of engineers from the Department of Culture to the practical work of excavation.

In archaeological terms, Bhutan is for the most part uncharted territory. That is, in determining procedures and making assessments, the excavation team had no previous comparative data or experiences to rely on. In this respect, each stage of the work was a step into the unknown and demanded exceptionally thorough documentation. Some correlations became clear only toward the end of the excavations. It was a tremendous advantage for the excavation directors to be completely autonomous in carrying out the project, needing only to attend to the local circumstances of weather, time frames, number of workers, and danger zones.

The vast extent of the compound—with its main fortress on the highest knoll of the hill, two lower-lying baileys, and a fortified settlement in the valley below, measuring in total 500 metres along the longitudinal axis—required a concentrated use of personnel, time, and finances. Work was thus confined to the excavation of the main fortress, which—in terms of the ground plan—the team was able to fully expose. A complete excavation, i.e., down to the natural substrate, of some of the buildings had to be foregone, not only due to lack of time, but above all for safety reasons. Some towering walls built of natural stone with clay as a binding agent were so deteriorated that they threatened to collapse if the debris holding them in place were to be removed; such an action would have posed an irresponsible risk to the safety of the workers.

Despite these limiting circumstances, the excavation team achieved some important results. They successfully established the chronological beginning and end of the compound—a major goal of the excavation—as well as the historical sequence of the construction. According to radiocarbon analyses, the construction of Drapham Dzong began in the mid-16th century and was completed in several stages. In the late 17th century the southern front and entrance area were renovated and extended. The abandonment of the complex can be dated to the early 18th century, and numerous findings imply violent destruction by a charging assault, looting, and arson. The suppositions voiced by historians that Drapham Dzong had fallen victim to the Tibetan invasion of 1676 were thus conclusively refuted.

A comparison of the excavated wall segments with analogous building components from other, preserved Dzongs enabled the team to prepare a rough graphic reconstruction of the main fortress, a further goal of the excavation.

The assessment of the finds and features elicited additional information beyond the basic history of Drapham Dzong's construction. The excavators also found traces of the plant- and animal-based diet of the fortress inhabitants, evidence of trade relations (Chinese porcelain!), and remnants of everyday life. The numerous ceramic remains could be categorized typologically, but due to the complete lack of comparative material, the question of the temporal and spatial validity of this provisional typology cannot be answered. Nevertheless, a beginning has been made.

It will be the task of Bhutan's historians to correlate the excavation's findings, especially the key expository data, with the vague and sometimes legend-imbued written sources. To summarize, the archaeological work at Drapham Dzong has made a significant and innovative contribution to the study of Bhutan's history.

ལས་འགུལ་བཅུད་དོན།

སྤྱི་ལོ་ ༢༠༠༨ དང་ ༢༠༡༠ ལོའི་གནམ་སེར་ཁའི་དུས་ལུ་ བཞི་རིག་ཉམས་སྲུང་སྡེ་ཚན་གྱི་ལས་འཆར་དང་འབྲེལ་ཏེ་ བུམ་ཐང་ཆོས་འཁོར་ལུ་ཡོད་པའི་ ཞིག་རལ་སོང་བའི་དགྲ་ཐམ་རྫོང་གི་མནའ་ཤུལ་ས་ཀོའི་ལས་འགུལ་འགོ་བཙུགས་ཡོདཔ་ཨིན། ས་ཀོའི་ལཱ་དེ་ཡང་ Swiss Liechtenstein Foundation for Archaeological Research Abroad (SLSA) གཞི་ཚོགས་ལུ་ འབྲུག་གཞུང་གིས་ཞུ་བ་འབད་དེ་ Helvetas Swiss དང་མཉམ་རུབ་འབད་དེ་ སྲོལ་འཛིན་ལས་ཁུངས་ཀྱི་བཞི་རིག་ཉམས་སྲུང་སྡེ་ཚན་གྱིས་ མནའ་ཤུལ་ས་ཀོའི་ལས་འགུལ་གཞི་བཙུགས་འབད་དེ་ཡོད། སུའིཛ་ལེནཌ་ལུ་ཡོད་པའི་ བཟླ་སེལ་གཙུག་སྡེའི་ རྒྱལ་རབས་ཀྱི་སྡེ་ཚན་ནང་ལུ་ཕྱག་ལཱ་གནང་མི་ མཁས་དབང་ Prof. Werner Meyer འདི་ ལས་འགུལ་གྱི་སྡེ་ཚན་འགོ་འཁྲིདཔ་སྦྲི་མཛད་ཡོདཔ་དང་ ལས་འགུལ་འདིའི་དམིགས་དོན་གཙོ་བོ་ར་ གཅིག་འབྲུག་ལུ་ཡོད་པའི་ཞིག་རལ་སོང་བའི་མནའ་ཤུལ་ཚུ་ ས་ཀོའི་ཐོག་ལས་མནའ་རབས་རྟགས་ཞིབ་འབད་ནི་དང་ གཞན་མི་འདི་ མནའ་ཤུལ་བརྟག་ཞིབ་ཀྱི་ལས་སྣའི་ནང་ལུ་ སྲོལ་འཛིན་ལས་ཁུངས་ཀྱི་བཟོ་རིག་པ་ཚུ་གྲལ་གཏོགས་འབད་དེ་ ཤུལ་ལས་མནའ་ཤུལ་བརྟག་ཞིབ་ཀྱི་མི་སྟོབས་ གོང་འཕེལ་གཏང་ནིའི་རེ་འདོད་ཨིན། འབྲུག་རྒྱལ་ཁབ་ཀྱི་ས་གནས་ཐེངམ་ཐེད་ཁ་ལུ་ མནའ་ཤུལ་གྱི་ས་ཁོངས་ཡོདཔ་ཨིན་རུང་ ད་མ་ལས་རྟགས་ཞིབ་འབད་ཐངས་ཀྱི་ཁྲིད་བསྟུར་གྱི་གོ་སྐབས་དང་ ཡང་ཅིན་ མནའ་ཤུལ་དང་འབྲེལ་བའི་ཁྲིད་རིག་གི་ཉམས་མྱོང་། དེ་ལས་ལཱ་འབད་ཐངས་ཀྱི་བྱ་རིམ་ཚུ་མེད་པར་ལུས་ཏེ་ཡོདཔ་ལས་བརྟེན་ ལཱ་གི་འགོ་རིམ་སོ་སོའི་གནས་སྟངས་ལུ་ལྟོད་ཚེ་ ད་མ་གོ་མ་མྱོང་པའི་དམིགས་བསལ་གྱི་ཞིབ་འཚོལ་གྱི་ཐོ་བཀོད་འབད་དགོཔ་འདུག མནའ་ཤུལ་ལ་ལུ་ཅིག ས་ཀོའི་བརྟག་ཞིབ་འབད་ཞིནམ་ལས་རྐྱངམ་ཅིག ཞིག་རལ་སོང་བའི་མནའ་ཤུལ་ཨིདམ་ཧིང་སངས་སངས་སྦྲི་ཤེས་ཚུགས་པས། ལས་འགུལ་འདི་གི་སྐོར་ལས་ཤེས་ནིའི་དོན་ལུ་ མནའ་ཤུལ་མཁས་དབང་གི་མདོ་ཆེན་ཚུ་གི་ལྷན་ཚོགས་ཆ་ཚང་གཅིག་དགོཔ་ཧ་ཅང་གི་ཁེ་ཕན་ཡོདཔ་ལས་ ས་གནས་ཀྱི་གནས་སྟངས་ དཔྱེ་སྦྲི་བ་ཅིན་ ཉེན་འཚུབ་ཀྱི་ཕྱོགས། ལས་མིའི་གྲངས་ཁ།ཞག་དུས། དེ་ལས་གནམ་གཤིས་ཚུ་ཤེས་ནིའི་དོན་ལུ་གྲལ་གཏོགས་འབད་དགོཔ་རྐྱངམ་ཅིག་ཨིན། མནའ་ཤུལ་གྱི་ས་ཁོངས་རྒྱ་ཆེའི་ཐད་ཁ་ རྫོང་གཞི་ཆགས་སའི་སྐད་དོག་སྒོམ་འདི་དང་ རྫོང་གི་ཕྱིའི་ལྕགས་རི་དམའ་སུ་ཡོད་མི་གཉིས། དེ་ལས་རྫོང་རགས་ཀྱི་གཡུས་ཚན་ཆགས་ཚུ་རྟེས་ཏེ་ ཡོངས་བསྡོམས་ ཡར་མར་གྱི་རིང་ཚད་ མི་ཏར་ ༥༠༠ ཙམ་ཡོདཔ་ཨིནམ་ལས་ མནའ་ཤུལ་ས་ཀོའི་ལཱ་རིགས་ཚུ་ཡང་རྫོང་ཤུལ་གྱི་མཐའ་སྐོར་ལུ་ར་འབད་ནིའི་དོན་ལུ་ ལཱ་འབད་མི་གི་མི་སྟོབས། དུས་ཚོད། རྒྱ་དངུལ་གྱི་རྒྱབ་སྐྱོར་གནང་དགོཔ་ གལ་གནད་ཅན་ཅིག་འབད་བྱུང་ཡོད། རྨང་གཞིའི་ལས་འཆར་གྱི་ཐད་ཁ་ལུ་ཡང་ རྫོང་ཤུལ་ཁོ་རའི་གཞི་འཁྲམ་འདི་ མངོན་གསལ་འབད་འབྱུང་འོང་ཟེར་ཞུ་ནི་ཨིན། ས་ཀོ་ཡོངས་རྫོགས་ཟེར་བའི་སྐབས་ལུ་ ཞིག་རལ་སོང་བའི་ཁང་རོའི་རྨང་གཞི་ཚུན་ཀོ་སྟེ་ ཁང་རོ་ཐལ་དགོ་པའི་གནད་དོན་ཚུ་ཡང་ གནམ་དང་དུས་ཚོད། ལྷག་པར་དུ་ཡང་ ཉེན་སྲུང་དོན་ལས་བྱུང་ཡོདཔ་ཨིནམས།རྫོང་གི་རྩིགས་རོ་མཐོ་དྲག་སྦྲི་ཡོད་མི་ཚུ་ཡང་ རང་བཞིན་ནས་བྱུང་པའི་ས་དང་རྡོ་ཚུ་ལས་ སྦྲིང་སྦྲིང་འབད་རྐྱབ་ཡོད་མི་ཚུ་གི་རྩི་ཚུ་ཡང་ཡལ་ཏེ་ གལ་སྲིད་རྩིགས་རྡོ་ཚུ་འཐོན་ཡར་སོང་པ་ཅིན་ ས་ཀོའི་ལས་བྱེད་པ་ཚུ་ལུ་ རྩིགས་པ་ཞིག་རལ་བྱུང་བའི་སྣང་མེད་ཀྱི་ཉེན་ཁ་སྒོམ་འབྱུང་ནི་ཨིན་པས། ནི་ཚུ་ ཚད་འཛིན་པའིགནས་སྟངས་ཅིག་ཨིན་རུང་ གྲུབ་འབྲས་ཚུ་མངོན་སུམ་འབྱུང་ནི་ཨིན་མས། རྫོང་ཤུལ་གྱི་ས་ཁོངས་ནང་ལུ་ ས་ཀོའི་ལཱ་ཚུ་ཡང་ མནའ་ཤུལ་ས་ཀོའི་དམིགས་གཏད་དང་ རྫོང་བཞེངས་ཀྱི་ལོ་རྒྱུས་རྒྱལ་རབས་དང་འབྲེལ་ཏེ་ དུས་རིམ་གྱིས་འབད་འགོ་བཙུགས་པའི་ས་གནས་ལས་ མཇུག་ཚུན་ཚོད་ལེགས་ཤོམ་འབད་གཞི་བཙུགས་འབད་དེ་ཡོད། མཚན་རིག་གི་འཕྲུལ་ཆས་ Radiocarbon ལག་ལེན་འཐབ་ཐོག་ལས་ ཞིབ་འཇུག་འབད་བལྟ་བའི་སྐབས་སུ་ དགྲ་ཐམ་རྫོང་འདི་ དུས་རབས་ ༡༦ བར་མཚམས་ལུ་བཞེངས་ནིའི་འགོ་བཙུགས་ཏེ་ རིམ་པ་བཞིན་དུ་རྒྱ་བསྐྱེད་འབད་སྟེ་ རྫོང་གཞི་ཅིག་ལུ་གྱུར་ནུག དེ་

ལས་ དུས་རབས་ ༡༧ པའི་ནང་ལུ་ ཉམས་གསོ་དང་ལྷོ་ཕྱོགས་མདུན་ངོས་ཀྱི་བཟོ་བཀོད་རྒྱ་བསྐྱེད་གཏངམ་མ་ཚད་ འཇུལ་སྒོ་ཚུ་ཡང་བཟོ་སྐྲུན་འབད་ནུག དོ་རུང་ སྐད་ཕྱོགས་ཀྱི་བཟོ་བཀོད་ཚུ་ དུས་རབས་ ༡༨ པ་སྟོད་མཚམས་ལུ་ཨིནམ་དང་ དེ་ཡང་ གལ་ཅན་གྱི་ཨང་གནས་དང་འཁྲིལ་བ་ཅིན་ རྫོང་དེ་ནང་ལུ་ གནོད་བཀལ་དང་རྐུ་ཧམ་འཕྲོག་པ་མེ་སྐྱོར་ལ་སོགས་པའི་རྐྱེན་སྦྱོད་ཀྱི་ཐོག་ལུ་ཉམས་རྐྱེན་ཤོར་ཡོདཔ་འབད་ཐོན་ནུག་རྒྱལ་རབས་ལོ་རྒྱུས་ཀྱི་ཞིབ་འཚོལ་པའི་ ཚོད་དཔག་དང་འཁྲིལ་བ་ཅིན་ དགྲ་ཕམ་རྫོང་འདི་སྤྱི་ལོ་༡༦༧༦ ལོར་བོད་དམང་གིས་ རླག་གཏོར་བཏང་པའི་ཞིབ་འཚོལ་གྲུབ་འབྲས་ལུ་ མནའ་ཤུལ་བརྟག་ཞིབ་མཁས་མཆོག་ཚུ་གིས་ ལོ་རྒྱུས་དེ་ཚུ་མི་བདེན་ཟེར་ཨིན་པས། ས་རྐོ་འབད་བའི་སྐབས་ལུ་ཐོབ་ཡོད་པའི་རྫིགས་ཤུལ་དེ་ཚུ་གིས་ འབྲུག་རྒྱལ་ཁབ་ཀྱི་ས་གནས་སོ་སོ་ཚུ་ནང་ལུ་ ཉམས་སྲུང་འབད་དེ་ཡོད་པའི་ རྫོང་གཞི་ཚུ་གི་འབྲེལ་ཡོད་བཟོ་བཀོད་ཀྱི་ཆ་ལག་ཚུ་དང་འདྲ་མཚུངས་ག་དེ་སྦེ་ཡོད་ག་དང་ རྫོང་གཞི་ཚུ་ཉམས་གསོ་ནམ་འབད་ཡོདཔ་ཨིན་ནའི་རགས་རྟེས་སྟོན་ཚུགས་ནི་ཨིནམ་ལས་ དེ་གིས་ མ་འོངས་པའི་མནའ་ཤུལ་ས་རྐོའི་ལས་འགུལ་ཚུ་གི་ དམིགས་དོན་ཚུ་ཡང་འགྲུབ་ཚུགས་ནི་ཨིན་པས། ང་བཅས་རའི་རྒྱལ་རབས་ལོ་རྒྱུས་ཀྱི་བདེན་ཁུངས་ལས་འདི་ ས་རྐོའི་ལས་འགུལ་ལས་ཐོབ་པའི་ ཞིབ་འཇུག་གི་གནས་ཚུལ་མངམ་འབད་ཐོབ་ཚུགས་པས། རྫོང་གི་མནའ་བོའི་རྗེས་ཤུལ་ཚུ་ཡང་ སྟོ་ཤིང་། སྒོ་ནོར་སེམས་ཅན་ཚུ་གིས་ཟ་བའི་རྫ་དང་ གཞན་ཡང་ ཚོང་འབྲེལ་འཐབ་པའི་ཅ་ཆས་(རྒྱ་ནག་གི་དཀར་ཡོལ།) ལ་སོགས་པའི་ དུས་རྒྱུན་གྱི་མི་ཚེའི་གནས་སྟངས་ཚུ་ལས་ད་གོ་ཚུགསཔ་ཨིན་རུང་ དཔེ་བསྡུར་འབད་ནིའི་གདམ་ཁ་མེད་མི་ལུ་བརྟེན་འདྲི་བ་ལེ་ཤ་ར་ལུས་ཏེ་ཡོད། དེ་གིས་སྦེ་ རྫོང་ཤུལ་དེ་ནང་ལུ་ ཆག་གྲུམ་ཤོར་བའི་རྫ་ཆས་ཀྱི་རིགས་ལུས་ཡོད་མི་ཚུ་ཡང་ དབྱེ་རིམ་གྱི་སྡེ་ཚན་ཁ་ལུ་འཕྱེ་ཚུགས་ནི་ཨིན་རུང་ འཕྲུལ་གྱི་འཇིག་རྟེན་དང་རང་བཞིན་གྱི་དུས་ཚོད་ཀྱི་ཆ་འཇོག་ཡུན་གནས་དང་ལྡན་པའི་ རྫ་ཆས་ཀྱི་རིགས་ཚུ་དབྱེ་རིམ་སྡེ་ཚན་ནང་ལུ་ཚུད་མི་ཚུད་སླབ་མི་ཚུགས་ནི་ཨིན་མས། མནའ་ཤུལ་ས་རྐོའི་ འགོ་བཙུགས་ཀྱི་ལཱ་ཚུ་འབད་ཚར་ཏེ་ཡོད་རུང་ དེ་དང་འབྲེལ་བའི་ འབྲུག་པའི་རྒྱལ་རབས་ལོ་རྒྱུས་ཀྱི་ཞིབ་འཚོལ་པ་ཚུ་གིས་ ཞིག་རལ་སོང་བའི་རྫོང་གཞིའི་མནའ་ཤུལ་གྱི་ ཞིབ་འཚོལ་སླབ་བྱེད་ཚུ་ལས་གཙོ་བོ་ར་ གནས་སྡུད་ཐབས་ཤེས་དང་སྦྲགས་ཏེ་ ལོ་རྒྱུས་དང་ལྡན་པའི་ཡིག་ཆ་ཚུ་འཚོལ་ཞིབ་འབད་ནིའི་ལཱ་འགན་ཕོགས་ནི་ཨིན་མས། བཅུད་བསྡུས་ཏེ་ཞུ་བ་ཅིན་ དགྲ་ཕམ་རྫོང་གི་མནའ་ཤུལ་ས་རྐོའི་ལས་འགུལ་དེ་ གལ་ཅན་གྱི་ལས་འགུལ་ཅིག་ལུ་གྱུར་ཡོདཔ་མ་ཚད་ འབྲུག་གི་རྒྱལ་རབས་ཀྱི་དོན་ལུ་ རིག་གསར་གྱི་ཐོག་ལས་གནས་ཚུལ་ཕུལ་ཚུགས་ཅི་ཟེར་ཞུ་ནི་ཨིན།

8. Appendix

8.1. Bibliography

M. ARIS, Bhutan, *The Early History of a Himalayan Kingdom*, Earminster 1979.

M. ARIS, *Sources for the History of Bhutan*. Introduction to this edition by J. A. Ardussi. Delhi 2009.

G. AVITABILE and S. GRAF VON DER SCHULENBURG, *Chinesisches Porzellan*. Frankfurt 1992.

R. BLUMER and L. BRAILLARD, *Forgotten Archaeological Sites of the Choskar Valleys in Central Bhutan: the Batpalathang Site Near Jakar and the Potential of Bhutan's Archaeological Heritage*. SLSA Annual Report 2000.

Drapham Dzong, Bumthang District, Bhutan. *Proposal for Conservation of the Site*. Submitted by the Division for Conservation of Architectural Heritage, Department of Culture, Ministry of Home and Cultural Affairs, Bhutan 2007.

E. FISCHER, *Proposal for a new SLSA Project in the Kingdom of Bhutan*. SLSA Annual Report 2006.

E. FISCHER and B. FISCHER, *Clay pots in Bumthang Dzongkhak (Central Bhutan)*. SLSA Annual Report 2008.

A. GANSSER, *Geology of the Bhutan Himalayas*. New York 1983.

A. GRUEN, H. EISENBEISS, M. BLAHA, M. SAUERBIER, P. FUX and NAMGYEL TSHERING, *UAV photogrammetry project Drapham Dzong, Bhutan*. SLSA Annual Report 2009.

Introduction to Traditional Architecture of Bhutan. Department of Works, Housing and Roads, Royal Government of Bhutan 1993.

D. J. LAROCCA with essays by J. Clarke, A. Heller and L. Jamspol, *Warriors of the Himalayas*. New York and London 2006.

U. LÜTOLF, *Medizinische Begleitung des archäologischen Teams bei Drapham Dzong, Bhutan*. SLSA Annual Report 2008.

M.C. MEYER et al., *Active Tectonics in Eastern Lunana (N.W. Bhutan). Implications for the Seismic and Glacial Hazard Potential of the Bhutan Himalayas*. Tectonics 25, 2006.

W. MEYER, *Bhutan-Swiss Archaeological Project Drapham Dzong 2008*. SLSA Annual Report 2008.

W. MEYER, *Bhutan-Swiss Archaeological Project Drapham Dzong 2008–2010*. Drapham Dzong, Bhutan Report 2009. SLSA Annual Report 2009.

W. MEYER, *Der Drapham Dzong. Grabungen auf einer Festung in Bhutan 2008–2010*. Burgen und Schlösser 52, 3, 2011.

W. MEYER, *Bhutan-Swiss Archaeological Project 2009–2010*. Drapham Dzong, Bhutan 2010. Excavations Results from Stage 3 (Autumn 2010). SLSA Annual Report 2010.

W. MEYER, *Drapham Dzong. Excavations of a Motte castle in Bhutan, 2008–2010*. Château Gaillard 25, Caen 2012.

NAGTSHO DORJI, E. FISCHER and NAMGYEL TSHERING. *The First Excavation Campaign at Drapham Dzong in Central Bhutan. Administrative Report*. SLSA Annual Report 2008.

B.C. OLSCHAK, U. GANSSER and A. GANSSER, *Bhutan, Land der verborgenen Schätze*. Bern and Stuttgart 1969.

B.C. OLSCHAK, A. GANSSER, A. GRUSCHKE and E. BÜHRER, *Himalya. Wachsende Berge, lebendige Mythen, wandernde Menschen*. Cologne 1996.

D. OPPLER, R.SOULIGNAC and V. SEMEELS, *Entdeckung einer metallurgischen Industrie am Fusse des Hochhimalayas*. Hochwald 2013.

F. POMMARET, *Bhutan*, Edition Erde Reiseführer Bremen 2006.

S. SCHEUERER and KUENGA WANGMO in collaboration with D. Oppler, J. Osatinsky, Sonam Tashi, G. Weber and V. Wyler, *Bhutan-Swiss Archaeological Project 2008–2010, Introduction*. SLSA Annual Report 2010.

C. SCHICKLGRUBER and F. POMMARET, *Bhutan, Festung der Götter*. Vienna 1997 and Basel 1998.

SLSA Annual Reports of the Swiss-Liechtenstein Foundation for Archaeological Research Abroad, 2000ff.

K. THINLEY and R. DAMPNIER. *The Folk Heritage Museum*. Thimpu 2006.

Topographic Maps 1:50,000. 78 I/10 (Trongsa, Bumthang), 1999 and 78 I/14 (Tongsa Province), 1967.

8.2. Participating Institutions

Office of Museums and Archaeology, Canton Basel-Landschaft, Liestal (Radiographic Analysis)

Centre of Isotope Research, Faculty of Mathematics and Natural Sciences, University of Groningen, J. van der Plicht (Radiocarbon Dating)

Institute of Prehistoric and Scientific Archaeology (IPNA), University of Basel, J. Schibler (Animal Bones), A. Schlumbaum (Plant Remains)

Department of History, University of Basel, Werner Meyer (Scientific Director).

Institute of Destruction-Free Analysis and Archaeometry (IfZAA). A. Burkardt, Herrliberg-Zurich (Metal Analysis)

Institute of Mineralogy and Petrography, University of Basel. S. Graeser (Mineral Analysis)